W9-ARI-014

Printers and Men of Capital

University of Pennsylvania Press
EARLY AMERICAN STUDIES

Richard S. Dunn,
Director, Philadelphia Center for Early American Studies,
Series Editor

Also in the series:
Aaron Spencer Fogleman. *Hopeful Journeys: German Immigration,
Settlement, and Political Culture in Colonial America, 1717–1775.*

Printers and Men of Capital

PHILADELPHIA BOOK PUBLISHERS

IN THE NEW REPUBLIC

ROSALIND REMER

PENN

University of Pennsylvania Press

Philadelphia

Copyright © 1996 by the University of Pennsylvania Press
All rights reserved
Printed in the United States of America

Library of Congress Cataloging-in-Publication Data

Remer, Rosalind, 1963–
    Printers and men of capital : Philadelphia book publishers in the
new republic / Rosalind Remer.
        p.   cm. — (Early American studies)
    Includes bibliographical references and index.
    ISBN 0-8122-3337-9 (cloth : alk. paper)
      1. Publishers and publishing—Pennsylvania—Philadelphia—
History—18th century.   2. Publishers and publishing—Pennsylvania—
Philadelphia—History—19th century.   I. Title.   II. Series.
Z478.6.P5R46 1996
    070.5'09748'11 — dc20   95-51384
                                                                        CIP

For Jim

Contents

List of Illustrations   ix

Acknowledgments   xi

List of Abbreviations   xv

Introduction   1

1
The First Century of Philadelphia Printing and Publishing   11

2
Politics, Patronage, and Publishing in the 1790s   24

3
"Young Adventurers," Master Printers, and "Men of Capital"   39

4
New Modes of Publishing in the Early Republic   69

5
Credit Networks and the New Publishers   100

6
"Forced Trade" and Distant Markets   125

Conclusion   149

Appendix   153

Notes   159

Bibliography   191

Index   205

Illustrations

Figure 1. *A Premium* (1803). Engraving of Johnson's shop.
Photo courtesy of the American Antiquarian Society.   74

Figure 2. Thomas Dobson receipt, 1790. Photo courtesy of
the Historical Society of Pennsylvania (Stauffer Collection).   76

Figure 3. Mathew Carey receipt, 1813. Photo courtesy of the
Library Company of Philadelphia (McAllister Papers).   77

Figure 4. M. Carey & Son receipt, 1818. Photo courtesy of the
Historical Society of Pennsylvania (Daniel Parker Papers).   78

Figure 5. Title page (v. 1), *Travels of Anacharsis the Younger
in Greece*. Photo courtesy of the Library Company of
Philadelphia.   89

Map 1. Areas reached by traveling salesmen, ministers, branch
stores, and wholesale accounts in the country trade, c. 1825.   131

Acknowledgments

THIS BOOK BEGAN AS A doctoral dissertation at UCLA, and through almost eight years of research and writing, I have incurred many debts, both intellectual and personal. It is with great pleasure that I compose these words of gratitude to those individuals and institutions who extended valuable criticism, financial support, and friendship.

My greatest intellectual debt is to Joyce Appleby, whose incisive reading and inspired criticism helped me to craft my ideas and research into a dissertation. I am especially grateful for the interest and respect she showed my work, even as she continued to advise and encourage. In her hospitality, energy, and wide-ranging interests, Professor Appleby has truly provided a role model for her graduate students in search of a life of the mind.

I am also grateful to other historians at the University of California. Edwin Gaustad and James Kettner sparked my early interest in history, while Gary Nash, whose knowledge of Philadelphia and Boston sources is unsurpassed, helped me hone my research skills and saw me through my first major research project in graduate school. Eric Monkonnen has been a true friend and a reliable source of sound advice.

A number of individuals have read all or portions of versions of this study, and I would like to thank them for their good suggestions, many of which I have followed: Robert Arner, Scott Casper, William Childs, Dan Cohen, Donald Farren, William Gilmore-Lehne, David Hall, John Hench, Christine Heyrman, Richard John, Susan Klepp, Isabelle Lehuu, Warren McDougall, Edwin Perkins, Richard Sher, Alan Taylor, Peter von Allmen, Michael Winship, Ronald Zboray, and Michael Zuckerman.

Several institutions have provided vital financial support. A Summer Research Fellowship at the Historical Society of Pennsylvania and the Library Company of Philadelphia allowed me to begin my research at those institutions in 1988. The time I spent in 1987 and 1988 as a Kate B. and Hall J. Peterson Fellow and as a participant in a Summer Seminar in the History of the Book at the American Antiquarian Society had an enormous impact on the shape of this study. I also received support from the Bibliographical Society of America, UCLA's Graduate Division, The Business

History Conference, the American Council of Learned Societies, and the Faculty and Research and Development Council of Moravian College.

The Philadelphia Center for Early American Studies at the University of Pennsylvania grants fellowships to graduate students working on dissertations, and I was fortunate to receive one. But the Center affords much more than office space and financial support. It is a place for discussing a wide variety of topics in early American history and for meeting an astonishing number of visiting historians. The Center's hospitable qualities are due in no small part to its director, Richard Dunn, who takes enormous interest in the scholars who pass through, acting as "dissertation director in residence," and going to great lengths to help them succeed. I have drawn steadily on Professor Dunn as a resource and am deeply grateful for his support and friendship. I am also appreciative of the interest that Richard Beeman, of the University of Pennsylvania, has taken in my work over the years; I like to think that I learned a thing or two about teaching from him.

I wish to especially thank the staffs of the libraries where I conducted my research. I am grateful for the help of Marcus McCorison, Georgia Barnhill, Nancy Burkett, Joanne Chaison, John Hench, Marie E. Lamoureux, and Dennis Laurie, of the American Antiquarian Society, as well as Barbara Trippel Simmons, former manuscripts curator there; Alan Degutis, the head of cataloging at the Antiquarian Society, who helped me navigate their North American Imprints Program Catalogue (sending me enormous printouts when I wondered how the imprints for, say, the year 1805 might look); Edward Carter II, Roy Goodman, and Beth Carroll Horrocks, of the American Philosophical Society; Connie King, of the Free Library of Philadelphia; Linda Stanley and Louise Jones, of the Historical Society of Pennsylvania; Ellen Dunlap, former director of the Rosenbach Museum and Library and current president of the Antiquarian Society; Leslie Morris, former curator at the Rosenbach; and Daniel Traister, of the University of Pennsylvania Libraries, Special Collections.

I wish to single out the Library Company because it proved to be a second home for me. To begin with, the late Edwin Wolf, who had retired as librarian a few years before I arrived, nevertheless took me under his wing and helped me appreciate the products the publishers put out: the books. His generosity and his faith in me have meant more than I can say. John Van Horne, the current librarian, and Ken Finkel, Mary Ann Hines, Phil Lapsansky, Denise Larabee, Karen Nipps, and Susan Oyama all shared with me their areas of expertise. The Library Company is also where I met Jim Green, the assistant librarian, to whom I dedicate this book. He has been my companion and mentor ever since we first began to talk of publishing history.

I have often heard the complaint that research and writing are lonely tasks. This has not been my experience, however. This project has continually brought me into contact with people who have kept me well-stocked with friendship. I would like to acknowledge the support of Rose Beiler, John Bidwell, Wayne Bodle, Susan Branson, Bruce Burnam, Hans Eicholz, Aaron Fogleman, Alison Games, Tom Ingersoll, Ben Keppel, Matthew Lee, David Lehman, Kim LoPrete, Roderick McDonald, Donna Rilling, Mildred Rivera-Martinez, Nancy Rosenberg, Ellen Slatkin, Steve Smith, Joe Torsella, Rick Vernier, Dan Wickburg, and Karin Wulf, all of whom ensured that the business of research and writing was far from a solitary affair.

I am grateful to my colleagues at Moravian College who offered encouragement of all kinds: Bonnie Falla, Dennis and Dorothy Glew, Curt Keim, Win Kohls, Janet Loengard, Roger Martin, Martha Reid, Michael Smith, Bettie Smolansky, Robert Stinson, and Jill Youngken. George Brower and Susan Overath Woolley both helped with a variety of computer and software problems, and Susan designed the map in Chapter 6.

I also wish to thank the *Journal of the Early Republic* for permission to incorporate portions of my Winter 1994 article, "Preachers, Peddlers, and Publishers: Philadelphia's Backcountry Book Trade, 1800–1830," into this book.

Finally, I wish to acknowledge my parents, Franklin and Alice Remer, who have read and commented on my work from the very beginning. They have been, quite simply, wonderful parents.

Abbreviations

LFC-HSP Lea and Febiger Collection, Historical Society of Pennsylvania

MDR-HSP McCarty and Davis Records, Historical Society of Pennsylvania

MDP-AAS McCarty and Davis Papers, American Antiquarian Society

SGC-HSP Simon Gratz Collection, Historical Society of Pennsylvania

Evans, Bristol, and Shaw and Shoemaker numbers are given along with citations of primary printed sources. These are drawn from Charles Evans's *American Bibliography*, Clifford K. Shipton's continuation of Evans's bibliography through 1800, Roger Bristol's *Supplement* to Evans, Ralph Shaw and Richard Shoemaker's *American Imprints*, and Shoemaker's continuation of that work.

Introduction

IN SEPTEMBER 1794, MATHEW CAREY, an Irish printer and bookseller who had immigrated to Philadelphia in the 1780s, reported on the state of the American economy to a relative in Ireland. "The human imagination can hardly reach to an idea of the prosperity and importance to which this country is rapidly verging," he wrote.[1] Credit was becoming easier to obtain, according to Carey, and state and federal governments alike sought ways to facilitate growth by building roads and canals. Eager for the new nation to fulfill its republican promise, Carey saw opportunity in every quarter. Agriculture would flourish and manufacturing would develop out of American ingenuity and the desire for progress. Carey marveled at the young nation's unique position to set a republican example to a world well-acquainted with tyranny.

Carey's political writings of the 1790s and his letters to friends and family in Ireland are filled with enthusiasm. In the former, he prescribed a balance of agrarian and manufacturing pursuits, all under the umbrella of republican government.[2] In the latter, he described his efforts to build a flourishing printing and bookselling business in his adopted country. This involved significant energy and risk: Carey hoped to provide the new nation with books. First, he needed to find titles that would meet with ready sale and to print them cheaply enough so they could compete with widely available imported books. He needed to develop a busy retail establishment from which to sell his books, and he would also have to strive to reach markets that extended beyond local boundaries and regions. A wide assortment of steady-selling books was key to success in early national publishing and bookselling, and Carey knew that cooperation with others in the trade could provide him with the assortment he needed. Carey was not the only aspiring publisher to face these formidable tasks. According to city directories and an analysis of surviving imprints, in 1790 Philadelphia was home to twenty-six printers who, like Carey, published books and pamphlets with their names appearing in the imprints. Five years later, the number of printers matching this description had risen to thirty-four. At decade's end, there were thirty-nine, and by 1805, fifty-one can be identified (see Appendix).[3]

The rapid growth in the printing trade had major implications for the development of publishing in early national Philadelphia because many printers of the 1790s acted as publishers when they took on the risk of producing works for their own sale. In the early years of the republic, the word "publisher" was hardly ever used in connection with publishing books; it was more commonly employed to describe those who published newspapers, commercial sheets, and city directories, suggesting that sustained, or at least ongoing, periodic publishing activity was required for the description of "publisher" to apply. The term "bookseller" was generally used to describe someone who published and sold books. It became increasingly common, however, for those who published books to refer to themselves as publishers in the later years of the new republic, when publishing houses came into being. For the sake of clarity — and with a nod to modern usage — I use "bookseller" when referring to the London publishers and the eighteenth-century Americans who made publishing just one of their many activities; I use "publisher" to refer to those who later made publishing their primary activity, even if they had not yet fixed on the term.

Printing and publishing comprised different economic activities requiring different levels of capital and time investment. For the majority of printing jobs — work printed for customers — the level of financial involvement for the printer was so low that in many cases he did not even have to buy the paper, the most expensive component of a printing job. If he did supply the paper, he charged his customer for it; otherwise, the customer was expected to procure it. The printer simply performed the tasks of setting type and pulling the press. His own costs consisted of labor, press, ink, and type. Stitching and binding were also separately charged items, to be passed on to the customer.[4] Publishers, on the other hand, combined judgment, capital, and marketing strategies with the craft of printing in an attempt to create and sell printed matter. Publishers had their hands in the creation, the financing, manufacturing, and distribution of printed material.[5] Profit from the sale of his own publications was the publisher's ultimate aim. Printers were not the only individuals to engage in publishing activity in the 1790s. Retail booksellers — those who may or may not have had a direct hand in printing the works they sold — also increased in number, from eight in 1790 to eleven five years later, and then held steady at sixteen between 1799 and 1805. Taken together, the printers who acted as publishers and the city's booksellers formed the nucleus of Philadelphia's early publishing trade.

In Philadelphia, throughout the period of this study, publishing was a function that could be performed by any number of individuals or groups in or out of the book trade: printers, booksellers, book binders, authors, civil or religious corporate bodies. Moreover, an individual could combine one or more of these roles with publishing in a variety of permutations. In the early years of the 1790s there were several members of the book trade who occasionally acted as publishers. By the 1820s and 1830s, some of these figures, most of them originally printers, had committed to publishing books on a more or less full-time basis, leaving the manufacturing and retailing to others. They formed an increasingly well-defined and tightly knit subgroup. These are the figures whose careers this study follows to the exclusion of many others, and it is they who effected a transition to large-scale nineteenth-century commercial publishing enterprises.

The focus of this study is the process by which a group of late eighteenth-century Philadelphia printers and booksellers evolved into nineteenth-century entrepreneurs of the book trade. This transformation did not occur overnight, nor was it fully complete by 1830. But the beginnings of the change can be traced to the 1790s, and over the next several decades the profession of "publisher" gained definition. Furthermore, the publishing profession did not emerge in neat, chronological phases; there appears to be no year or decade when printers began acting solely as publishers.

The printers and booksellers whose careers this study follows can be seen as transitional. Even as they struggled to move beyond the financial constraints of their craft and to develop markets, they continued to employ many traditional eighteenth-century business practices: they managed their own businesses, employing few clerks to help them in the day-to-day management of their concerns; they had a direct hand in the production of their publications, even when some had abandoned printing; they combined retailing and wholesaling; and, unlike their successors, they did not have the railroad to rely on for distribution of their books. Stereotype plate printing and printing by steam were just gaining recognition and widespread use in the late 1820s, so the production of books during the years of the early republic remained costly, time-consuming, and labor intensive.[6] Innovations in papermaking and binding would also produce important changes in the production of books, but they too, came a little too late for the publishers of the early republic.

Yet these publishers were not colonial craftsmen caught in the wrong century. Their business strategies reflected the intensity of a rapidly changing and growing society and suggest that their methods were far from backward. To begin with, those in the business of publishing books were flexible. Most only made small-scale efforts to specialize, as the market for books was not developed enough to support specialty publishers. This flexibility led to innovation and a keen recognition of the need to efficiently combine competition with cooperation. Collusion was common among the early publishers, who understood the reality of overproduction and the difficulties of reaching far-flung and often limited markets. Other ways to function in this competitive world of all-purpose publishing suggested themselves as well. Attempts to control production and costs came in the form of vertical integration and consolidation, activities usually associated with big business in the later decades of the century.[7] Finally, the nature of the publishing business made these entrepreneurs unique. Their products were diverse: each book represented a separate investment strategy and a distinct risk. Even publishers who specialized to a degree — religious publishing, say, or schoolbooks — still saw each title as a discrete product. One steady seller could provide the bedrock of a publisher's good fortune, while one uncompetitive book could cause enormous problems. Even if, as was typical, average sellers made up a publisher's list, each book had its own identity. Clearly, notions of interchangeability and specialization could not mean for publishers what they came to mean for other businesses in the nineteenth century.

*   *   *

Colonial printers operated very much within the confines of British mercantilism. They entertained notions of publishing only as long as they could guarantee for themselves relatively low risks in the undertaking. In the colonial period, this was most often done by publishing books either by subscription or under the aegis of governmental or religious institutions. Printers could also publish inexpensive books, pamphlets, and newspapers which, for a variety of reasons, London booksellers would not or could not produce.[8] Many printers sold books, stationery, and other goods to help keep them afloat. An assortment of English books and locally printed works could usually be found in late eighteenth-century American printing shops.[9] The colonial printer, therefore, tended to produce material of local interest and sponsorship for local markets. While commodities such as molasses, tobacco, and humans linked colonial regions, printed matter was not considered a particularly valuable commodity for trade. It would take a relative degree of political and economic unity, as seen in the Revolutionary crisis and the years of the Confederation, before printers could see the utility in *re*printing works published in other American regions; only with an increasingly national political and economic orientation did members of the trade begin producing printed material for distant markets.

The Revolutionary era saw a significant increase in the role of the press in politics, and the connection between the two grew more intimate with the formation of political parties in the 1790s. These events, combined with the relocation of the federal government to Philadelphia in 1790, contributed to a flood of printed matter from the presses of that city. Much of this publishing was political in nature, and some printers seized on patronage opportunities, becoming party spokesmen through their newspapers and other publications. The political publishing trade was enriched by French émigrés, British radicals, and Irish dissidents who flocked to Philadelphia in the 1780s and 1790s, many taking up the trade of printing for political purposes or continuing in the trade after having been trained in their home countries. These immigrants had an impact on the trade itself and on the politicization of its members.[10] As the 1790s drew to a close, political publishing had become something of a profession unto itself. Those engaged in it had begun to move away from bookselling and job printing, focusing instead on politics.

Nonpolitical book publishing also emerged in the years of the early republic. Domestic and international economic developments in the years following the ratification of the Constitution provided printers with more opportunities to act as book publishers than their colonial counterparts had enjoyed. The funding of the revolutionary debt and the accompanying assumption of the state debts, as well as the creation of the Bank of the United States and other banks, generated new pools of capital for speculation and investment. America's economic growth was phenomenal, particularly from 1793 to the turn of the century, when agricultural exports rose dramatically to meet the needs of war-torn Europe. Earnings from imports and re-exports left the new nation with almost no trade deficit.[11] As part of what Thomas Doerflinger has termed an "efflorescence of mercantile innovation," Philadelphia's merchant community engaged in high-risk trade and investment in the decades following the Revolution, and speculation was at an all-time high. This included speculation in publishing. Population growth and mobility also played a major role in the burgeoning book publishing business. The movement of people to the west and southwest in the early decades of the new republic increased the need for printed matter over a larger area than before and stirred Philadelphia printers with visions of new markets for books. Further, the interregional flow of capital and the establishment of country presses and book stores were integral to establishing far-flung markets for books.[12] Beginning in the 1790s, a number of Philadelphia printers saw opportunities to expand their book publishing activities; and their efforts to muster credit, seek specialized markets, and find creative ways to speculate in books produced a sort of merchant class among printers. Increasingly, these individuals reduced or eliminated printing in their own shops, choosing instead to have the work executed by others.

Scholars of the early national period have examined subjects related to publishing such as literacy, the rise of the novel as a literary form, social and cultural changes relating to the dissemination of print, and the democratization of knowledge.[13] Cultural, economic, and political development in the new republic were intertwined with the development of early national publishing. Dramatic changes in the nature of print culture and the uses of literacy altered American society in the late eighteenth century and the first half of the nineteenth century. Referred to by some historians and literary critics as the "reading revolution," these changes took the form of widening literacy, readership, and consumption. At the same time, historians have argued, religion and communication underwent a process of democratization, and the ranks of the genteel middle class expanded. Members of an aspiring working class also sought self-improvement through knowledge and organized themselves around the printed word.[14] Most scholars agree that a commercial economy developed in tandem with a broad reading culture, and many assert that books became inexpensive and widely available early in the nineteenth century. The popularization of print, whether effected by evangelical preachers, Bible societies, and a growing religious press, or by wider participation in local, state, and national economies and politics, encouraged printer-booksellers to create and pursue markets for books.

Concerns about education and citizenship in Philadelphia led to the relatively early establishment of public schools there, and the growth of public education and accompanying rise in literacy translated into an expanded reading market. Prominent Philadelphia printers Mathew Carey and William Duane were both active in the debate over public education, on the side of expansion and greater access. Their role was no doubt in accordance with the Controllers of the Public Schools' larger aim to prepare young citizens for participation in a republican society, but they did not lose sight of the fact that education required books and that the needs of American education would best be served by American schoolbooks.[15] Indeed, reprinted English and domestic schoolbooks became the bread and butter of the infant American publishing trade.

The history of printing in America has not been neglected by historians and bibliographers, but while there are excellent studies of colonial printers and printing, none has been concerned with the publishers of books in the early national period, when book publishing began to be a viable economic activity.[16] Scholars have generally been more attracted to mid-nineteenth-century publishing. This interest comes out of the study of authorship and literature on one hand, and developments in transportation and communication, on the other.[17] The very existence of house histories for many major publishing firms has influenced the periodization of publishing history, drawing our focus to the middle years of the nineteenth century. For the period in between, however, we still lack a basic understanding of who produced books, how they were financed, how publishers' credit and exchange networks worked, and how books found their way into the hands of American consumers.

A case study of early national book publishing in America could take as its site any of the major urban areas of the early republic. As in Philadelphia, the printing and publishing trades of Boston and New York were dynamic, with growing numbers of tradesmen. Baltimore, Charleston, Hartford, and Albany also boasted active publishing trades. In addition, publishing did take place in smaller towns, but many publications of small-town presses were financed by authors, local governments, church bodies, and other institutions, making *them*, rather than the craftsmen who printed the work, the publishers. An interest in early Philadelphia publishing flows quite naturally from the diversity of its presses' output in the eighteenth century. It has been argued that printers in Philadelphia produced the widest variety of printed matter throughout the colonies.[18] The printing trade gained extra sustenance when the new nation's capital moved from New York to Philadelphia in 1790, and printers there expected to benefit quite directly from the proximity to the chambers of the federal government. Until 1800, when the capital moved to Washington, D.C., Philadelphia was alive with political publishing and publishing schemes directly connected to political patronage. But some members of the trade were equally active in their attempts to publish nonpolitical works, and there was a dramatic rise in the number of general works published during that decade. The momentum did not let up until the late 1820s and 1830s, when the publishing houses of New York and Boston gained ascendancy over Philadelphia's trade.

A picture of Philadelphia's early national publishing trade emerges through analysis of the enormous cache of records that some of its members left behind. To begin with, this study could not have been undertaken without publishers' surviving publications. It is possible, even assuming low survival rates, to count and analyze the products of the Philadelphia presses, something that would be difficult, at best, to do with other types of goods. From an economic standpoint, books are consumables, but they are unique in that they are often preserved by people and libraries, making them available for historians not only to read, but to assess as sources of material culture evidence. The books from Philadelphia's publishing firms survive in great numbers in libraries. In addition, both the publishers' high level of literacy and the risky nature of their endeavors are evident in their extensive correspondence and bookkeeping; the many account books, letterbooks, and collections of business correspondence from Philadelphia publishing firms that survive in libraries, archives, and historical societies make it possible to form an understanding of their operations. Some firms are better represented than others in the archives. Letters and accounts are particularly rich for Benjamin Franklin Bache, the Bailey printing family, the Bradfords, Mathew Carey and his successors, Johnson and Warner, McCarty and Davis, and William W. Woodward. Their business practices become, of necessity, representative of the activities of the trade as a whole.

There are, of course, many things this study does *not* attempt to accomplish. This examination of the development of publishing in Philadelphia focuses mainly on book publishers and the publication of books. The many newspaper and periodical publishers of the early nineteenth century deserve separate treatment, and I argue that they engaged in quite different activities from those in the book trade, as described here. The same can be said about job printers, who, by the end of the 1790s, were becoming increasingly separate from publishers in terms of their business activities and their role in the trade. The forms that this division and specialization took in the 1790s and early years of the new century are explored, but by about 1810, when this process was more or less complete, attention is turned to the publishers of books. This study also does not attempt to bring into focus the book trade in Boston or New York, or any other major publishing center. The cast of characters and the trade practices in each of these important hubs cry out for studies of their own, from which, it is hoped, a larger, national picture can be constructed.[19] The products of German language printing and publishing were ubiquitous in colonial and early national Pennsylvania, but the German trade is only referred to in passing in this study. I have relied on, among other sources, an excellent study of the trade in Robert E. Cazden's *A Social History of the German Book Trade in America to the Civil War*.[20] Finally, this study makes no attempt to analyze consumption patterns, readership or literacy, all essential elements of a larger understanding of the history of the book in America. It is hoped, however, that this examination of the ways in which Philadelphia's publishers financed, produced, and distributed books will shed light on these other areas of inquiry.

The generation of publishers that followed immediately on the heels of this study's subjects viewed their trade and the market with new eyes. Less than fifty years after Carey penned his optimistic letters to Ireland, book publishing and publishers had changed considerably. Many mid-century publishers had no experience in the printing trade at all. With the growth of American literature, publishing houses were becoming identified with particular American authors and specific areas of literature, and publishers began to issue catalogues that showed their increasing specialization — lists of novels, or religious works, or medical texts. Most mid-century publishers were operating primarily as wholesalers and distributors of the titles they published, rather than tying up capital in retail stock or other publishers' books. The railroads aided them in reaching a national market, and the technologies of steam printing and printing from stereotype plates were critical to the mass production of the literature in which they were engaged.

The story of early national publishing, then, is not one of unimpeded progress. Most of the Philadelphia publishers examined in this study were born in the middle decades of the eighteenth century and reached adulthood during the years of Revolution and the 1780s and 1790s. While the new nation was being formed and defined, these men were seeking to establish themselves in their trade. They set out to build a publishing industry and to create and serve new markets for books. Like many entrepreneurs of the early republic their vision of a truly national market remained somewhat limited, as population growth and geographical expansion outstripped the nation's communication, transportation, and financial capacities. The early publishers were often faced with markets that were difficult to penetrate. In the very places in which books were not readily available, most books were not yet considered necessities. Nevertheless, it is the intention of this study to bring this important transition in the history of publishing to life and, in so doing, to shed new light on the formative years of an industry and a nation.

I

The First Century of Philadelphia Printing and Publishing

To UNDERSTAND THE RISE of the publisher in early national Philadelphia, it is necessary to consider both the business culture of colonial printing and the publishing strategies of colonial printers. For most of the eighteenth century, printers in America engaged in a variety of printing-related occupations. In addition to printing job work, they imported and sold books and other goods, both retail and wholesale; they occasionally published small or otherwise low-risk books; and most printed newspapers at some point in their careers. Many also engaged in book binding, and some were involved in the papermaking business. Depending on circumstances, a printer would engage in all or some of these activities. Not until the end of the century did the trade begin to diversify.

In London, this process of specialization had already occurred by the seventeenth century, when the book trade had divided distinctly into printers and publishers, known as booksellers. By the middle of the eighteenth century, London booksellers were the entrepreneurs who mobilized the capital, evaluated the market, and employed printers and binders to execute the work. These booksellers used their economic leverage, gained by the aggressive acquisition of copy, to control printers. Printers were relegated to earning their living by printing for the booksellers or by moving to less crowded and competitive settings in English provincial towns or in the colonies.[1]

During the colonial period, American printing developed as a part of the British book trade and early American printers functioned much like their English provincial counterparts. However, the lapse of the Licensing Act in 1695, which had restricted the numbers of printers admitted to the trade, and the increasing specialization of the London trade, encouraged the growth of provincial printing and bookselling.[2] The proliferation of presses in towns like Edinburgh, Glasgow, Newcastle, and York was mir-

rored in eighteenth-century Boston, New York, and Philadelphia, as well as
in some market towns throughout the colonies. Irish booksellers were extremely quick to reprint London books and boldly sell them at very competitive prices. The same can be said of some members of the Scottish trade.
However, during the first half of the eighteenth century, American printers
and booksellers did not regularly engage in the high-risk, intensive publishing activities characteristic of the London trade, or even of the Irish and
Scottish reprint trade. Colonial markets were not highly developed or diverse, and importing a few copies of a book cost less than producing a
whole edition locally.[3]

The Colonial Printer as Book Importer

The limitations of the American market, and the nature of the mercantilist
relationship between Britain and her colonies, made it difficult for early
American printers to prosper from simply pulling the press. The printers'
craft made it logical for them to be involved in the dissemination of printed
matter, and indeed, printers, acting as booksellers, figured prominently in
book sales and distribution throughout the colonies. There were a number
of ways American colonists could obtain the books they wanted to buy. A
small minority of colonists with reliable correspondents in England could
obtain books at "gentleman's prices," a small discount allowed to steady customers with good credit, and thus bypass local booksellers.[4] Colonial printers usually kept stocks of imported books in their shops, and shopkeepers
who sold dry goods often carried a selection of inexpensive books as well.
In addition, some booksellers who were not necessarily in the printing
business, acted as importers of British and European books and stationery.

The American colonial market for books was not small—it made up
almost half of British book exports—but it was easily glutted. Colonial
booksellers wanted an assortment of salable books, rather than many copies
of one title.[5] British booksellers, hoping to exploit the American market by
selling to colonial retailers, maximized their profits by sending books whose
copyrights they partially or fully owned. Only by doing this could they
allow a large enough discount or long enough credit to make importation
by colonial booksellers worthwhile. Therefore, the needs of the English
booksellers and the American retailers were often at odds. Colonial dealers
complained that their English suppliers were not sending what was most
salable in America but rather the books rejected by the British market. By
the 1760s, English booksellers agressively began to dump their slow-selling

titles onto the American market, following a trend in the British trade of remaindering, or selling "rum books" — unsalable, overstocked titles — cheaply.[6] These practices, hardly sensitive to colonial book-buying and reading needs, had the effect of flooding the colonial market with some books while others remained scarce.

Colonial printers were hardly willing simply to sacrifice all power in their relationships with British booksellers, however. David Hall, Benjamin Franklin's printing partner and a large-scale importer of British books, arrived at one method to attain an equal footing with his suppliers in London and Edinburgh. He knew that, as a colonist, he could not beat the British exporting system, so he endeavored to work within it. He cultivated excellent relationships with British booksellers and carefully maintained these contacts, always making sure to pay on time. In exchange, he gained favorable terms of credit and, equally important, significant respect and cooperation from a number of prominent English and Scottish booksellers. Cooperation meant that he was less likely to receive rum books than others with more tenuous ties. But Hall took no chances; he was particularly exacting in his demands, never ceasing to remind his correspondents of his reputation as a large-scale buyer and prompt remitter. In an order to the Edinburgh firm of Hamilton and Balfour, Hall enumerated all the sorts of books he did *not* want sent, as well as the terms he expected:

Remember Divinity is a most dull Article here. Send nothing relating to Scots Affairs, such as Pitscottie, Hathorndon, Guthrie, Fletcher &c. no Plutarch's Lives, Knights of Malta, and such like. And you must send everything on the best and lowest Terms.[7]

Most of these books would be Scottish favorites, but Hall knew they would not meet with ready sale in the colonies. Yet the seemingly endless lists of books he did order are a powerful reminder of his position in the trade. He continued to flex his muscles when the bankrupt London bookseller James Rivington moved to New York in 1760 to begin business anew. Rivington informed his American competitors that "[t]here never was a Bookseller on the Continent till he came" and that the colonial printers "know nothing about Books, nor the Prices of them." Rivington claimed that the British booksellers were "picking the pockets" of their American wholesale customers.[8] Hall's response was to write immediately to all of his British trading partners to demand satisfaction on this point, thus attaining written guarantees of the lowest terms possible, as well as tarnishing further his new competitor's reputation.

Other printers besides Hall turned to alternative means to make ends meet. Competition in the trade, as well as the basic economic difficulties that all craftsmen faced in the eighteenth century, made enterprising printers seek out ways to augment their incomes.[9] Soliciting government support was a standard practice for colonial printers. Benjamin Franklin wasted no time in securing the favor of the Pennsylvania General Assembly. "My first Promotion [in Philadelphia]," he later wrote, "was my being chosen in 1736 Clerk of the General Assembly," a paid position to be sure, but more importantly, one that gave him the advantage in bidding for government publications. The government printing and the "other occasional Jobs for the Public" proved to be "on the whole . . . very profitable," and Franklin found that he could persuade the assembly of the commonwealth's needs for compilations of acts and other expensive jobs.[10] The importance of government-sponsored publications to the printer's success should not be underestimated. By "profitable," Franklin meant not only that he was given paying jobs by the assembly, but that his recognition and position in society were bound up in this very visible form of patronage. David Hall kept careful accounts in a separate book titled "Account Currant Book for Printing work done for the Province of Pennsylvania and Governments of the Counties of New Castle, Kent, and Sussex on Delaware, 1756–69" for the purpose of keeping track of this important and lucrative part of their trade.[11]

Along with imported books, the products of their own presses, and their job printing, many printers stocked stationery and other goods in retail stores attached to their printing shops. Printing blank legal forms was a lucrative business. They sold all sorts of imported dry goods and medicines, invested in real estate, bound books, and erected paper mills. Franklin and others advertised standard stationery supplies such as "Slates, Pensils, Ink and Ink-Powder, blank Accompt-Books and Pocket-Books, Writing Paper of several Sorts, blank Bonds, Indentures, and all other Blanks in Use, with other Stationary Ware. Also very good Chocolate, and coarse and fine Edgings."[12] Rare was the printer who did not follow an advertised list of books with an enumeration of other items for sale, usually, but not limited to, stationery sundries. Consider one of William Bradford's ads of 1742:

Also a curious Parcel of fine Pictures, either painted on Glass, Mezzetinto or otherwise, such as Cartoons, the 7 Works of Mercy, Sea Pieces, Views of the most Magnificent Buildings in Europe, sets of fine Horses and a Variety of other Sorts.[13]

As odd as this collection of goods might seem, Bradford's competitor, Franklin, would not be caught without at least some of these very same items, as his accounts with Bradford indicate that he bought a number of the "mezzetinto pictures" to sell in his own shop that same year.[14] Commercial activities such as these were typical among British provincial printers of the time and had been common in the London trade a century earlier, so there was nothing exceptional about this form of diversification.[15]

And, of course, printers printed. There was a lot of job printing—commissioned printing—that needed to be done in the colonies—enough to keep fifty-one Philadelphia printers busy throughout the century following the establishment of Pennsylvania's first printing press in 1685. Nine of these fifty-one printers opened before 1740.[16] Jobs could range from printing legal forms, contracts, and licenses, to government printing, broadsides, sermons, and other pamphlet-sized material. It is impossible to determine the number of items printed that had no imprint—forms, contracts, and licenses, for example—but surviving works that contain Philadelphia imprints rose dramatically throughout the eighteenth century. The following table shows how many imprints survive for the first year of each decade, offering some indication of the steady growth in Philadelphia's output from the earliest printing to 1800.[17]

Philadelphia Imprints, 1690–1800 (decennial).

	1680	1690	1700	1710	1720	1730	1740	1750	1760	1770	1780	1790
Number of surviving imprints	0	4	7	3	3	17	65	31	68	119	114	230
Printers with imprints	0	1	1	1	1	3	3	5	6	15	16	26

Sources: North American Imprints Program Catalogue (NAIP), American Antiquarian Society, and H. Glenn Brown, Maude O. Brown, *A Directory of the Book-Arts and Book Trade in Philadelphia to 1820*.

Despite the amount of available job work and their other commercial activities, many printers kept their eyes open for opportunities to publish books, an activity that could make their presses more profitable. Yet book publishing was risky. There were relatively few safe opportunities for colonial printers to act as publishers of books. Printing was capital- and labor-intensive, which meant that publishers had to produce editions large enough to spread the cost of composition over as many copies as possible. Cost-effectiveness often required book edition sizes too large for local colonial markets, making it basically impossible for American printers to sell most books as cheaply as they could be imported from Britain and Europe. Book publishing was also risky because it tied up capital for long periods of time. The central problem of book publishing has remained constant: the publisher of a book never knows how quickly or steadily it will sell or, indeed, if it will find a market at all. Nevertheless, the relative lack of printing regulations and censorship and the unenforceability of British copyright law in the colonies, combined with the distance between the mother country and the colonies, made it possible for printers occasionally to act as publishers, if not as publishers of major books.

Colonial Publishing

Although they were discouraged from undertaking major publishing projects, printers in colonial Philadelphia did publish work that required only small amounts of capital, paper, and type. Broadsides could be published with minimal risk. Consisting of only one sheet of paper and requiring small amounts of type, broadsides automatically involved lower investment of capital than longer works. Furthermore, the broadside format lent itself distinctly to subjects of high, if temporary, interest, enabling them to meet with ready sale. If the broadside printer miscalculated, however, and produced a sheet that did not sell, it was not likely to be a major loss, and he would know this immediately. There would be no agonizing wait with large amounts of capital tied up, books gathering dust on the shelves, and creditors impatient for payment.

Books and pamphlets, consisting mainly of political tracts, catechisms, primers, collections of ballads, and chapbooks, were relatively inexpensive to print and to buy. Chapbooks were pamphlet-sized books, usually containing popular tales, ballads, poems, short plays, and jokes. Small, both in format and number of pages, they were generally bound in boards (a form of cardboard) or merely stitched in paper wrappers (a sewn antecedent of modern day paperbacks).[18] Pamphlets and chapbooks did not require fine paper or a great deal of type to produce. They could thus be printed in large, cost-effective editions and sold cheaply. These inexpensive productions were obviously attractive to the would-be publisher concerned about financial risk.

By far, the most appealing publishing investments were to be found in small books that had proven to be steady sellers. Steady sellers were not

necessarily "best sellers" in the modern sense. Rather, they were books or
pamphlets that provided a reasonably reliable source of income for the publisher. They would not, by nature, be highly topical or political, as such
publications would prove of fleeting interest, and, in any case, pamphlets
of this sort were usually financed by their authors or other interested spon-
sors. While published frequently, sermons and political pamphlets were not
steady sellers. The former were almost all subscribed for by congregations
or families who wished to see their ministers' words in print. Election day
sermons were published at the behest of the local governments. And politically controversial pamphlets were usually paid for by their authors or authors' supporters. The printer might take copies of such works to sell in lieu
of, or more usually, in addition to, being paid.

Almanacs, on the other hand, provided the perfect steady seller. They
were one of the most common types of books published in the colonies,
because their astronomical calculations pertained to the locale in which they
would be used; by the same reasoning, imported almanacs were clearly un-
suitable for the local colonial markets. A publisher could know from the
previous year's sales roughly how many to produce, giving almanacs a sort
of built-in mechanism for "market research." Colonial printers quickly and
in great numbers jumped to sew up this obvious hole in the net of British
imports.[19] According to one scholar, "almanac publications during the seventeenth and eighteenth centuries actually outnumbered all other books
combined — religious included."[20] Almanacs had a few extra advantages
as well: They provided valuable name recognition for printers, and the illustrations and complicated tables found therein advertised the craft and
skills of their producers. Between 1764 and 1783, Pennsylvania printers published almost 30 percent of all American almanacs, far exceeding the number produced in either New York or Massachusetts.[21]

Broadsides, almanacs and other pamphlets, schoolbooks, chapbooks,
and small devotional works had the additional advantage of being relatively
easy to distribute throughout the countryside. Colonial peddlers hawked
them along with other wares. Peddlers bought their supplies in cities and
radiated out to country towns and rural areas to resell them.[22] In short,
their cheap production and easy sale and distribution made pamphlets well
suited to the American printing trade, just as they were to the British provincial trade.[23] No matter who underwrote the cost, publishing these inexpensive productions suited the authors, the trade, and the market.[24] From
1690 to 1770, small publications fitting these descriptions made up about
75 percent of Philadelphia publishing.[25] While it may seem to modern

eyes—and perhaps may have seemed to members of the London book trade—that such pamphlets were ephemera hardly meriting the trouble of production and distribution, they represented the bulk of locally produced reading matter for most American colonists. These products of the colonial presses were the stuff of which early American publishing was made.

Colonial printers did occasionally publish more expensive books, although the ways in which they did so confirm the importance of risk as a factor in their decision making.[26] Collecting advance subscriptions was one way to publish books without governmental or religious institutional sponsorship.[27] This entailed issuing a proposal to publish a title, which would usually include the terms of publication, the price to subscribers, and the timetable for payment. Proposals would indicate whether the work was to be published serially, how many volumes the whole would be, and the expected completion date. Subscription publishing was a common practice in eighteenth-century England. Sometimes it was the author who, unable to convince a publisher to take the risk, solicited subscriptions as a means of subvention. Most commonly, however, publishers resorted to subscription plans to gauge the market and to capitalize expensive projects.[28]

The earliest instance of a colonial subscription plan was Bradford's proposal to publish "a large house-Bible" in 1688. He explained that publishing certain books by subscription was necessary, "for the printing of large Volumns [*sic*], because Printing is very chargeable."[29] As was the case with many proposed publications, Bradford's Bible was never printed. Usually, proposed works did not appear due to insufficient numbers of subscribers. Literally hundreds of books were proposed in the colonial period, with only a portion of them ever seeing print. This further emphasized to printers the limits of the colonial market and the constant need to test that market before plunging into publishing. One scholar has pointed out that colonial Americans were accustomed to subscriptions of all sorts. The developing status of British North America made it particularly suited to subscription plans and lotteries, whether for building roads, exploration, mining, church construction, or the numerous societies and associations that formed at mid-century.[30] Anything that involved large amounts of capital or substantial risk took on an aspect of collectivity, and book publishing was no exception.

As the eighteenth century wore on, subscription schemes fell into some disrepute because many proposed books never made it to press. Subscribers were all too often disappointed by printers' decisions to abandon publications that had not received enough advance support. Proposals increasingly cautioned that the work would only "go forward" if sufficient numbers of subscribers were gathered. Nevertheless, subscription remained through the 1790s, in the words of Franklin's grandson, "the most usual & safest mode" of publishing.[31] English booksellers had turned increasingly to credit networks within the trade to finance their publications in the eighteenth century, making subscriptions less necessary. True to form, by the beginning of the nineteenth century, their American counterparts followed suit.[32]

Some colonial tradesmen actively engaged in more daring publishing activities. Benjamin Franklin provided a prototype for the pre-Revolutionary printer who wanted to turn publisher. He acted as publisher when he took the financial risks of printing books such as Isaac Watts's *The Psalms of David, imitated* and George Whitefield's *A Journey of a Voyage from Gibraltar to Georgia.*[33] Franklin took risks in publishing only when firmly convinced that his investment would be returned. Whitefield's popularity in the colonies made the publication by subscription of his *Journal* a safe bet, but Franklin's calculations went awry with Watts's *Psalms,* which lay on his hands for almost two years.[34]

Franklin's decision to act as a publisher may also have been bolstered by the printing network he devised, made up of family members and trusted former apprentices. His intention in creating this network was motivated by at least two considerations. First, by farming out to distant places the men he trained, he kept them from setting up in competition with him, as he had done when he left Samuel Keimer's shop and set up shop on his own. Second, thinking of economies of scale, he could use the network to create and then supply markets throughout the colonies. He could thus avoid the problems of oversupplying his local market with his publications. Other colonial printers developed similar connections for distributing books throughout the colonies.[35] These methods would be copied and refined later when other printers acted as publishers during the years of the early republic.[36]

Early American Newspaper Publishing

If ambitious colonial printers avoided publishing risky books, they were less hindered in publishing newspapers, something most printers throughout the colonial period attempted. Newspapers and literary periodicals were popular publishing choices for printers in early eighteenth-century England. Periodical literature offered greater financial control to publishers. Newspapers provided steady work and, when they were successful, brought their publishers a degree of financial stability and public recognition.[37] In fact, the practice of subscription book publishing had borrowed its methodology from newspaper publishing: subscribers were solicited and expected to pay on a regular basis.[38] Printing advertisements, of course, was also a significant way to offset the costs of newspaper publishing. In addition, there were other ways to decrease risk, the simplest of which involved altering the numbers of copies printed to match the number of subscribers; if subscriptions declined, it was not necessary to continue to print larger numbers. In this way, the printer could avoid the common book publishing problem of overstock remainders. The popularity of English newspapers was matched in the colonies, and as the eighteenth century progressed, newspapers took on increasing importance as the ubiquitous and locally produced reading matter for colonial Americans.[39] Between 1719, when the first newspaper was published in Phildelphia, and the 1760s, practically every successful Philadelphia printer, at one time or another, printed a newspaper.

Newspapers also served to increase name recognition for printers and their printing shops. Advertising in their own papers not only helped to finance the newspapers, but also promoted the sale of books and other goods they plied from their shops. Keimer, Franklin's first employer and later competitor, made sure that the readers of his *Pennsylvania Gazette* knew they could simply apply to the office of the newspaper to acquire "choice melasses, very cheap," as well as "choice Nutgalls, Fine Gum Arabick," "Ruggs, Blankets, [and] Broadcloaths" recently imported from Ireland.[40] He also took the enterprising, if logical, step of acting as a consignee of goods sold through classified ads in his paper. He offered to "faithfully [sell goods] with exact Justice, unwearied Diligence, and profound Secrecy." In the sellers' favor was the fact that the goods would be advertised in the "Gazette, Two Hundred and Fifty of which are printed every week."[41] The colophon of Franklin's newspaper read: "Printed by B. FRANKLIN, POSTMASTER, at the New Printing-Office near the Market. Where Advertisements are taken in, and Book-Binding is done reasonably, in the best manner."[42] In short, the publishers of newspapers used them to promote their businesses, to generate money through advertisements, and to establish themselves as central figures in colonial commercial life. Publishing newspapers became an imperative for printers of any ambition; in fact, once a competitor began to produce a newspaper, it was practically impossible for others not to follow suit. James Green has argued that competition among printers, both in job printing and in newspaper publishing, was a prerequisite for the development of publishing as an entrepreneurial activity in the colonial period. In Philadelphia, Franklin's arrival on the scene spurred Bradford and Keimer to new levels of innovation. Franklin's lively, well-written newspaper prompted Bradford to look for more interesting news for his own publication. Ultimately, Franklin proved the most innovative and competitive, driving Keimer out of business and significantly reducing Bradford's market share.[43]

While most colonial newspaper printers sought some level of public recognition through their papers, many were wary of drawing the wrong sort of attention. They feared alienating patrons and customers. In an important study of colonial printers, Stephen Botein argued that they were "meer mechanics," attempting to remain neutral and inoffensive in order not to jeopardize their businesses.[44] Economic exigencies drove printers' decisions about the content of their own publications. According to Botein, the proprietorship of newspapers allowed American printers to "take pride in the intellectual dimensions of their craft," but, ultimately, a printer's success in the colonies required "neutrality" and a comfortable relationship with governmental authority. Such neutrality would ensure contracts for printing paper money, laws, and other official work.[45]

Franklin was acutely aware of this delicate relationship between printer, patrons, and politics, to the point where he could claim that his newspaper could not guarantee freedom of expression to contributors who would have his paper become overtly political. He later explained this position in his *Autobiography*:

In the Conduct of my Newspaper I carefully excluded all Libelling and Personal Abuse, which is of late Years become so disgraceful to our country. Whenever I was solicited to insert any thing of that kind, and the Writers pleaded as they generally did, the Liberty of the Press, and that a Newspaper was like a Stage Coach in which any one who would pay had a right to a Place, my Answer was, that I would print the Piece separately [in pamphlet form] if desired, and the Author might have as many Copies as he pleased to distribute himself.[46]

In Franklin's mind, "liberty of the press" as understood by some had at least the potential to deny printers their daily bread. Rather than granting access to the newspaper, which carried no one's name but his own, he offered to political commentators the anonymity, safety, and liberty of the *real* press, the "stagecoach" with platen and frisket. Franklin obviously saw nothing wrong with being a printer and being political; however, it is worth pointing out that he had largely retired from the printing business before his official political career got underway.[47]

In no small part because of Franklin's aversion to political fighting in the newspaper press, Philadelphia newspapers may have been less politically charged than their counterparts in New York and Boston, but the political press was not dormant in the Quaker city, as Franklin's "stagecoach" statement suggests. Fiery pamphlet wars broke out over the Logan-Lloyd power struggle as well as other disputes in the early years of the eighteenth century.[48] Political pamphlets, as Franklin pointed out, offered greater anonymity for author and printer alike. And the printers of pamphlets, if they were known, were not so readily blamed for offensive content as the publishers of newspapers. This was largely because of the prevailing view that to print was to perform a job for another; to publish was to take on risk and responsibility. In essence, publishing a newspaper made a printer an editor and entrepreneur, and publishing a political newspaper committed the publisher to the opinions expressed therein.

Historians have seen the development of a political press in the first half of the century as a prelude to the flood of political publishing during the Revolutionary struggle.[49] The steady rise in numbers of newspapers published in the colonies, and their increasingly political nature in the second half of the eighteenth century, indicate that printers were beginning to see their role in society as more important than simply that of craftsman.[50] Largely through their newspapers, printers became increasingly public figures, and this affected how they perceived themselves and their trade, as well as the kinds of publishing decisions they made. They were increasingly willing to take on the role of publisher in both a financial and social sense. Pauline Maier has argued that the politicization of printers, as seen in their memberships in the Sons of Liberty, made their newspapers the "prime vehicle of uniting the population."[51] The Revolution and the partisan divisions among colonial printers, according to Botein, "reshaped the self-imagery, or 'occupational ideology,' of the printing trade," turning printers into individuals who were conscious of the role they played in forming political discourse.[52]

Throughout the Revolution, and in the 1780s and 1790s, this relationship between printers and politics became even more complicated. As Pennsylvanians clashed over the nature of the commonwealth's constitution, and as struggles for power and party dominance gripped the new state, the recognition that there was room for conflicting views in political publishing began to sink in. Staying neutral or choosing sides were no longer primary issues. Instead, there was a shift toward the ways printers of newspapers handled their roles as political "speakers." In the 1780s and 1790s, many of the printers who published overtly political newspapers became political figures themselves as they immersed themselves in the heady atmosphere of political intrigue. Readers were hungry for political commentary and debate, and politicians were eager to have their views publicized and to gain as much control of the press as possible. For printers this meant an abundance of opportunities for starting up newspapers, gaining favor in influential circles, and operating within the merchants' and gentlemen's world of credit, speculation, and politics.

2

Politics, Patronage, and Publishing
in the 1790s

As WE HAVE SEEN, colonial printers in Philadelphia engaged in a complex of activities including job printing, bookselling, and occasional book publishing. For the most prominent members of the trade, printing a newspaper was the mainstay of their businesses, providing steady work and income and a venue for advertisements. This combination of activities remained largely unchanged from the time when Franklin began to compete with Bradford and Keimer through the 1780s. In the 1790s the trade began to experience an increased division of labor and diversification, and the traditional roles of the colonial printer were no longer necessarily embodied in the same person. Two categories emerged: those who printed newspapers and those who did not. For those who did, the newspapers dominated their time and energies. Most of the major newspapers of the 1790s appeared daily or triweekly, leaving little time for their printers to engage in other print-trade activities. The specialization can be partly attributed to growth and increased competition in the trade. Clearly, not all printers could viably publish newspapers, as even in times of great political foment there were only so many newspapers the market could bear. It is important to note, however, that these categories remained fairly fluid; at least some of the time, or in succession, most individuals engaged in more than one type of printing-related activity.

Political developments also led to increased specialization. It is well-documented that the newspaper press grew increasingly political in the 1790s and that incipient party politics and the growing importance of public opinion played enormous roles in this transformation.[1] This had profound effects on the individuals who supplied Philadelphia with its daily printed matter. Printers who used their presses *and* editorial pens became, in the process, specialized political publishers and editors who acted as hired guns for party interests. This chapter examines some of the connections between politics and publishing in the 1790s and looks more closely at the role of political patronage and the business decisions that led to the development of specialization within the trade.

American newspaper publishing underwent dramatic growth in the 1790s. There were fewer than one hundred papers in 1790 and more than 230 by 1800. In Philadelphia the number of newspapers rose from nineteen published during the 1780s, to forty-two in the 1790s, an increase of 120 percent.[2] Most papers survived only short periods of time — sometimes producing only a single issue. But the number of attempts is nonetheless impressive. Not all newspapers were politically oriented, but those that were served as central forums for political debate. The papers were political not merely because of their publishers' positions, but because the politicians of the period directly supplied them with their news copy.

The mode of political publishing described in the previous chapter and the prestige accorded to newspaper publishers continued and gained in intensity in the 1790s. Newspaper publishers often launched themselves into the thick of political controversies. Even as they occasionally avowed, in the longstanding tradition, that their papers were open to all parties, they were aware that their partisanship attracted readers. In addition, and perhaps more importantly, their partisanship was expected by their political patrons. This is not to suggest that political activism in the press was without its risks. Printers knew in the 1790s what they had known throughout the colonial period: political partisanship drew both positive and negative attention, affecting patronage, credit, and the state of their finances. Yet the political environment had changed since the colonial and Revolutionary periods. Political factions — soon to be identified as parties — were gathering momentum in the Federalist era, with opposing views on economic development, international affairs, and domestic politics. It was becoming increasingly clear that contesting sides could effectively use the press to try to achieve ascendancy. The recognition that opposition, as well as administration views, had an important role to play in the press was a source of inspiration for printers and politicians alike. This was especially the case as the Republican party, under Jefferson's leadership, began to take shape during Washington's second term and throughout Adams's presidency.

The rise of political parties both gave life to and was sustained by the rapid establishment of politically charged newspapers in Philadelphia.[3] William Cobbett, John Fenno, Philip Freneau, Andrew Brown, Benjamin Franklin Bache, and William Duane were the main figures in political publishing in the 1790s, and their careers are relatively well known. Cobbett was the young Englishman who, shortly after arriving in America in 1792, took on the persona of Peter Porcupine, "a prickly defender of all things British, and a powerful opponent of any form of radicalism."[4] Cobbett's pamphlets and his newspaper, *Porcupine's Gazette*, were the vehicles for his antirepublican rhetoric, and thus his role in the political press of the decade is important. However, Cobbett was not formally associated with the Federalist party, and his monarchist opinions were generally more extreme than most of the Federalists' positions. The other major political printers had closer party connections. In New York in the 1780s, John Fenno made a name for himself as an effective writer, and in 1789, when he proposed to publish a newspaper that would represent the Constitution and Washington's administration in a favorable light, the Federalists were quick to lend their support. Fenno moved his paper to Philadelphia in 1791 to be near the newly relocated seat of government. Alexander Hamilton was a frequent contributor to his *Gazette of the United States*. In the two years during which Fenno's paper circulated, his main foe was Philip Freneau, the poet and editor of the *National Gazette*. Freneau started his paper as an antidote to Fenno's; accordingly, he was sponsored by Jefferson, who had appointed him translating clerk of the Department of State in 1791 as a way of providing him with a steady income while he published the paper.

Several other newspapers were backed and manipulated by Jefferson. While the government was still in New York, Jefferson made Fenno the publisher of the federal laws in return for the editor's agreement to publish news from a Dutch paper whose republican bent Jefferson trusted. With this, Jefferson hoped to keep Fenno's paper balanced. Yet the *Gazette of the United States* became more Federalist than ever, and when Fenno moved to Philadelphia, Jefferson sought out another printer to whom he could grant the publication of the laws. Benjamin Franklin Bache and his republican newspaper, the Philadelphia *General Advertiser* (later named the *Aurora*), were already securely in Jefferson's camp, so Jefferson offered the laws to Andrew Brown, publisher of the *Federal Gazette* and an editor well worth having on the Republican side.[5]

Surviving records and excellent scholarly work on Bache's short career provide a picture of a printer turned political publisher and editor who, acting as a spokesman for the newly forming Republican party, had little time for other printing-related activities. Bache had been taught much about his craft by his grandfather, Benjamin Franklin, and had also learned from the aged printer and statesman the virtues of impartial reporting. To this end, Bache promised that his new newspaper, the *General Advertiser*, would maintain "the strictest impartiality . . . in the publication of pieces offered," and that the paper would be "open, for the discussion of political, or any other interesting subjects, to such as deliver their sentiments with temper and decency, and whose motive appears to be, *the public good*."[6]

There were those who either doubted the sincerity of Bache's intentions to publish an impartial paper or who knew that he would quickly cave in to polemics. Writing from New York, the powerful and politically savvy United States senator Robert Morris warned Bache: "Some of your friends here are rather sorry for your intention of printing a News Paper. There are already too many of them published in Philadelphia, and in these days of Scurrility it is difficult for a Press of such Reputation as you would choose yours to be, to maintain the Character of Freedom & Impartiality, connected with purity."[7] Morris's advice fell on deaf ears. By 1798, the year of Bache's untimely death from the yellow fever, he had become so absorbed in republican politics that his newspaper was the prime organ for Jeffersonian republicanism.

Bache's increasingly personal involvement in politics, beginning with his fervent attack on Jay's Treaty with the British, created problems for his printing and newspaper business. Instead of simply capitalizing on the news of the treaty, as Mathew Carey did when he rushed the document into print (albeit with a negative slant), Bache felt compelled to campaign against it. The treaty's terms seemed to many to subvert America's independence, doing little to protect American trade or expansion. The controversy surrounding the treaty did much to stir up republican, anti-British sentiment and to cement opposition to Washington's administration. Bache published a summary of the treaty's points, followed by excerpts of earlier debates in Senate, all of which cast the treaty in an unfavorable light. He took his publication to New York, Boston, and Providence to sell.[8] By the time he reached New York, his first stop, he realized that he would be unable to make "a rapid sale [as] two of the morning papers have published [the Treaty]."[9] He gave up on the stated purpose of his trip and instead threw himself energetically into the business of attending town meetings and polling fellow citizens on the treaty and on the government in general. Carey noted later that Bache's paper had been successful at the outset and that its publisher had been "popular on account of his amiable manners and his descent from Dr. Franklin," but the *Aurora*'s stepped-up attacks not only on Federalist policies but on Washington himself "blasted Bache's popularity, and almost ruined the paper. Subscribers withdrew in crowds — and the advertising custom sank to insignificance."[10]

As much as Bache tried to follow in his grandfather's footsteps, and as much as he admired and even espoused Franklin's principles, he did not have Franklin's keen ability to see when business and politics did not mix *profitably*. And times had changed: The newspaper business in the 1790s was competitive and cutthroat; although Benjamin Franklin had been well-acquainted with competition and how to deal with it, his brand of gentlemanly journalism would have seemed out of place during his grandson's time at the editor's desk. Indeed, Franklin had been concerned about the unrestrained direction the press seemed to be taking in the late 1780s, shortly before his death at the beginning of the new decade.[11] Still, from the beginning of his short career, Bache worried that perhaps he was not cut out to be a businessman at all. He fretted that he was not suitably trained in the ways of business (although he was certainly trained in the ways of printing and typefounding), that he was too young and inexperienced, that his competition was far more experienced, and that he was not as "steady" and industrious as his great mentor had been. He attempted, in touching imitation of his grandfather, to set down "A Notebook of Resolutions and plan for self-improvement," in which he noted "A Difference in our Sentiments [which] will occasion some slight Deviation from [Franklin's] Plan."[12] But Bache was not Franklin; the young man spent enormous energy daydreaming about and courting Margaret Hartman Markoe, as well as convincing his father that as soon as he could marry her and become "settled in life," he would have "more weight to promote [my business]."[13] But marriage did little to cool his political urges.

One indicator that Bache was functioning outside normal trade practices is the way he dealt with the prominent London bookseller, Charles Debrett. Instead of the usual practice of ordering books on credit or enclosing a bill of exchange for the books desired, he sent along five hundred copies of his own publication on the treaty and admitted that,

It is so uncommon to send books from this side of the water where labour is dear to yours where it is cheaper, that I am at a loss to say at what price the work should be sold in London. It sells here in blue boards at 2 dolls and a half and the two volumes I pay 8/100 of a doll a copy for the folding, collating and pressing. From these data I leave it to you to fix the price, or rather fix it from the sight of the volume and the nature of its contents.[14]

It may well have been that Bache's republican tracts were welcome and well-received in London, but what is striking about this episode is Bache's desire to disseminate the pamphlets, no matter what the arrangement might bring in payment or response. Bache then asked Debrett to pay for the unsolicited books by settling some debts for him in England. Once Debrett had done so, he could send Bache "the residue, or the whole if you cannot possibly advance any Money," in books of a "particular description."

Of a particular description, I say, because I am not absolutely in the book selling line. I publish a newspaper *and have connected with it* pamphlets and books of a political cast. Any thing of merit in the line of political novelty or a republican cast will be most acceptable.[15]

With this, Bache clearly defined himself as someone other than a traditional printer who sold books and published a newspaper. The newspaper, and its role as a party organ, was his primary concern and occupation. The books he sold were only of a certain type, a kind of specialization that few other bookselling-printers engaged in. Other booksellers interested in politics, like Mathew Carey and Thomas Dobson, did not limit their shops' assortment to suit their politics, or even to politics in general. It made bad business sense to do so. Printers who sold books had to be willing to *sell* political treatises of all stripes, even if they were only willing to *publish* narrowly. Publishing could be an act of political self-definition; selling far less so.

Even if Bache were to offer a more balanced assortment of political writings for sale, he was still taking a risk by selling strictly political works. Some booksellers were unwilling to take the chance of offending customers, and avoiding controversial pamphlets was one way to limit risk. For example, when Robert Bailey, a young Philadelphia printer, set about distributing "A Pill for Porcupine," an anonymous pamphlet (attributed to Mathew Carey's younger brother, James) attacking Cobbett (Porcupine), Bailey sent it off to exchange with other booksellers throughout the country.[16] Most accepted it and included it in their inventories. One bookseller who would not sell it was William Spotswood, who had just moved to Boston from Philadelphia. Spotswood explained that he would have been happy to stock it, but worried that as a newcomer to Federalist New England it might be too risky to vend a piece that "borders too much on personalities." Still, Spotswood immediately found another bookseller to take the pamphlets and added his private and, quite vehement, support for "The Pill":

I could wish it had been such a Pill or even a Bolus that I might have assisted in administering to the author of Peter Porcupine—no matter how severe, whether emetic, diuretic, or cathartic, as I would have cheerfully acceded in working him at all points, such is my opinion of that author and his writings.[17]

Spotswood's belief that his business would suffer by the sale of one satirical political tract underscores the precariousness of reputation under which purveyors of print labored. Spotswood's business sense stayed his enthusiasm for Porcupine's medicine, and customers would have to search other Boston bookstores for the piece.

Despite Bache's risky strategy, he was not working without a net. He had prominent supporters in Thomas Jefferson, Thomas Paine, James Monroe, and Robert Morris. Yet even these connections did little for him financially. In fact, they may well have led him further to subordinate his business concerns to ideological ones. Jefferson hoped to turn Bache's paper into a political organ that would devote itself solely to republican political principles, leaving no room even for the paper's lifeblood. "The advertisements [in the country edition]," he wrote Bache, "[are] perfectly useless there, occupying one half the paper, [and] render the transportation too embarrassing." Jefferson wondered somewhat impractically whether the advertisements "could be thrown into the last half sheet (say pages 3 & 4) which might be torn off or omitted for distant customers." Jefferson's desire to see "a purely republican vehicle of news established between the seat of government & all its parts," meant that the *Aurora* had to rely on republican rather than commercial patronage.[18] A comparison of the *Aurora* with several other Philadelphia newspapers of the time shows that in Bache's paper the ads became sparse and small while in other papers they grew more elaborate and ever more numerous. Bache took Jefferson's suggestion to create a tear-off sheet of advertisements, but before long his paper was in dire economic straits.[19] In fact, Jefferson's political patronage had never extended to direct financial support of the paper; Jefferson knew that Bache's paper could be counted upon to uphold republican views.

Another political patron who failed to understand the fiscal realities of the printing trade was Thomas Paine, who made it clear to Bache that the most important aspect of his writings was their dissemination, not their profitability. Writing from Paris in 1795, Paine told Bache that he wished to hold the copyright for the publication of the second half of his *Age of Reason* not because he hoped for greater monetary return but because he wanted greater control and a richer *political* harvest.[20] He was concerned that "unauthorized" editions had changed the meaning of his original text and that, in any case, they were all too expensive. The first part, he wrote, suffered from frequent reprinting "in the several states, [in which] I am made to say what I never wrote . . . and besides this, it has been sold higher than I expected or intended." Paine stipulated that the second part should sell "no higher than a third of a dollar by the single copy," so that more people could afford to buy it.[21] Bache's profits, however, would be cut into by this scheme, as he was Paine's agent for marketing and distributing the work.

James Monroe was more sensitive to the young publisher's financial needs when he commissioned him to publish and sell his narrative of his mission to France.[22] Monroe wished Bache to take on the risk (and copyright) of the publication, but offered to provide him with a loan to begin the project. Still, he wanted to be repaid soon, as "I want money much, having to pay out the freight on my furniture from France soon and being in consequence of a bad note, obliged to borrow it." Monroe wished that Bache would "be amply compensated for [his] trouble, worries &c.," but added that "after the whole edition is sold and you amply repaid, that the copy right might be given up to the world, and that the price be moderate."[23]

The limitations of political patronage were felt not only by political newspaper publishers like Bache. If Bache's example shows that patrons did not always have their printer's best interests in mind, it remains that he could have called on his supporters for help if he were about to fail. With the exception of Paine, the republicans with whom he associated could have, if necessary, kept him afloat by extending him credit. Yet the patronage of someone who, unlike Jefferson, was on the decline in political and public favor could bring about financial ruin to an unwary publisher. In other words, it little mattered if one published a newspaper or a political work of another kind; what mattered was choosing the right patron. Edmund Hogan, a publisher of city directories in Philadelphia, had as a patron John Nicholson, the comptroller general of Pennsylvania and a well-known land speculator. Nicholson's career and financial dealings have been studied from many angles, but the network of printers who became entangled with this politician-financier suggests that one man whose fortunes rose and fell could easily affect the workings of an entire trade that was peculiarly dependent on political gifts. Hogan failed to see the writing on the wall, and when in 1793 Nicholson appeared before the state Senate, accused of financial wrongdoing, he stood fast by his "personal" publisher, Hogan, and requested that he publish the trial proceedings. Hogan duly attended the trial, issued press releases favorable to the defense, and gathered the material necessary to publish a complete account of the proceedings, convinced that the comptroller would be exonerated. Nicholson was forced from office, however, and Hogan suffered the consequences. "When

I undertook to publish your trial," he complained to Nicholson, "you promised to provide for me, [but] I have created more enemies by that publication, than I could have foreseen. Many of the books are on hand and many are delivered to subscribers who will not pay."[24] In this case, two business decisions came back to haunt Hogan: betting on the wrong patron and publishing work that, because of the outcome of the case, was found to be offensive even to those subscribers already obligated to buy it.

Nicholson's downfall affected a number of other members of the printing trade as well. He had underwritten the bilingual paper published by Pierre Egron, an entrepreneurial Frenchman who emigrated from Santo Domingo, and had hoped to establish a mercantile sheet that would have an international economic and political scope as its selling points.[25] As a man of business, Nicholson was willing to support the paper for the promises Egron made him of the most up-to-date international import and export information. Egron engaged a young printer, William W. Woodward, to print the paper, and when Nicholson fell from grace, it was Woodward who was the most injured. He tried to recover the money for the ongoing printing job, but Egron merely referred him to his generous patron. Woodward then turned to Nicholson directly and pleaded with him to make good on the work he had done. The printer told Nicholson that he was responsible for feeding and clothing a household of ten, and added that "I am but young in business, and should I fail in my bank engagements it may be of great detriment to me in the future day."[26] In this case, Nicholson did settle his debts, albeit gradually, so that Woodward ended up avoiding the credit catastrophe he expected.

Francis Bailey, a prominent Philadelphia printer, became involved with Nicholson perhaps even more deeply than had Egron or Hogan. Bailey requested Nicholson to pull strings in order to obtain the contract for printing an edition of the laws of the United States in 1790: "Your kind letter in my favour to Mr. Morris, led him frankly to offer me every service in his power, and I find his influence great. My application to Congress, has been referred to Mr. Hamilton, and before him it now lies, much depends on his report."[27] On the basis of Nicholson's promises and recommendations, Bailey took on numerous printing jobs on Nicholson's account, yet after Nicholson's departure from office, Bailey's chances of being paid grew dim. Nicholson had by this time entered into his infamous land speculation partnership with Robert Morris, but he kept Bailey hanging on, despite the latter's claims that "it is out of my power either to pay my journeymen, who are poor, my paper maker who is now at a stand or to go on with business without your assistance."[28] Finally, in the winter of 1799, when Nicholson entered debtors' prison, Bailey's son, Robert, helped him further by printing and distributing for him a small, short-lived newspaper called *The Supporter or Daily Repast*. It was Nicholson's last-ditch effort to raise some money, even as he sat in jail, but in June of 1800, the young Bailey wrote agitatedly to the prisoner: "I hold you as firmly bound for last week's work as for any hitherto published . . . and a type shall never be lifted in this office on the paper, unless paid & for what is already done, or secured in the payment of it."[29]

Nicholson's newspaper brought him into contact with other printers, such as Thomas Dobson, Robert Aitken, Abraham Small, and John Thompson. Dobson wisely eschewed close involvement with the prisoner turned publisher. After placing one ad, he informed Nicholson that he would no longer need his services, noting that "the other papers circulate most among my customers." He also counseled the abandonment of the project: "I was pleased to hear that you was [*sic*] going to drop the paper, as I thought you must sink money by it. If it is continued you will please to discontinue mine merely because it is of no use to me."[30] Despite Bailey's waning sympathy and Dobson's practicality, William Woodward, who by 1800 had developed a sizable printing and bookselling establishment, submitted several book advertisements to Nicholson's paper, noting that "I shall be happy to do every thing in my power for one for whom I entertain the highest esteem."[31] It seems Woodward had not forgotten that Nicholson had saved him from disaster — even if the disaster was Nicholson's own doing — some five years earlier.

With the increasing politicization of printers in the 1790s, the whole meaning of political patronage for the press changed. The kind of patronage that political publishers sought and were given was different from that in Benjamin Franklin's time, when lobbying the government for printing contracts reaped tangible rewards. As Franklin pointed out, seeking patronage was a perfectly reasonable and wise business strategy, but in the new world of national party politics, the nature of political power was nebulous and often based on promises of future rewards if a person or party were helped into office. Patronage was dispensed promiscuously, and the number of individuals with real power, who could deliver what they promised was small. Therefore, the politicization of print in this new political environment made seeking patronage a much riskier strategy than before the rise of political parties.

Nevertheless, seeking patronage was something most printers felt compelled to do. The difference lay in what type of patronage they sought, and while printing for individual patrons, or relying on party support brought risks as well as rewards, government printing contracts still provided safety nets and prestige for printers, much as they had done in the colonial period. Government contracts were more than just promises of support: they meant real income. If party patronage was promissory, like credit, government printing was more like cash.

Some of the political printers did obtain practical patronage. When John Fenno's creditors pressed him in 1793, Hamilton raised a subscription of two thousand dollars to help bail him out. Jefferson performed a similar deed for William Duane when he was floundering in debt in 1811. Jefferson also granted the paid translating post to Freneau, although it did not go far in covering the costs of his newspaper. But the most practical patronage came directly from government printing jobs. When the nation's capital moved from New York City to Philadelphia in 1790, Philadelphia printers who bid successfully for government printing received a windfall of jobs. In 1789, six New York printers shared the United States printing jobs, printing among them over twenty-six official publications, including acts of Congress, bills passed, speeches, the *Congressional Register*, *Journals of the House of Representatives*, and a variety of broadsides and proclamations. In 1791, after the capital's move to Philadelphia, eight Philadelphia printers (including Francis Childs and John Swaine of New York, who retained the majority of the U.S. printing and opened shop in Philadelphia), shared seventy-three U.S. printing jobs. In 1795, U.S. government printing jobs in Philadelphia numbered 131.[32]

Philadelphia printers like Francis Bailey, John Bioren, Mathew Carey, Benjamin Franklin Bache, and others hoped to gain from their city's new central role, as can be seen from their lobbying attempts. The removal of the capital to Philadelphia pitted printers against each other as they scrambled for patronage. It also meant that those in political power needed to work on behalf of printers who were their friends and constituents, or who were sympathetic to their party's cause. Robert Morris surreptitiously slipped information to Bache about who might be appointed as official printers to Congress once the move took place. Morris, the powerful financier and U.S. senator from Pennsylvania, noted that while he wished he could promote Bache's interest, it would be difficult because "early as you think your application[,] others have been before you." One of the "others" was the Federalist John Fenno who, according to Morris's intelligence, "set up his press with the avowed intention of being always at the Seat of Government. Consequently he will remove to Philadelphia with Congress and claim the Continuance of that employ which he has already obtained." Still, Morris felt that, armed with this information, Bache could press his case and that "the removal of Congress gives every one in Philadelphia a justifiable pretension on which to ground such an application."[33] As we have seen, Bache did not end up with an official appointment; Morris had little of real value to offer.

The lobbying did not end with the government's move to Philadelphia. Printers remained in stiff competition for large government jobs and in their petitions often advised the governing bodies that editions of laws and other government publications ought to be large enough so that every politician would have a copy. Francis Bailey, who had moved to Lancaster, Pennsylvania, at the turn of the century, acted as an agent for Mathew Carey and John Bioren, who sought the Pennsylvania state government contract to publish an edition of the laws of Pennsylvania. He informed Carey of the daily progress of his petition as he saw it through the State House of Representatives, remarking at the end that Carey almost lost out to "that vagabond [George] Helmbold who offered to print for seven Dollars a sett." Bailey's reward for securing the contract was the printing job itself, which Carey, acting as publisher, gave to him to execute at his printing shop in Lancaster.[34]

The decade of the 1790s was a transitional period for the printing trade in Philadelphia. The nation's capital moved from Philadelphia to Washington, D.C., in 1800, thus relocating the site of national political attention. With this shift, members of the printing trade who hoped to continue to gain government patronage either left Philadelphia for Washington or worked harder to gain state-level patronage. William Duane moved to the new capital to stay close to Jefferson's administration. He had been given to expect a large share of printing and stationery contracts from the government, but this prospect fell through. Nevertheless, Jefferson stuck by Duane, appointing him lieutenant-colonel of rifles in 1808 and helping him out of debt in 1811. Mathew Carey not only lobbied for state publishing business, he also vigorously sought an appointment to the board of directors of the Bank of Pennsylvania, something he finally achieved in 1802.

The shift in power and its focal point dispersed and decentralized political newspaper publishing, leaving Philadelphia's press in a position no different than that of any other major urban center. This dispersal was also certainly due to the remarkably low survival rate of the publishers of Philadelphia's most visible political newspapers of the 1790s. Fenno's paper failed

to bring in enough money, and he faced bankruptcy in 1793. He was forced
to suspend the paper, although his main patron, Alexander Hamilton, took
up a subscription to raise money for the financially pressed editor. Fenno
succumbed to the yellow fever in 1798, and his son, John Ward Fenno,
whom Carey later referred to as a "rash, thoughtless, and imprudent young
man," ran his father's paper until 1800, when he sold it.[35] Bache was also
carried off by the yellow fever; his paper was continued by his widow and
William Duane, and, later, by Duane's son William J. Duane. The *Aurora*
was the only significant paper of the 1790s to continue its life as an actively
partisan paper. Andrew Brown was killed in a fire in 1797; his son published
the *Federal Gazette* for only about a year after his father's death. Freneau's
paper fell onto hard economic times in 1793 and was suspended. When Jefferson resigned as Secretary of State at the end of that year, his protégé had
to give up his position as translator as well. He edited several other papers
in New Jersey and New York for the next few years before retiring from
journalism altogether. Cobbett returned to England in 1800.

Yet there is evidence that changes in attitude as well as personnel had
occurred. When Duane took over the *Aurora* upon Bache's death and mar-
ried Bache's widow, he managed to turn the paper's fortunes around. Although Duane continued to run the paper as a Republican organ, his
previous newspaper experience in England and India had left him better
trained as a writer and a more careful editor than his predecessor.[36] Duane
was a stricter and more attentive business manager, too, and he was somewhat more guarded in his political expression. Despite his high profile during what he and other Republicans called Adams's "reign of terror,"—he
was imprisoned under both the Alien and Sedition Acts—he emerged at
the end of the decade believing that political publishers needed to turn
down the volume of their rhetoric.[37] By 1802, he thought it wise for Republican newspapers to pursue a "calm and forbearing course," as it was not
as though the "Blues of Macpherson were once more breaking our windows."[38] It was perhaps easy for Duane at this stage in his career to be
circumspect. Jefferson—his president—was in office and Duane, never one
to miss an opportunity, had moved to the nation's new capital to seek government patronage there. Nevertheless, his comparison of the early years of
the new century to the days of intimidation under the previous administration is instructive. His advice to Republican newspapers was a form of political strategy, but his advice to printers who published books followed
similar lines. Duane was aware that politics and book publishing did not
necessarily mix. He advised a bookseller in Boston to steer clear of "mere"

politics in a proposed geography text. "I do not mean," he added, "thereby the desertion of truth or correct principles such as were laid down by Locke and Rousseau. But such as are merely of a party nature."[39]

Mathew Carey's career shows that he, like Duane, went through stages of political activism both in and out of print, only to redirect his energies toward sustaining a viable publishing business.[40] Carey's original intentions were to publish a political newspaper, but his *Pennsylvania Herald*, begun in 1785, served up unwelcome competition and unpalatable politics to Eleazer Oswald, the publisher of the *Independent Gazetteer*. Oswald and Carey tangled over state politics and immigration issues — Oswald was a nativist and Carey believed the Test Acts of Pennsylvania's constitution to be an infraction against civil government and rights — but their antipathy quickly grew personal. The result was a duel in 1786 in which Carey was shot in the leg. In 1787 Carey abandoned the newspaper press and began publishing the *American Museum*, a magazine that supported ratification of the United States Constitution. Gradually, however, his sympathies became more closely linked with the ideals of the newly forming Republican party, and his alliances with prominent Republicans, as well as difficulties with disseminating the magazine, led to its demise in 1792. It was not until he was baited by William Cobbett in 1798 that he left his "retirement" from politics to take Cobbett on in a pamphlet war. When Carey first became aware that he and his political opposite and bookselling competitor might duel with their pens, Carey worried about the consequences, fearing "the great influence [Cobbett] had on public opinion — and the danger of his injuring me in my business and in my standing in society."[41] Yet when Cobbett published a scathing pamphlet in 1798 titled *Detection of a Conspiracy formed by the United Irishmen, with the evident intention of aiding the tyrants of France in subverting the Government of the United States*, in which he named Carey as one of many subversives, Carey answered with his *A Plumb Pudding for . . . Peter Porcupine* (1799).[42] Thus, according to Carey, Cobbett's attacks on him in print dragged him into the fray. However it started, there is no doubt that Carey took much glee in sparring with his "formidable antagonist," and with *Plumb Pudding* Carey "handled him with great severity in his own abusive style."[43]

Carey's war with Cobbett, unlike his scrape with Oswald a decade earlier, ended in triumph for Carey, partly because his *Plumb Pudding* really was damaging to Cobbett and partly because of a successful libel suit brought against Cobbett by Benjamin Rush.[44] Both of these blows against Cobbett contributed to his departure for England in 1800. As political as

Carey was, his two bad experiences left him eager to remain above party politics and to keep his political activities separate from his business. He continued the search for political patronage, but through practical routes, not through party politics, thus he lobbied for the job of publishing the state laws and for the post at the Bank of Pennsylvania. In the end, the heated 1810–1811 debate over the rechartering of the Bank of the United States left Carey a man without a party, as he found himself running counter to the Republican party's anti-bank position.[45]

Party politics had played a major role in the professional lives and development of Philadelphia's political publishers in the 1790s, leading, ultimately, to a distinction between them and other printers. Meanwhile, other printers during that decade concentrated their energies on areas of the printing trade that had little or nothing to do with politics and newspapers. And some, like Carey, moved in and out of the realm of political publishing. The political publishers are the most readily recognizable figures in the printing trade during the Federalist years, but they were pursuing the most visible course. While they battled furiously on behalf of party interests, William Woodward and Thomas Dobson became major publishers of books; Francis Bailey combined printing and book publishing until his death in 1815; John Ormrod also printed and published throughout the 1790s. And within only a few years after the turn of the century, new printer-publishers entered the picture whose names cannot be linked to the political drama of the 1790s at all: John Conrad had been a printer throughout the second half of the 1790s but, with his brothers, stepped up his book publishing ventures after 1800; Patrick Byrne, an Irish printer and bookseller, relocated to Philadelphia around 1800 and became a major bookselling force there; and Abraham Small began as a printer in 1799 and became, in the next twenty years, a significant contributor to Philadelphia publishing. Like the political newspaper publishers, these individuals, throughout the 1790s and the early decades of the new century, began to direct their energies away from the traditional complex of activities associated with printing. But these members of the trade turned their attention to the business of publishing books for the new nation. In the chapter that follows, we shall see how the early national publishers distinguished themselves from job printers, and how their entrepreneurial activities fit into the development of a domestic economy and culture.

3

"Young Adventurers," Master Printers, and "Men of Capital"

THE STRUCTURE OF THE PRINTING TRADE underwent significant changes in the 1790s and the early years of the new century. Along with party politics and economic growth, increasing competition in the trade played an important role in defining these changes. Throughout the decade, printers and booksellers who began to devote large portions of their businesses to publishing produced a flurry of competition among master printers who vied for the job work. Efforts to underbid one another led printers to streamline their shops by taking on more apprentices and limiting the numbers of journeymen who worked for them on a steady basis. The ranks of the journeymen increased as the apprentices completed their contracts, thus adding to the problem of underemployment among journeymen. Journeymen sought to address these problems through the formation of craft associations, but some, recognizing that their chances of reaching master status were slimmer than ever, approached the problem by acting as publishers themselves.[1] As for masters, their attempts at cost-efficiency often left them unprepared for big publishing jobs, as the large pool of journeymen was highly mobile. Understandably, journeymen went where work could be found and this often meant moving from city to city and state to state. All of these changes suggest that the trade was growing increasingly diverse: those who published began to exercise significant control over the trade as they sought the lowest bids for printing their publications; master printers who did little or no publishing emerged as a class of tradesmen who worked increasingly for those who published; and journeymen struggled to become either master printers or publishers, sometimes concluding that the latter occupation, if riskier, could offer better rewards.

At the same time, competition among publishers became fierce. The rush of publishing activity throughout the decade ran ahead of the real market for books, with dramatic increases in the most commonly published genres.

Philadelphia Imprints by Genre, 1781–1800.

Genre	1781–1790	1791–1800	% Change
Devotional	93	114	22.58
Poetry	135	186	37.78
Almanacs	120	182	51.67
Schoolbooks	87	144	65.52
Sermons	56	102	82.14
Broadsides	305	566	85.57
Bibles/psalms	45	87	93.33
Plays	21	72	242.86
Novels	14	62	342.86
Median			82.14

Source: North American Imprints Program Catalogue (NAIP), American Antiquarian Society.

Publishers in Philadelphia, New York, Boston, and Baltimore were even churning out competing editions of the same books. The first U.S. Copyright Law, enacted in 1790, protected only books written by Americans, which before 1800 made up a small proportion of books published in America.[2] Unlike in England, where London remained the undisputed center of the British book trade, there was no one city in America that controlled or monopolized the national trade. This ultimately forced the new publishers of the early republic to form inter-urban trading networks and to cooperate broadly with one another in an effort to create and serve a national market. These new networks, while not always successful or free from difficulties, played a key role in the development of book publishing activity in America, further distancing the entrepreneurs of the trade from the craftsmen. By the end of the first decade of the new century, printers who had achieved some measure of success in publishing saw themselves as divorced from — and in some cases, at odds with — "their" printers. While many publishers of the early nineteenth century carried with them a sort of genealogical and nostalgic zeal for their craft, their actions often spoke otherwise.

The Role of "Traditional" Journeymen

Philadelphia print trade regulations were practically nonexistent in the early republic. While there were relatively few formal rules and regulations governing the American trade, there was also little fluidity within the labor market.[3] Opportunities for journeymen to advance without master patronage were slim, and the pool of journeymen who did not advance to master status grew disproportionately. In addition, master printers increasingly took on apprentices as cheap labor, instead of training them properly in the trade — a practice that clearly heightened the journeymen's anxiety. This was a trend throughout the rest of the nation as well. As Ebenezer T. Andrews, partner with Isaiah Thomas in Worcester, sniffed:

I am almost sick of Journeymen, they are in general so poor workmen. We have got a very good set of lads [apprentices], and I think I shall be able to do all our work without any, or with very few Journeymen — we have 12 lads in the office.[4]

With the increased use of apprentices and unskilled labor, journeymen found themselves in an untenable position: their work was diminishing, and so were their chances of reaching master status. It was increasingly common for American journeymen to work their entire lives without becoming proprietors of their own businesses.[5] The perception of this reality as a new form of hardship must have been great. It may not have been uncommon for English journeymen to have experienced limited upward mobility because of the role of guilds in the English trade, but in the American colonial trade, the move from journeyman to master had been more assured.[6] Now the journeymen were caught in a tangle of wage struggles and job competition.

This lack of job security and advancement led journeymen to move about from one situation to another, rarely staying in one place. In 1790, Carey reported to his partner, James Stewart, on the state of the shop and its workers:

Business goes on pretty well, though Lang has gone to Dobson — Haswell to New York — and Tate has quit in a fit of drunkenness. Davis, who formerly worked at Mr. James's is on the Bible, with an apprentice whom Bailey turned over to us. They can easily execute a half sheet a day. I have engaged one Springer, a decent, quiet, industrious pressman & Brackstone I have been once more obliged to employ. I have taken two apprentices since your departure — both very decent lads . . . we have therefore six apprentices in the house: and if they be possessed of but a moderate portion of honour & honesty, we may on your return execute a vast deal of work with them.[7]

These personnel changes left Carey's shop with three journeymen (Davis, Springer, and the temporarily employed Brackstone) and six apprentices. Clearly, Carey relied heavily on apprentices to perform the lion's share of the shop's work.

The situation had not improved in the early years of the new century. Another master printer, John Bioren, left an extraordinary log recording his impressions of the journeymen he employed which suggests that journeymen were highly mobile, moving about from one situation to another, seeking higher pay and different masters, or even a chance to set up on their own. In the short time between October 1809 and April 1810, Bioren employed seventeen journeymen, each of whom worked an average of only twenty-eight days for the printer. He described individual workers variously as "a whimsical unsteady fellow," "a proud conceited fellow, gone to set up in New York," "a slow workman," "a monstrous hypocrite," "a good workman but a drunkard," "as cunning as his name [Fox] and a hypocrite," and "a gambler and lazy fellow who loves his cards & bottle better than he does his wife & children. Went off without giving notice." In 1810, Bioren went through even greater numbers of journeymen he considered lacking in either industriousness or sobriety.[8] Bioren was not the only master printer to go through large numbers of journeymen, and it is not clear that his personality was the sole cause of the rapid turnover in his shop. One of Philadelphia's busiest nineteenth-century job printers was Lydia R. Bailey, whose payroll accounts show that from 1808 to 1855 she employed 167 men. She inspired loyalty in some, who remained in and out of her employ for twenty or more years, while others set type and pulled the presses in her shop for only short periods of time.[9]

In response to the growing pressures within the trade, the journeymen attempted to organize numerous times to demand higher pay, to set prices for piece work, and to institute stricter rules governing apprentices and their contracts.[10] They also approached their employers directly, as did the journeymen compositors and pressmen working at the *Aurora* office. They addressed their grievances to Margaret Bache, Benjamin Franklin Bache's widow, who still owned the paper in 1799. According to their petition, William Duane, who had taken over the editorship, had informed them that their pay would be reduced to seven dollars per week (most likely from $7.50), "believing that sum to be a sufficient compensation for their labour and support." The aggrieved journeymen appealed to Mrs. Bache to consider "the rights of man . . . the feelings of nature—and [the] dictates of humanity." On a more pragmatic level, they argued that their health was jeopardized by the fact the shop was understaffed—Duane had refused to hire a fourth pressman—and that they often worked after dark (unlike competing newspaper workers who "seldom, if ever, light candle"). In addition, the rising cost of living and their "depressed spirits, and a worn appearance" led them to plead for their former salaries and another worker.[11]

Mrs. Bache responded that she trusted Duane to run the shop as he saw fit. A few days later, however, Duane flew into a rage and fired a worker who had suggested a suitable candidate for the job of fourth pressman. In protest and solidarity, the *Aurora*'s five compositors and remaining two pressmen quit: "We have pledged ourselves to each other, that if a reasonable cause was not assigned, for one of us being discharged, we all would be obliged to quit our employ."[12] Mrs. Bache's next communication to her disgruntled employees was addressed to "the *late* Pressmen & Compositors of the *Aurora*." In it she firmly responded that "the *Aurora* Office is entirely under the direction of Mr. Duane," and that she "cannot interfere in any shape whatever."[13]

The end of the year 1800 saw the formation of the Asylum Company of Journeymen Printers which, two years later, became the Philadelphia Typographical Society. Both organizations called for minimum wages for composition and presswork as well as for more protective duties on imported books. In addition, journeymen who made up these associations limited their ranks to those who had served out the full term specified in their apprenticeship agreements. Ultimately, the goal of the journeymen was to attain a competence from their craft, even if they held little hope of becoming masters: "Indeed, we cherish a hope, that the time is not far distant, when the *employers* and the *employed* will vie with each other, the one *allowing* a competent salary, the other, in *deserving* it."[14] An 1810 list of prices and rules established by a meeting of journeymen printers stipulated that "no pressmen shall teach an apprentice press work without the benefit of his work 13 weeks nor shall he teach an apprentice who is more than 18 years old, and who is bound for less than three years." This effort at organization and exclusivity floundered, as similar attempts by the Typographical Society had. Lydia Bailey watched the journeymen closely in 1810, recorded their ultimata in her memo book, and finally noted with satisfaction that "the Journeymen did not succeed in [their proposed] turnout."[15] The activities and rhetoric of the journeymen's associations suggest that they understood their relative position in the trade to be basically unchangeable, and that they lobbied instead for better conditions within their ranks.

There are a number of reasons the journeymen had difficulties organizing. First, they were transient. Journeymen simply could not afford to stay in one place long enough to establish stable connections with the few craft organizations that were established; however, they did not give up the idea of organizing. Studies have shown that the same names show up on different organization lists in numerous cities and towns. Their position was also weakened by competition in their ranks for journey work and by the increased use of apprentices. William McCulloch, a printer and observer of the trade, related a story about one member of a journeymen's association who, having just come from a meeting at which the journeymen present had "entered into an obligation to each other, to print at such and such prices," offered to print for the bookseller Robert Campbell at far less than the agreed upon prices.[16] This kind of scrambling for steady work undermined their power to organize. Another factor that may have threatened solidarity among their ranks was that a number of them chose to quit journey work and become publishers. By breaking into the world of speculation and finance, they acted not as craftsmen but as entrepreneurs. It is not likely that such ambitious journeymen wished to devote energy to strengthening the position of a class from which they expected to rise.

Journeymen as Publishers

On June 1, 1790, a young Scottish immigrant who had recently arrived in Philadelphia wrote to his parents in Edinburgh, describing the dismal job prospects for an educated young man in America. "In this country," he explained, "[clerks] may be employed for 2 or 3 months in the year and idle the rest . . . in consequence of which, I resolved with the advice of my friends, to go to a trade which is the most . . . secure way of bread." The trade his friends recommended to the eighteen-year-old Robert Simpson was printing, a business which Simpson cheerfully described as "the genteelist and most flourishing in this country."[17] Completely untrained, Simpson contracted with Andrew Brown, the publisher of the *Federal Gazette and Philadelphia Daily Advertiser*, to serve an abbreviated apprenticeship in the printing trade.[18] At the end of his three-year apprenticeship, which was filled with acrimony between his master and him, Simpson worked for a number of master printers in Philadelphia as a journeyman printer. After leaving Brown's shop, Simpson found that he could make six to seven dollars per week at most shops and eight dollars as the overseeing journeyman in John Fenno's newspaper office. He reported that Fenno "is very much of a gentleman, and I am extremely happy."[19] Still, only six months later, he begun expressing doubts about his new employment.[20]

One of Simpson's concerns was competition in the printing trade. Apparently without irony, he pointed to a commonly cited source of extra trade competition: immigration. He wrote to his parents of the huge influxes of immigrant tradesmen who made work harder to get, drove wages down, and, in his estimation, brought about skyrocket inflation.[21] He surmised that "at the close of the [Revolutionary] war, . . . this was really a good country for tradesmen of every description, when there were high wages and provisions cheap; but the knowledge of this has brought tradesmen of every description to this country in such numbers, [and] that time is now gone."[22] If the pressures of inflation and increased competition from other tradesmen were not enough, his fear that he might never be able to reach master status in America *or* in Scotland led him to make alternate plans for his future. He complained that in America, master printers relied too heavily on apprentice work, shutting journeymen out of the system, and that "a vast many [masters] do with nothing but apprentices, there being no rules or regulations to restrain them."[23] Furthermore, while some American printers set up trusted journeymen in other parts of the country, this generally required a long and favorable association with a master printer, something his experiences with Andrew Brown did not provide him. Trade rules and regulations, however, would ironically prevent him from becoming a journeyman or master in Scotland, as his short apprenticeship would not be considered sufficient at home: "I would probably be despised as a person, who not having served an equal term of years, was unworthy of employment."[24]

Had he arrived in Philadelphia a generation earlier, rather than during the formative years of the new republic, he might have more easily continued on to become a master printer after performing journey work for a number of years. Given the circumstances, however, he chose to leap ahead to uncharted territory, leaving behind the familiar if increasingly unsure path of apprentice-to-journeyman-to-master. He believed that publishing might give him enough of an advantage to rise above the swarms of printers competing for jobs. Simpson and a couple of his journeymen friends decided to become publishers.

"[T]hinking the time of youth the best," Simpson, James Key, and J. H. Dobelbower agreed that if they undertook to publish a book, it would advance their ambitions "much better than working journey work, and if it does not, we have at least the consolation that it was an honest endeavour to do for the best."[25] They published an eight-volume book titled *The World Displayed, or A Curious Collection of Voyages and Travels.*[26] While optimistic about the venture, Simpson was aware that his transformation from printer to publisher was "a bold undertaking." He projected that they would spend almost two thousand pounds sterling. The partners published the book by subscription. Indeed, without the option of subscription publishing, these entrepreneurs would have had little chance to see *The World Displayed* into print. The partners advertised their proposed work in the major newspapers, requesting that interested patrons reserve their copies by signing up at any of "the principal booksellers in this city."[27] No payment was required in advance, but payment would be taken when each weekly number appeared. In all, there would be forty-eight parts, consisting of eighty pages each. The subscriber's price for the whole work was a rather hefty twelve dollars, or about three pounds sterling.[28] When a book was sold in parts by subscription, it offered an even greater security to the publishers. Using their list of subscribers, the publishers really only needed to secure enough credit for the first part, and when payments began to come in, they would be applied to the subsequent parts. Further, paper, the most expensive aspect of publishing, could be bought on time, enabling them to spread out the payments to the papermaker.

Once the partners had gathered enough signatures—they vowed not to proceed with fewer than four hundred—they could begin production. Armed with the assurance of their subscribers' signatures, the young entrepreneurs could then obtain the necessary materials and labor for the project. The list of subscribers served as a sort of collateral for the papermakers, engravers, and printer. Simpson, Key, and Dobelbower recognized that buying a press and materials and renting a shop would be prohibitive, so like true publishers, they hired a printer who already had the required equipment. That three journeymen printers would see no utility in buying their own equipment suggests that *The World Displayed* was an investment in the beginning of a publishing career, not a stepping stone to a printing career.

The book proved a success: the publishers obtained 1,463 subscribers and probably printed at least 1,500 copies, all of which were eventually disposed of (some were sold at auction for bids that would have been significantly lower than the original prices). At this rate, the three partners could have seen a total profit of around two thousand pounds, or eight thousand dollars. Encouraged by their success, Simpson and Key published another book, *Carver's Travels*, by subscription in 1796. This work was a logical extension of their first publication, which consisted of travels from around the world, excluding North America. Printed by the same printer and in the same type, the book consisted of Captain Jonathan Carver's travels "through the Interior Parts of North America, for more than five thousand miles," making it the appropriate companion or bookend to their first publication.[29] If *The World Displayed* brought the old world to American readers, *Carver's Travels* added America to that world. The second project also made sense, as the publishers could have easily advertised it and raised subscriptions while they were delivering the numbers of the first book, thus working to reinvest their earnings as they brought them in. *Carver's Travels* was not a major investment when compared with *The World Displayed*; it was one-eighth the size of the first work and was a proven seller, as three other Philadelphia editions appeared and had sold out in the 1780s and in 1792. Viewed together, these publications clearly contributed to building a reputation for the new publishers.

However, as early as January of that year, Simpson began to look for ways to return home. He had tired of America, and his only wish was to convey his earnings safely to his homeland in order to have enough money to buy a farm. He was also concerned about the threat of war with Great Britain and the increasing hostilities between France and England. Feeling he had to justify to his father his retirement from a successful business in America, he observed that the economy of the new nation "has undergone a strange alteration since I last wrote, [with] . . . a scarcity of cash to an alarming degree, business of every kind at a stand with the war, so many American vessels being captured by both French & English, [and] provisions and living of all kinds treble their former prices."[30]

Simpson's trepidation about staying in America was underscored by several realizations about the nature of the early national publishing trade. The only way to really make money in publishing was to sustain a steady level of publishing activity, something that Simpson seemed unwilling to do. As he readied for his departure back to Edinburgh, he wrote to his father, explaining what he would need to do to continue as a publisher:

When I first landed in this country it was . . . to endeavour . . . to better my fortune and embrace the first opportunity of returning to my native country . . . I have no doubt but if I were to continue in the line I am at present of printing books & being successful in getting subscribers but in a few years I might get something handsome.[31]

Simpson was correct to assume that perseverance in publishing—"printing books & being successful in getting subscribers"—would require more time than the year in the publishing business he had allowed. But success also required much more. It required that publishers assess markets for books, and that they turn books into credit and credit into books. They also needed to develop exchange networks that would provide them with assortments of books to sell.

Simpson and his partners were not alone in their ambitions to "better their fortunes," and, obviously, not all intended to publish for only a short while. Dobelbower undertook a number of new publishing projects, beginning with William Alexander's *The History of Women* in 1796. John Thompson, the newly arrived British printer employed by Simpson and his partners to print *The World Displayed*, soon embarked on an ambitious publication with another young man, Abraham Small. Thompson had only been printing in America for less than a year when he and Small took subscriptions and published an extraordinarily lavish Bible, which sold for a whopping twenty dollars. In 1796, another group of journeymen with the same idea published by subscription William Burkitt's *Expository Notes, with Practical Observations on the New Testament*.[32] Subscription publishing was central to the journeymen's publishing schemes because it was the only practicable way to finance expensive publications. Yet by the middle of the 1790s, this method of publishing had come under fire and the public, tired of financing inferior books and proposed books that never saw the light of day, rebelled by refusing to sign for books in advance. Simpson recognized this dilemma when he described to his father the glut of subscription books. He believed that his successful example was in no small way responsible:

> [E]ven the report of our little success has set all the printers into the way of publishing proposals for books, till such a time that they are become a perfect drug, and nobody will hardly look at them, having been so deceived by a fine description in the proposals and when the books come out, they were often not worth half the money.[33]

Nevertheless, the allure of publishing was that it offered a chance at financial success that could exceed a printer's competence. It tempted with the vision of a self-reliant man of business, a man who answered to nobody and who was not chained to a press.

Mathew Carey's brother James was hounded by such dreams. He moved from Baltimore to Richmond seeking the "right" setting in which to publish. Yet from Richmond, he wrote his brother that he would have to move again. "The objects that present themselves to my mind's eye," he explained, "are either a removal to Charleston in pursuit of wealth, or to some considerable back town in pursuit of competence and ease."[34] In the meantime, he supported himself by job printing and by publishing short-lived newspapers. Then from Charleston, overrun with competitive book-stores, he wrote that he might finally have to content himself with printing: "I do not wish to embarrass myself with a variety of business; and as the printing is my favorite and most profitable one . . . I mean to confine myself entirely to it." But he could not give up the idea of making a fortune at publishing either newspapers or books, because he soon moved to Savannah to try yet again. He gradually began to recognize his relentless "bad luck," something his older brother saw as a character flaw. Mathew lectured James that "nothing but perseverance will do in so arduous an undertaking as the Establishment of a News Paper, and I am fearful that you do not possess enough of that Quality to secure you from wandering."[35] Whatever James's character, he was never able to succeed as a publisher, and during one of his many low turns, he despaired, noting that "[s]hould my Savannah expedition also fail, I may possibly fall into the more humble and obscure walks of life—still contenting myself with the solacing idea, that although unsuccessful, I have made the necessary efforts to obtain consequence—I meant to say *competence*—however let them both stand."[36]

If the journeyman-publishers did not become the major publishers of the early nineteenth century, it was not for lack of trying. Nevertheless, the operators with the greatest chance of success were those who were already established in the printing trade. Master printers relied, as we shall see, on extensive and complicated networks both for credit and books. Their dealings with papermakers, printers, and binders were frequent and developed into long-standing relationships in which credit played an enormous role. The journeymen-publishers could finance their works by subscription publishing, but this could be taken only so far. The prominent publishers of the early republic came predominantly from the ranks of master printers, but the incidence of journeymen acting as publishers serves to highlight the developing diversity within the trade. In this peculiar environment, the economic advancement that master status conferred was constricted, even as the activities of publishing seemed to offer promise.

Printers as Publishers

As relatively unknown would-be publishers like Simpson, Key, Dobelbower, Thompson, Small, and James Carey leapt into the business of pub-

lishing, other, more seasoned printers, including the elder Carey, John
Bioren, Thomas Dobson, William W. Woodward, David Hogan, John
Ormrod, and Patrick Byrne, were acting to transform their businesses from
printing and bookselling to publishing. For most of them, this transformation would involve printing less or, as in Carey's case, giving up job
printing altogether.

In the 1790s and early years of the nineteenth century, Mathew Carey
steered his already established printing business in an entirely different direction from that which he had adopted when he opened shop in Philadelphia in the 1780s. By 1792, the *American Museum*, the periodical Carey had
begun in 1787, had become a financial albatross. At first he was unable to
attract enough subscribers, and when interest rose in the magazine, he faced
the difficulties of sending issues to the often remote places where his customers lived. Discouraged, he wrote to his brother James in 1792 that he
wished to drop the project altogether. He explained that "half the slavery
& trouble employed in that work, will suffice for other work, more profitable." [37] In his autobiography, Carey described the steps that led to his subsequent success in publishing:

When I relinquished the ill-fated *Museum*, I commenced bookselling and printing
on a small scale. My store, or rather my shop, was of moderate dimensions; but
small as it was, I had not full-bound books enough to fill the shelves — a considerable
portion of them were occupied by spelling books. I procured a credit at Bank, which
enabled me to extend my business; and by care, indefatigable industry, the most
rigid punctuality, and frugality, I gradually advanced in the world. [38]

Carey's account highlights the importance of assortment and credit for a
would-be publisher. To address the first problem, he began importing large
numbers of Irish, Scottish, and English books — "without which I cannot
have a proper assortment" — to sell in his Philadelphia store. [39] The second
problem, though very much connected, was addressed by his application to
the bank.

Carey jobbed out to other printers the printing of most of the books
and pamphlets he published. He used local printers, as well as those in the
countryside. By June 1794, Carey had begun the process by which he would
transform himself from a reasonably successful printer and bookseller to a
prosperous publisher. He sold imported books, American books he obtained through exchanges with other booksellers, and books of his own
publication. "The rumors you heard," he wrote to his brother, "respecting
the increase of my business, are, thank God, true. I do nearly as much as

any Bookseller in the City. I at this moment have five or six Books printing [being printing by other printers]. I have totally sold my office."[40] A few days later, he wrote to his father that "I have lately quitted the printing business, finding it impossible to pay the necessary attention to it and the bookselling."[41] Having sold his presses, he could turn his attention to his quest for a successful location from which to sell books.

As more and more individuals decided to take their chances with publishing, the market was often flooded with several editions of the same books, or with many books on the same subjects. Because of their proximity to one another, Philadelphia publishers could generally avoid publishing a work that was already in press in Philadelphia. However, the chances of duplicating the efforts of a New York or Boston publisher were far greater. This note from James Rivington of New York to Carey is fairly typical of how publishers checked on the competition and determined what was available for publication:

Do you propose to carry through your remembrancer the whole of Camillus's Defence of the Treaty with Great Britain, and afterwards print it in a volume when the whole of the writer's object is complete, for if you do not effect the latter I conjecture one of our printers may aim at it. This suggestion is for your government.[42]

Although publishers from the different cities were in contact with one another, this system of correspondence far from eliminated the chance of infringements. Sometimes publishers were unaware of competing editions until so alerted by anxious authors. James T. Callender, the republican writer from Scotland, informed Carey that Rivington was about to bring out "a new Edition of [Callender's] the political Progress of Britain," and requested that Carey "call on this man & tell him that a new Edition of the Pamphlet is in the Press and will be published in a few days, & that if he goes further he will be prosecuted." Just to be safe, Callender inserted an advertisement "to this purpose in Mr. Brown's paper this day," in order to give weight to his claim.[43]

To cope with the problems of competition, and to ensure a market for one's books, it was essential to plan carefully the publication of any book. A publisher would decide first on a book to publish or reprint. He next would consult with publishers in his area and elsewhere to see if any competing editions were at press. He might ask their opinions of a work; he might solicit "experts" to see if the work being considered was the latest and best of its kind. He would determine the amount of type and paper needed. If he did not intend to print it himself, or was not a printer, he would have this done by the printer he intended to use, or take bids by having various printers cast off and report to him. Then he would advertise. Advertising might mean sending circular letters announcing the publication of the book to gentlemen, libraries, and other publishers. Circulating subscription proposals was another form of announcement. Publishers often announced their intention to publish a book by placing ads in newspapers, providing information about how and when the work would appear.

All of these steps were necessary for the publisher to undertake publication. But following these steps did not guarantee success, or stave off the competition. It was considered part of the "courtesy of the trade" that the first to advertise would have the "right" to undertake the publication. But often simultaneous ads would appear or, more commonly, a publisher would neglect to make his intentions public enough and would discover that another edition was being published at the same time.

Publishing Decisions

The essence of the publishers' risk lay in the decisions they needed to make as to what and how much to publish. With an unblushing Franklinian didacticism, Carey noted in his autobiography that the key to success in early American publishing was to publish in moderation. Yet Carey was always in debt because of overproduction. "I printed and published above twice as many books as were necessary for the extent of my business," he wrote, "and, in consequence, incurred oppressive debts to banks — was laid under contribution for interest to them, and to usurers, which not only swallowed up my profits — but kept me in a constant state of penury."[44] Overproduction meant not only publishing too many copies of a particular book, but publishing too many titles. Ultimately, Carey made his fortune — the independence he derived from publishing — by publishing Bibles in various formats, leaving the type standing so that he could print copies practically as they were needed.[45] Thus his financial success came from one book, a book that would always find a market and which, when produced cheaply — as he managed to do with the standing type — could compete with British imports.

Some publications were clearly meant for speedy sale, however, and when Carey first thought to write and publish an account of the yellow fever epidemic of 1793, his hopes for its sales were grand. But by February

1794, he revised his opinion: "From the present state of the market, glutted as it is with a variety of productions on the same subject, I am convinced that my expectations will be miserably disappointed, and that the sale of the work will be extremely slow, and probably a large proportion will be totally unsold."[46] Although his pamphlet was cheap and therefore a fairly safe risk, such publications suffered from competition, and their subject matter often captured the public's interest for only a short time.

In an environment where books written by Americans were still relatively rare — and where "steady sellers" paved the surest route to publishing success — the factor that most inhibited sales was keen competition. Printers in the 1790s knew well the kinds of books Americans desired; they had been importing them and, in a more limited way, reprinting them for years. Because the first American copyright law in 1790 did not protect foreign titles, printer-booksellers raced to get copies of popular foreign works as quickly as they were imported so that they could be the first to reprint them. Any foreign text could be reprinted, but to protect it under the new copyright law, editorial changes "to suit American readers" were sometimes made, rendering it different enough from the original to be considered "American."

In the 1790s American-written works were mostly political or practical in nature — political pamphlets, essays on American manufacturing and improvements, discussions of economy, banking, and American exploration, and so on. British titles reprinted by Americans ran from schoolbooks, religious writings, and medical and legal books to novels, plays, and other standard works. From June 1, 1795, to October 1, 1795, for example, Philadelphia newspapers ran advertisements for 276 titles that were sold by the city's printers and booksellers. Of 138, or half of those sampled, fifty-seven were written by English authors, eighteen by Scots, six by Irish, fourteen by French, one by Italian, and thirty-three by American writers; nine were not identifiable by nationality. The foreign works were either reprints or imports.[47]

The race to get books out quickly was essential for a printer-bookseller's success in the 1790s. Publishing a book was in some ways analogous to the land speculation of the 1790s, and the new publishers eagerly sought out appropriate titles on which to risk capital. The New York printer-bookseller James Rivington tried to make a business out of recommending books to other printers, arguing that his superior knowledge of the British trade and his long career gave him a particularly fine instinct when it came to publishing decisions. His letters to other printer-booksellers invariably mentioned that he had just received shipment of the latest British books. If his correspondents wished, he would send these "early" copies so that they could be speedily reprinted. His price for consultation and for sending newly acquired books was a share in the books his clients reprinted. It is unknown whether or not anyone bought Rivington's advice and early copies, but Carey, for one, was outraged by Rivington's methods, replying that he did not believe that "the mere act of giving an opinion, [as to] which article would probably be salable, gives claim to any number of copies of the work when printed." Carey suggested that Rivington's advice was not needed in his shop: "Though not so experienced in the book business as you are, yet we know sufficient of it, to be able to fix upon as many books which would certainly be well & generally received." Furthermore, Carey's shop received spring and fall shipments of imported books — "from one half dozen to twenty" — and he could "never agree to pay so high a premium for the opinion of any man."[48]

The early book publishing industry developed in a competitive atmosphere. The growing number of publishers and their scramble to reprint imported books lent a sense of urgency to the publisher's business. Competition was also manifested in the ways books could be distributed and how territories would be divided up by the new publishers. Mason Locke Weems wrote to Carey that if he did not act quickly to form a partnership with William Prentiss of Petersburg, Virginia, the Virginia printer planned "to form a partnership with Campbell, Dobson and the Capital Booksellers of Philadelphia."[49] In another instance, Carey unsuccessfully negotiated with Noah Webster to print and sell Webster's speller in 1791 because Webster would offer no assurance of territorial rights. Carey wrote to him that "if the contract you offer us be only for the printing, while Tom, Dick, & Harry may vend within our district, it would not suit us on any terms whatever." But if Webster were to offer Carey the exclusive right to print *and* sell the work "within the limits prescribed," then Carey felt he could accept. After all, Carey noted, "the expression 'West of the Hudson,'" used by Webster in his proposed contract, "do[es] not appear sufficiently clear. Do they mean throughout the whole of the United States, south of New Jersey, as well as the country situated to the West of that River?" If not, he reasoned, he would not even be allowed Pennsylvania, something he obviously could not accept.[50]

Webster's speller was one of the very few copyright American books reprinted frequently enough to become an object of contention and competition. In fact, since the first appearance of his speller in 1783, Webster had tried to control the printing and selling of the book. He sold licenses to printers around the country and attempted in his various contracts to control where the books could be vended. The publishers' informal cooperative networks served to undermine Webster's plans, and the spellers circulated and were sold by the thousands by unlicensed booksellers. When Congress passed the copyright law in 1790, Webster finally conceded that he could not enforce specific areas of sale, but he comforted himself by drawing up new contracts with his licensed printers which allowed him a percentage of each copy printed. The new arrangements Webster made, however, were less acceptable to Carey, who actually wanted Webster to assert territorial boundaries to help him fend off competitors.[51]

Competition and Cooperation

Territorial disputes evaded solution either by the copyright law or any other legal measure. "Courtesy of the trade," an amorphous term loosely denoting trade cooperation—or, in modern terms, collusion—exerted pressure on printer-booksellers not to interfere in each other's markets. Ultimately, formal and informal cooperation determined much about what publishers chose to publish and prevented the early national book trade from becoming prohibitively competitive.

Printer-booksellers realized that the best way to alleviate the financial burdens of publishing and the tension of competition was to band together in both informal and formal ways. Shareholding was a type of cooperation that many publishers used increasingly in the 1790s by which a publisher offered to sell shares in a proposed book to other booksellers. This usually meant that shareholders would commit themselves to taking a certain number of copies of the work and pay for the book during production or on its completion. Shareholders generally bought their books at trade discounts, though this practice varied according to different circumstances. Shareholding was not an American innovation: London booksellers already employed this sort of arrangement, which became most pervasive in the eighteenth century after the Stationers' Company formally began to keep records of publishers' share agreements.[52]

Carey offered shares in books he published to other major printer-booksellers in the country. Writing to David West of Boston, he explained that "I am desirous of lightening the burden of the very heavy edition of Goldsmith, which I am printing by dividing it with two or three booksellers. I therefore offer you 500 copies at paper and print . . . I hope you will find it your interest to take a share in this work." As further inducement, Carey informed West that, excluding Thomas and Andrews, he had not offered shares to anyone else in Boston.[53] It seems apparent that, without shareholders, Carey and others would have had to bear too much of the financial burden for books that were expensive to produce. Shareholding may have cut into individual profits, but cooperation meant that many expensive books that formerly had been imported could be published in America.

Shares could also be sold by authors who took out the copyrights for their own books instead of leaving that task to the printer-bookseller. Astute authors like Webster and Jedediah Morse guarded their copyrights and sold shares of them to various printer-booksellers. In this way, they controlled the financing of the book as well as its distribution. Morse offered Carey, along with Thomas and Andrews of Boston, shares in his geography text, a proposal to which Carey would agree if no other bookseller, beyond Thomas and Andrews, were allowed in.[54] Ever concerned about territories, another of Carey's stipulations confined Thomas and Andrews's sales "to New England & part of New York, New Jersey, & perhaps some parts of Connecticut," while Carey's territory would be the southern states, to which he intended to send Mason Locke Weems to peddle the books.[55]

The shareholding process defrayed the cost of production for the primary publisher and ensured a supply of the book to the "secondary" publishers, or shareholders. In addition, owning a share often meant that the title page of the book would include the shareholders' names and locations. Sometimes, a shareholder was given permission by the primary publisher to print a new title page altogether, with his own imprint.

In 1796 the printer-bookseller Thomas Bradford proposed to publish a mercantile newspaper on a plan inspired by shareholder-publishing. His proposed *Merchant's Advertiser* would be "established on the principle of the merchants, traders and other citizens becoming its proprietors, and each of them as a proprietor to be entitled to the [news]paper at prime cost." The shareholders or proprietors of such a paper would also benefit from access to the paper for their advertisements at a "sum merely sufficient to defray the actual expence of printing." The content too, could be controlled by the proprietors, as "the literary department of the paper should be entrusted to men of their own choice; a circumstance that must afford the highest degree of assurance that the paper would be conducted with propriety." The proprietors would pay annual subscription fees, out of which the costs of "rent, labour, paper, ink, fire, candles, [ink] balls, skins, parchment, brushes, and other small contingencies attached to the printing" would be drawn. Bradford's proposal was for a perpetual-motion machine in the form of a newspaper that would guarantee him ongoing printing business, keep his compositors and pressmen with constant work, and provide him with access to a mercantile paper. Best of all, the plan required little or no risk on his part.[56]

For publishers, cooperation in the trade was part of their over-arching concern in developing the domestic market for printed matter, and this meant that members of the trade needed each other to share risks and help build up their stocks. As printers began to publish more, they also began to give their work to printers who did not focus on bookselling. In order to interest other booksellers in buying shares, booksellers needed to get the best printing prices possible. This pressure led them to set printers against each other in competition for jobs. The booksellers, many of whom still identified themselves with printing, were now in the odd position of driving wages down within their own craft. In this way, the seeds of division and discontent were sown, and printer-booksellers began to turn to one another to establish and solidify formally their new positions as employers of the trade.

The earliest signs that the trade was undergoing diversification came when a group of printers and booksellers formed the Philadelphia Company of Printers and Booksellers, which met for the first time on July 4, 1791. On that Independence Day the members of the new organization hammered out a constitution that declared "a union among the Printers and Booksellers of this city," in order to produce "solid advantages, in extending their business." The company was established as a risk-sharing venture for printers who published or who wished to become more involved in publishing. As members, they were entitled to subscribe for shares in each other's books and to participate in joint-publication schemes sponsored by the company. This agreement was intended to enforce a standard for shareholding, ensuring that all members paid the same amount for shares and that small groups of investors did not shut out others. The constitution of the organization also stipulated fixed prices for books sold by members, whether "to the trade, to shopkeepers, [or] to the public at large." Any member caught underselling would be expelled from the association.[57]

Nineteen members of the print trade joined the company. Of these, fourteen were listed simply as printers in city directories from 1790, 1795, and 1799. Seven considered themselves printer-booksellers. In addition, one member was listed as a bookseller and another as a bookseller-stationer. Five of the members published newspapers in addition to printing and bookselling. Only a handful of company members published books in a consistent fashion during the 1790s: Mathew Carey, Joseph Crukshank, Thomas Dobson, Benjamin Johnson, Henry and Patrick Rice, and William Young. All of these men were listed as printer-booksellers or bookseller-stationers in the directories.

While most of Philadelphia's booksellers joined the company, two notable members of the trade declined membership. Robert Campbell, a bookseller who was known for his cheap reprints of popular English titles, was proposed for publication by the company in April 1792, but sent word by another member that he refused the nomination.[58] The repercussions of this rebuff were immediate. At that year's October meeting, when the members of the company were informed that Campbell would not join, they passed new resolutions that could not have been any more pointed:

Resolved, That if any printer or bookseller, not a member of this company, shall print any book, of which the copy-right is vested in this company, or in any individual thereof,—this company will retaliate on such printer or bookseller, by reprinting such of his books, as they may see fit.

Resolved, That none of the members of this company, shall exchange books with printers or booksellers residing in this city, not belonging to the company.

Campbell, "a principal bookseller in the City," had specific reasons to avoid formal associations that legislated prices and assumed de facto copyrights. He regularly undersold the other booksellers—a tactic the company was formed, in part, to discourage—and he seemed to be able to get the kinds of bids from printers that allowed him to keep his costs down. In addition, he had developed an efficient importing network with his brother Samuel of New York, and it is likely that he felt they were quite capable of gaining access to the best-selling English books faster than others could, and that sharing this advantage would cut unnecessarily into their profits.

Another printer-bookseller, William McCulloch, refused to join the company. As he remarked some years later, "these associations, as far as they have come under my view, have been useless, if not pernicious." According to McCulloch, the interests of individuals could never be forced to conform with the perceived interests of a group, however united in a common goal. Pointing to the failure of trade associations to keep overly ambitious members in check, McCulloch capped his point with:

There is no faith in man's obdurate heart.
It does not feel for man.
The nat'ral bond
Of brotherhood sever'd.[59]

The following year, the company proposed even more severe reprisals
for noncooperation, resolving that "no account shall be kept with any
booksellers resident in Philadelphia, not being members of this company;
nor shall they be made the usual discount allowed to members of the company." It is significant that in the company's minutes the term "printer" was
dropped from most of the discussion. Indeed the association did not truly
serve the interests of the printers, who were the majority of its members.
The leadership of the company consisted of those men who did the greatest
amount of publishing and bookselling: William Young was the president,
Thomas Dobson was treasurer, and Carey was on the acting committee.

If tension existed between the interests of the members who were
printers and those who published, it was heightened by the new resolutions
made at the company's April 1793 meeting when Carey, Crukshank, and
Johnson, three of the leading booksellers, were all absent. These new rules
called for more stringent control over the practice of exchanging. According
to the minutes, those present agreed that members should not be allowed
to participate in exchanges or any other commercial transaction for books
printed in Pennsylvania or the other states if any of the titles were available
from members of the group. The practice of exchanging books and selling
them on commission to other booksellers, however, had already introduced
Philadelphia printer-booksellers into trade relationships with their counterparts elsewhere. Severing such ties would be foolhardy for the publisher
who wished to sell his books in any place other than Philadelphia. Furthermore, even when certain titles were available in Philadelphia, a member
might be able to strike a better deal with a trading partner in another part
of the country. The publishing members knew all too well how essential
was the practice of exchanging and maintaining accounts with other publishers. Closing off these channels would make their trade more provincial
instead of widening its influence and sources of supply.

Ultimately, the company proved to be unsatisfactory. The acting committee chose to publish schoolbooks in Latin, none of which seems to have
taken the American book market by storm. Committee members also
drafted petitions to Congress "to take the duty off on paper" as well as rags
imported for domestic paper manufacturing, but they reported that the

"prayer of their petition was not granted." The company had difficulty maintaining a quorum of nine members at their quarterly meetings, a sign that these formal gatherings, at least, were affairs to be avoided; and the company's draconian measures could not be enforced, even by those most devoted to the idea of the formal association. Records of any meetings after the middle of 1794 do not survive.

In February 1802, the leaders of Philadelphia's bookselling community formed a new association, this time consisting of men whose primary interests lay in publishing and bookselling. Dropping the word "printers" from the association's name, the group met at Hardy's Inn to organize the Philadelphia Company of Booksellers. Of the twenty-two members of this association, only six remained from the earlier company: Carey, Crukshank, Dobson, Johnson, and the Rice brothers.[60] Three of the twenty-two were printers, with the rest listed in the city directories as printer-booksellers, booksellers, bookseller-stationers, and printer-stationers. The newspaper publishers were reduced from five to two, indicating that the primary interest of this company was book publishing, and that newspaper publishers were less involved in bookselling than they had been ten years earlier.

The chief object of the association was for members to "unite in the risque of publishing such books as they may agree upon."[61] The booksellers decided on what titles to publish, subscribed for the numbers each was willing to underwrite, and appointed printers to execute the work. The printers of the company's books were not members, but they entered bids for the printing jobs. The members were to pay for their shares on delivery, either in cash or by note, and the title pages would, as with the earlier company, reflect that the book was printed as a joint venture.

This company's aim represented something more than merely a formalized version of shareholder-publishing. The company vested itself with powers to control the trade in whatever ways it could: It prohibited exchanges with any nonmember Philadelphian, it set prices at which books were to be sold; it claimed the privilege of reprinting books formerly reserved by individual members; and it sought to punish those on the outside who, in refusing to join or refusing to join under the rules of the constitution, operated individually, eschewing corporate identification.

When several members of the company nominated for membership John Bioren, an ambitious printer-bookseller, the company voted to postpone his election until he would promise to honor its constitution. The secretary informed Bioren of his contingent election, telling him that in order to be accepted he "must give up the sole privilege of printing such books as he has printed, which were printed before by members of the company after the present editions are sold."[62] Bioren sent word that he declined membership and in so doing rejected the assumed power of this corporate "cooperative" body. Soon after Bioren spurned the company, the members resolved that they would boycott any Philadelphia publications printed by nonmembers which members had already printed, either individually or as a group. This was an effort not only to censure Bioren but to bring him into line with the rest of the Philadelphia publishing establishment. All Philadelphia publishers would suffer in the national market if they were beset by infighting and local piracy, because competing editions of any book would dilute that work's market for exchange as well as its local sales.

The company also published its own periodical devoted to advertising the member's stock and intended publications. The paper was distributed to members of the trade outside Philadelphia in an effort to make their scope more national. While it contained nothing but ads and a few poorly disguised literary puff pieces, the paper's aim, from its opening statement, was grand and nationalistic, if somewhat unfocused:

The growing interests of LITERATURE in this rising Empire, have, for some time, appeared to the Booksellers of Philadelphia to demand a vehicle to communicate literary information, as well of Books already published, as of those contemplated to be executed. Under this idea, they have commenced the present Paper, printed at their joint expense, and to be distributed to persons likely to afford patronage to the productions of the Press — whether those merely calculated to afford amusement to the passing hour, or those which unfold the doors of the Temple of Learning.[63]

While the company intended to bring growth to the trade by encouraging publishing through risk-sharing, its practice was still largely defensive. The concerns of its members were focused on local competition and personalities. The association fostered the promotion of American book arts by offering prizes for paper and ink innovations. As with the earlier organization, the books that appeared under the company's aegis were hardly exotic, consisting mainly of Latin schoolbooks. Some of the titles the company proposed to publish were researched by appointed committees and found to be unpopular and too expensive to produce.[64] The last meeting to be recorded, held, as usual, at Hardy's Inn, convened in October 1804, less than three years after the company's founding.[65] The booksellers were already turning their attention to national markets for their books, but the company served, during its short life, to further separate the printers from the publishers at the local level.

Later in the same year the Philadelphia Company of Booksellers was founded, Philadelphia publishers had a chance to participate in a truly national trade event. America's first literary fair was held in New York in the summer of 1802 under the auspices of a new company known as the American Company of Booksellers. This company consisted of members from the major cities, all of whom had to be full-fledged booksellers. The company's constitution stipulated that members had to have "served a regular apprenticeship of not less than 5 years to the Bookselling business or have been 2 years immediately preceding his application a regular Bookseller." This rule would exclude printers who did not engage in bookselling; in addition, printers who only occasionally published were effectively excluded because membership meant getting access to the fairs, the events where the primary business of exchange took place. Without a full "list of all the Books he intends offering for exchange," the occasional publisher would have no business at the fairs. The constitution's definition of a "regular Bookseller" could include booksellers who had never been printers, thus further ensuring that the membership of the new company would be entrepreneurial rather than craft-oriented.[66]

The brainchild of Mathew Carey, the American literary fair was an imitation of those held by the booksellers in Leipzig. At these fairs, booksellers would congregate to exchange publications. In June, booksellers from New York, Philadelphia, and Boston met for this purpose and congratulated themselves for overcoming the greatest impediments to the growth of the American trade, namely, cutthroat competition and "the want of previously fixed regulations [and] the remoteness of traveling."[67] Hugh Gaine, a venerable New York printer-bookseller, addressed the congregated tradesmen and reminded them that their interest lay in "the literary welfare of the country." He expressed the hope that "mean and narrow jealousies, which have too long prevailed," would give way to "generous emotions of mutual good will" and act to reestablish the brotherhood of the trade, which in recent years had been sorely tested. With an image of the booksellers as brave soldiers, Gaine pled with his "troops" to protect the virtue and best interests of their nation:

'Tis ours, to fill the vacant moments that do so much for virtue or her foes, — to guard the passes to the mind, and stand in the gap between our country and the torrent of impiety which rages to overwhelm her! . . . Let us meet it as men, — and *spurn* any whisper of private and pitiful advantage, which would draw us from our station, and sink the patriot into the dealer. Let us join as one man to raise the name of American literature: and by uniting in support of each other's undertakings, give a *strength* to our social compact.[68]

After the fair, one attendee concluded that the American booksellers had "rivalled and perhaps surpassed the experience and wisdom of the old world," and that their effort "has been equal to all other efforts, founded on a deliberate study of society in the United States." How did they achieve what they believed were such stunning results? Through the establishment of wider credit and exchange networks. "The simple operation of exchange" allowed "many thousand volumes [to be] brought into circulation which might otherwise have lain on the shelves for years." By meeting at the fair, exchanging books, and giving life "to dormant capital," the booksellers fostered new connections that if maintained, would lead to "more extensive and certain trade," which would in turn give "additional sustenance" and vigor to the trade.[69]

The booksellers who met that summer had more in mind than simply "networking" and frantically exchanging books, however. They apparently took seriously Gaine's orders to the troops to consider the state of the market and of America's literature. At the meeting, the participants discussed how best to create American markets, how to find readers, and how, ultimately, to get books to them. Creating markets meant more than simply producing books and sending them around the country. According to Gaine, it meant the "progress of refinement in morals and taste . . . the growth of wealth and the advancement of science . . . the prosperity of commerce."[70] It also meant publishing books that were "suitable" as well as salable. According to one of their number, nothing could be worse for a fledgling nation and industry than the promulgation of bad morals, and to this end, the booksellers were reminded that they should avoid publishing books "such as sap the foundations of virtue and morality, the pillars of individual and national happiness." Moreover, this observer suggested that booksellers refrain from circulating such books.[71] The improvement of the book arts too, according to this member of the trade, was essential to the success of publishing. In a statement that was both a jab at printers and an assertion of a publisher's pride, he noted that the "credit of printing one incorrect book often extends itself to the succeeding labours of the publisher." Similarly, American binding needed to be brought up to higher standards as "books, like men, are often judged by their external appearance."

The booksellers' concerns for themselves, their trade, and their country led them to adopt several resolutions. First, they promised to avoid "any interference with the interests of each other, by the republication of Books already printed in the United States, of which there is a sufficient supply to be had on reasonable terms." Second, the members of the first literary fair left New York resolved to "discontinue the importation of all Books, of which good and correct editions are printed in this country, and on which a liberal discount is made by the publishers."[72] The qualifications in both these resolutions would leave plenty of room for both importing and "interference," and were probably intended to allow for the fact that many books were still not published or publishable in America, and that "sufficient supply" was indeed a variable.

The literary fair, unlike the local associations, called for cooperation that was not particularly coercive. Perhaps the organizers and participants knew that coercion, hardly successful on a local level, could not but fail dramatically on a national scale. But it is also notable that the language used in Gaine's oration and in the address printed at the conclusion of the fair was the language of boosterism. The rhetoric rallied the troops of booksellers, asking them to see themselves as the nation's providers of literary and artistic standards as well as its guardians of morality. This morale-building view of the trade was both more inspirational and pragmatic than the defensive local attempts at cooperation. It gave a sense of unity of purpose to the booksellers while leaving ample room for the aggressive pursuit of individual gain.

The literary fair also produced the acknowledgment among booksellers that they saw themselves as "publishers" and their trade as "publishing." The promotion of the book arts, which included printing, paper-making, binding, and engraving, was essential to the further development of publishing; and it is abundantly clear that while those who attended the literary fair hoped to promote the book arts, they distinguished themselves from the craftsmen who worked in these aspects of the trade.

Philadelphia publishers no doubt tailored their businesses and acted according to the ground rules set up by the literary fairs that convened biannually from 1802 to about 1805. Their entrepreneurial instincts and their keen desire to promote a national market led to ventures like William Poyntell's Classic Press. The year following the first fair, Poyntell, a Philadelphia stationer and bookseller, began a publishing operation that would reprint "the most valuable European books," sold on a wholesale basis. Poyntell's aim was to produce books that would be "at least equal, if not superior in quality to the London editions" at prices lower than their imported counterparts. The Classic Press, he hoped, would "unite in calling forth the talents and Industry of the Artist, and . . . encourage the investment of American capital." Poyntell, who had himself probably never printed, saw no reason to tout the promotion of the printing trade, as had the companies of printers and booksellers of the 1790s. Rather, he wished to "add to the common stock of American manufactures" in order to eliminate foreign competition. His appeal to the trade to buy his Classic Press books at attractive wholesale prices was aimed at the bookselling members of the trade rather than at printers who kept small bookstores. This is made clear by the fact that he would only extend credit to individuals buying twenty-five copies or more of any title, with the terms improving significantly for orders of titles that exceeded fifty in number. Poyntell's plan was successful, and his Classic Press turned out a number of schoolbooks from 1804 to 1806.[73]

Publishers versus Printers

Informal and formal attempts at trade cooperation derived in part from the growing competition of the 1790s, but also from a self-conscious, if increasingly nostalgic, pride in the craft of printing and from protectionist and patriotic impulses. Despite the fact that many printer-booksellers were phasing out printing from their businesses, a feeling of craft brotherhood, part nostalgic and part political, kept them from seeing themselves as capitalists, even if they were acting as such. The craft of printing had always been vested with special status. To begin with, printers were by and large literate. When they published newspapers, they could become well known. As the creators and disseminators of printed matter, whether they were publishers or not, they stood at the heart of society's expression of social, political, and religious ideas. Throughout the history of printing, although not in early America, printing guilds had made the craft exclusive, and an apprenticeship in printing carried more solemn weight and prestige than many other crafts. In addition, printers throughout history had access to presses and, if so moved, could use their skill to publish — or make public — their own or others' ideas.

The lore and tradition of the printing craft's exceptionalism was passed on from generation to generation by such well-known printers as Franklin and Isaiah Thomas, but also in printing shops everywhere. Innovation came naturally to these craftsmen who not only were relatively educated but often had mechanical skills. Presses, ink, and type underwent constant minor improvements through the insistent tinkering of mechanically inclined printers.

Printers' self-conscious exceptionalism led many to innovate. It also infused in them a desire to cooperate for the purposes of personal gain, protection of the trade, patriotism, and exclusivity. As we have seen, their modes of cooperation served these purposes variously. But printers also promoted and underscored divisions in the trade. Those who had cast printing aside in favor of bookselling still spoke of "the brethren" of printers and the specialness of their craft, but their actions spoke differently. They were now employers and entrepreneurs.

The Philadelphia Company of Booksellers, the national literary fairs, and enterprises like Poyntell's all reflected the growing gulf between master printers and booksellers. The printers were, to use one business historian's term, "maintainers" who opted to print jobs rather than to publish.[74] Aversion to risk and satisfaction with a "competence" could easily explain certain printers' decisions to stick closely to their craft, deviating only rarely if at all, into bookselling and publishing. Robert Aitken is one such printer who, during the Revolution, lost a great deal of money on a Bible he had published. After the Revolution, Aitken resolved never again to take that kind of risk and, in fact, could hardly be persuaded to accept large printing jobs for risk-taking publishers. When Carey brought him a Catholic book to print, Aitken was said to have pointed to his shelves full of unsold Bibles and said, "If you would even make good that loss, I would not print your book. I would sooner print the *Woman of Pleasure*."[75] Printers who published newspapers may have felt that their papers tied up capital and provided enough of an investment to discourage further speculation in publishing. Some may simply have found themselves unequal to or disdainful of the task of securing credit. Others may have been adverse to being part of an increasingly structured and hierarchical network. Whatever the reason, some printers remained tied to their craft. Perhaps out of their desire to remain independent, they did not form corporate bodies, as did the booksellers and journeymen.

In 1804, the members of the Philadelphia Company of Booksellers became concerned about a debate in the pages of the *Aurora* in which "the Booksellers are charged with ill treating their Printers."[76] The tensions inherent in the Philadelphia Company of Booksellers, and the success of the literary fairs, served to segregate master printers further from the world of the booksellers. Writing as "Cato," a master printer complained in the newspaper that what he understood to be the original intent of the literary fair had been undermined by the powerful booksellers: "I imagined that the printers or booksellers of small capital would thereby be encouraged to publish small works, without having them lying dead stock upon their hands." This could certainly have been construed by the constitutional stipulation that members had to have many titles to exchange. In addition, the fair was to allow "the humble printer or bookseller, with small capital . . . [to] . . . participate in the profit by exchange, with the more opulent capitalist." Yet after only two years, grumbled Cato, the fairs, which met alternately in New York and Philadelphia, had developed "into a mere monopoly, a combination of rich *booksellers* against *authors and printers*." [77] According to this master printer, the literary fair accelerated the differentiation between printer and bookseller, as "not only have *printers* been denied the privileges of sale or exchange, and even of admission to the fair, but a conspiracy has been formed also to deprive those printers, of bread, who shall *attempt to publish!*" The master printers were "the sport of the booksellers," argued the critic; their livelihood was threatened by the "barbarous monopoly," whose members first encouraged them by promising large jobs, telling them to buy presses and type and to take on more apprentices, and then "suddenly withdraw[ing] their employment by which the apprentices are thrown idle and the high rents bring them to the brink of ruin." The pressure exerted on printers by booksellers to keep prices low were countered by the demands of journeymen who, through "another combination against us . . . keep up the price of wages." [78] The only recourse, according to this exasperated printer, was for the printers to form an association "in their own defense," to establish their own literary fair, and to "unite bookselling with their printing business, even as it were but in a small way." All of these steps, if taken, would "prevent them from becoming so very dependent on the booksellers." [79]

The only known respondent to Cato's complaints, however, did not come from the membership of the American Company of Booksellers but from a journeyman who took offense at the printer's comments about journeymen's attempts to organize. If the printers found combinations so abhorrent, the journeyman asked, why would they consider resorting to such a device themselves? "On the one hand," he continued, "we hear complaints of combinations to oppress the *young adventurer* and oppose his honest endeavours to obtain a living — and immediately after, advice is given to pursue the same measures which have just been condemned!" Furthermore, the master printers had already undertaken at least one concerted effort to oppose journeymen's increasing demands when a group of them resolved to defeat the journeymen's typographical association by blacklisting journeymen who were members. [80]

Cato dismissed the journeyman's protests, however, noting that he had

not intended to offend the journeymen — "their combination was only no-
ticed as a thing of course" — and that his aim was still the booksellers. "I fly
at higher game," he responded, and "like the falcon who has in view a covey
of partridges, will not be diverted from my pursuit by a sparrow that may
fall in my way."[81] With this poetic touch the controversy in the pages of the
Aurora died.

The structure of the book trade had undergone an important transformation by the end of the first decade of the nineteenth century. Diversity
characterized the trade. Some members of the trade devoted larger and
larger proportions of their time and resources to publishing. They decided
what to publish and hired printers for the jobs. They were coming to represent what the angry printer in the *Aurora* called "*the man of capital*," or
the "opulent capitalist."[82] In addition, many printers still made occasional
forays into publishing and continued to bid for jobs and sell books. The
journeymen, more desperate than most established printers, sought relief
from the increase in their numbers and from diminishing work opportunities. This relief took shape in journeymen's associations and in their seemingly endless migration from one position to another. For some — the
"young adventurers" — speculating in book publishing seemed a risk well
worth taking.

4

New Modes of Publishing
in the Early Republic

PRINTERS DID NOT BECOME PUBLISHERS overnight, nor did members of the printing trade experience uniformly the shift from craft work to non-manual enterprises. The categories of journeyman, master printer, and publisher blend when we examine the work activities of the early nineteenth-century printing and book trades. Most of the individuals considered in this study were born in the 1770s, became printers' apprentices in the late 1780s, and became journeymen or proprietors in the 1790s. In this last decade of the century, some connected with the printing trade sought to achieve through publishing a comfortable competence and a status higher than that of mechanic. Indeed, most master printers of the 1790s, as well as some journeymen, experimented at least occasionally in newspaper, pamphlet, or book publishing. For some, there was no turning back; the rest of their careers were spent in publishing or in a combination of printing and publishing. Others returned to their craft, or never fully abandoned it, building up prosperous and long-lived printing establishments. When the master printer "Cato" railed against the "man of capital" and the "opulent capitalist" of the printing trade, he was in fact denouncing the publisher. Men of capital, of course, were not all publishers, but all publishers were men of some capital. In practical terms, this meant that publishers began to attempt to control and direct all aspects of book production and the book trade itself. Historically, printers had been the focal point of the book trade. By the first decades of the new century, they made up only one very important segment of a capitalistic and venture-oriented profession.

Early national publishing revolved around the promotion of book sales on a wider scale. An analysis of wholesaling, combination publishing, and investing in ancillary branches of their trade makes clear that publishers recognized that their local markets were not sufficient to support their fledgling enterprises, and they developed strategies to gain access to markets outside Philadelphia. This chapter, and the chapters that follow, will examine the ways in which Philadelphia publishers approached the problems of and opportunities for reaching wider markets for their books.

Of the almost forty master printers in Philadelphia at the turn of the century, ten individuals made the transition from printer to publisher most completely. They stand out for the length of their careers and the volume of work they published. John Bioren, Samuel Bradford, Mathew Carey, John Conrad, Thomas Dobson, David Hogan, John Ormrod, Abraham Small, Thomas Stephens, and William W. Woodward all began their printing careers in the 1780s and 1790s.[1] Throughout the 1790s they printed jobs for others and published books, pamphlets, and, in some cases, newspapers and periodicals. By the early years of the nineteenth century, they began to have others print their publications instead of maintaining full printing shops of their own. In 1794 Carey gave up printing entirely in favor of publishing and bookselling. The others only gradually did so, with some, like Bioren, Dobson, Small, and Woodward, maintaining printing shops throughout their careers. Their printing shops, however, diminished in scale and importance as their concerns in publishing and bookselling increased. Those with sons, like Woodward and Dobson, used their presses as resources for training and employing the next generation. Carey's son, Henry Charles, was trained from a very early age in bookselling and publishing.

A number of printers published only occasionally or on a limited basis. Thomas S. Manning was one such printer who acted as publisher only when others joined with him as partners in publication. William Fry, Joseph Kammerer, and Hugh Maxwell published newspapers or periodicals. Francis Bailey produced almanacs and a smattering of books that caught his fancy, such as the religious writings of Emanuel Swedenborg. However, most prominent early national printers built their businesses around job printing for publishers, and they printed for institutions and individuals, much as their colonial predecessors had done. Abel Dickinson and Francis Wrigley were two such "pure" printers.

Some new publishers of the early republic had not trained as printers at all. Beginning as teachers, clerks, ministers, and merchants, these individuals usually found their ways into publishing through bookselling. John Conrad and his three brothers fit this description, as did Benjamin Davies, Emmor Kimber, John Inskeep, and Benjamin Kite. Because their finances and energies were not absorbed with running printing shops, they published a great number of titles. Conrad headed a family of bookselling brothers in Philadelphia, Baltimore, Petersburg, Virginia, and Norfolk who published schoolbooks, literature, and a wide array of miscellaneous imprints. By the time of the Conrads' spectacular bankruptcy in 1813, they had become one of America's most prolific publishers. Benjamin Davies entered into publishing in the 1790s as a bookseller whose political sympathies lay with William Cobbett. After publishing some of Cobbett's writings, Davies continued to publish more generally for almost a decade into the new century.

Still other non-printers had partners who were printers. Thus the merchant John Inskeep joined with Samuel F. Bradford, a member of the famous Philadelphia printing family. Together they published a steady stream of literary and political works from 1807 to 1815. Emmor Kimber, a bookseller and Quaker minister, made up half of the publishing firm of Kimber and Conrad with the printer Solomon W. Conrad (apparently not a member of the Conrad publishing family). Kimber and Conrad operated a flourishing publishing and bookselling enterprise from 1803 until well into the 1820s. Benjamin Warner, a Quaker merchant and bookseller, became a partner with Jacob Johnson, a printer, bookseller, and inkmaker. The firm of Johnson and Warner specialized early in publishing children's books.

While the most obvious distinction between printers and publishers had to do with financial risk-taking, a residential pattern had developed that further distinguished the two types of tradesmen. In the colonial period, as we have seen, printers generally sold books and other goods from their printing shops. This required them to locate along commercial, centrally located streets where foot traffic would bring them a steady flow of customers. In addition, colonial printers usually lived near to or in the same building as their shops. In the 1790s, this began to change. As the trade divided more distinctly into printers and publishers, new geographical patterns emerged. The respective functions of printers and publishers defined where they worked and lived. As they eliminated bookselling from their businesses, printers gradually moved farther away from the commerical center of Philadelphia. Publishers, on the other hand, assumed positions of higher visibility from which to vend books.

Printers who did little or no publishing operated, as did many other nineteenth-century mechanics, out of shops in narrow alleys and courts, well out of the flow of foot traffic. Throughout most of the eighteenth century, printers' shops doubled as retail outlets for books and stationery (requiring prominent locations), but by 1820, over two-thirds of Philadelphia's printing firms were located in out-of-the-way locations. Some continued to sell books and stationery in a limited way, while others stopped altogether. Their new locations and the shift away from retail business indicate that these craftsmen were now functioning largely to serve the developing publishing trade; the direct link to the public that colonial printers had experienced was on the decline.

The main change in the spatial organization of these mechanics was that few of them lived on the premises of their workshops, as in former times. If they were heads of families, they might buy or rent the recently constructed small rowhouses in east-west streets to the north or south of downtown Philadelphia. If they were single, they often roomed with friends or family, or in the scores of boardinghouse rooms available in almost any price range.[2] As independent artisans who nevertheless had fewer and fewer contacts with the consumer public, these printers fit into the growing urban mechanic class of the nineteenth century.[3]

In about 1806, Abel Dickinson, a non-bookselling printer, moved his printing shop from 92 North 8th Street to Whitehall, a suburb in the Northern Liberties section of Philadelphia. Even as a major job printer, he had no need to be located in the commercial heart of the city. Robert Bailey printed and published at an address on High (Market) Street during the 1790s and the first few years of the nineteenth century, but when he died in 1808 his widow, Lydia, who concentrated almost solely on printing rather than publishing, moved the shop to North Alley, a street of only one block tucked between Fifth and Sixth streets and a block north of High Street. In her career of more than fifty years, Lydia Bailey printed for the government, institutions, associations, and almost every major publisher in the city. Similarly, Francis Wrigley, a printer and inkmaker, began business in 1785 on South Street between Second and Third streets, a location that was only a few blocks south of the city's commercial streets. In those early days, he sold books and stationery in addition to taking printing jobs. As the years passed, however, he abandoned retailing altogether and moved to more obscure locations, in small alleys to the west and south of the downtown area. Wrigley took a prominent location on Chestnut Street for only two years, in the 1790s, when he was in partnership with Jacob Berriman. This enterprising pair took advantage of the explosion of political publishing in the mid-1790s and located their printing shop close to the publishers who needed books and pamphlets speedily published. By the time he died in 1829, Wrigley, "one of the oldest printers in the United States," had his colophon on hundreds of books published by others as well as by the United States government.[4]

Publishers, in contrast with printers, concentrated on retail and wholesale sales. They commanded prime storefronts for their bookstores alongside dry goods stores, china shops, and dressmakers. While they situated their places of business on the main thoroughfares of Market, Chestnut, and Walnut, these retailers made their homes in the nearby residential neighborhoods — in the mid-sized, three-story townhouses of the smaller east-west streets, or the numbered streets — that most Philadelphia merchants called home. Indeed, the printer-booksellers, or publishers, were very much a part of Philadelphia's growing merchant middle class, a class whose members began to separate their places of work from their domestic settings with even greater regularity than did the mechanics.[5]

William Woodward, who began business as a printer in 1793, took a location at 33 Union Street, away from the city center. During the 1790s he relocated four times, edging ever closer to Second and Chestnut, one of the busiest corners and a location that became known for its high concentration of booksellers. By 1802 he took over the southwest corner of Second and Chestnut, and there he remained until he retired in the early 1830s. At about the time he arrived at Second and Chestnut, he also began to list a separate dwelling address a block away on Second Street, and later at 21 Zane Street, a residential street with good-sized three-story brick houses. Mathew Carey too gravitated toward Chestnut, with stops along the way on Front and Market streets. Writing to his father in 1794 he complained about his unfashonable location: "My stand is not well calculated for business: and I have been in vain in quest of a better a long time past."[6] Once his bookselling establishment was settled at 126 Chestnut Street, however, he gradually absorbed the storefronts at 124 and 128 Chestnut, making his business one of the largest wholesale and retail bookselling concerns in Philadelphia.

If the booksellers desired increased visibility and more walk-in business, they also knew they would need to stay in one place for longer periods in order to build up public recognition and stable reputations. By the early years of the new century, most Philadelphia booksellers settled down into semi-permanent quarters. They began to identify their shops as landmarks in and of themselves. Whereas in the colonial period a printer might advertise his shop as "near the Post-Office," the booksellers of the early republic tried to fashion their shops into well-known destinations. An engraving

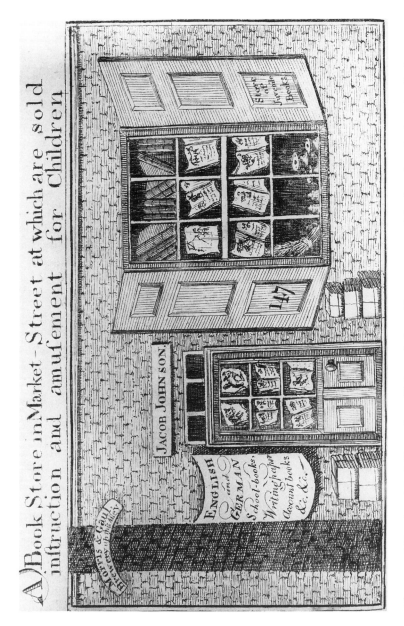

Figure 1. *A Premium* (1803). Engraving of Johnson's shop. Photo courtesy of the American Antiquarian Society.

depicting Johnson's "Juvenile Bookstore" at 147 Market Street was featured as an illustration in many of the children's books he published. Clearly, this early form of graphic advertising in books was designed to make their shop a readily recognizable symbol to customers of all ages. In newspaper ads and city directories of the early 1790s, Thomas Dobson identified his bookstore as the "New Stone House at the Corner of Second and Chestnut street." Soon he did not even need to give his address: he simply directed people to "The Stone House" for all of their book-buying needs. Dobson's shop even became known as an ideal place to "lounge away an hour," according to one British traveler who wrote of Dobson's use of his store as a kind of salon. The writer described Dobson as "a very liberal intelligent man, [who] will inform you on most subjects."[7] Surely Dobson's reputation for whiling away time with customers accelerated his stone building's rise to landmark status. Bookseller's receipts, too, began to feature elegant engravings of their storefronts or buildings. No longer did customers go away with slips of paper with their purchases recorded in a hurried scrawl. The larger, illustrated receipts symbolized the establishment's permanence and lofty image. By the beginning of the nineteenth century, Philadelphia's booksellers had become established. Their bookstores provided books, stationery, and even some intellectual conversation. Such conversation, or simply quiet browsing, went on undisturbed by the bustle of printers in inky aprons, for the site of labor was moving steadily away from the locus of commerce.

If the bookseller's locations and style of conducting business seemed less and less like those of printers, there is one other very important way in which publishers and printers differed. Even "non-bookselling" printers occasionally sold books or kept small stocks of almanacs, primers, and stationery, much as present-day drugstores carry diaries, calendars, and paperbacks. Similarly, as we have seen, many printers occasionally took financial risks in publications. What these craftsmen did *not* engage in, however, was large-scale wholesale bookselling and distribution. This type of wholesaling consisted mainly of selling in quantity to other members of the trade. Above all else, wholesaling activities distinguished publishers from printers. Most publishers of the early republic engaged in active wholesale businesses in addition to their retail concerns. The three most common forms of wholesale activity for publishers in the early national period involved a widespread system of exchange, the sale of large quantities of books on commission, and the sale of quantities of books at discounts to retailers of various descriptions.

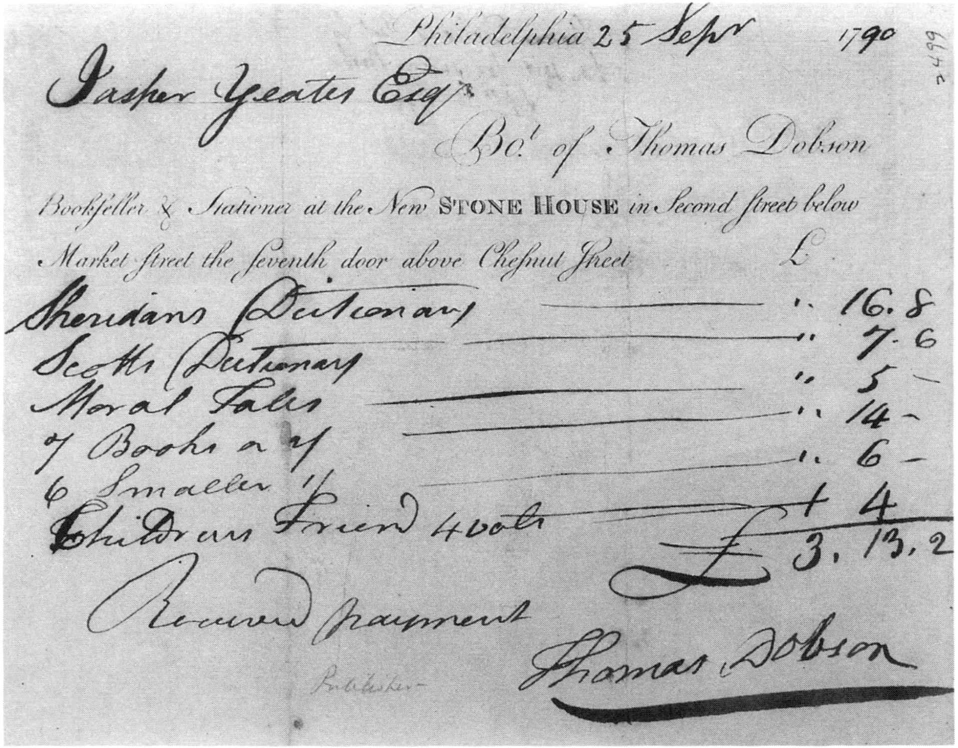

Philadelphia 25 Sepr 1790

Jasper Yeates Esqr

Bot. of Thomas Dobson

Bookseller & Stationer at the New STONE HOUSE in Second street below

Market street the seventh door above Chesnut Street

	£
Sheridans Dictionary	.. 16.8
Scotts Dictionary	.. 7.6
Moral Tales	.. 5
7 Books a 2/	.. 14
6 Smaller 1/	.. 6
Childrens Friend 4 vols	1 4
	£ 3. 13. 2

Received payment

Thomas Dobson

Figure 2. Thomas Dobson receipt, 1790. Photo courtesy of the Historical Society of Pennsylvania (Stauffer Collection).

Figure 3. Mathew Carey receipt, 1813. Photo courtesy of the Library Company of Philadelphia (McAllister Papers).

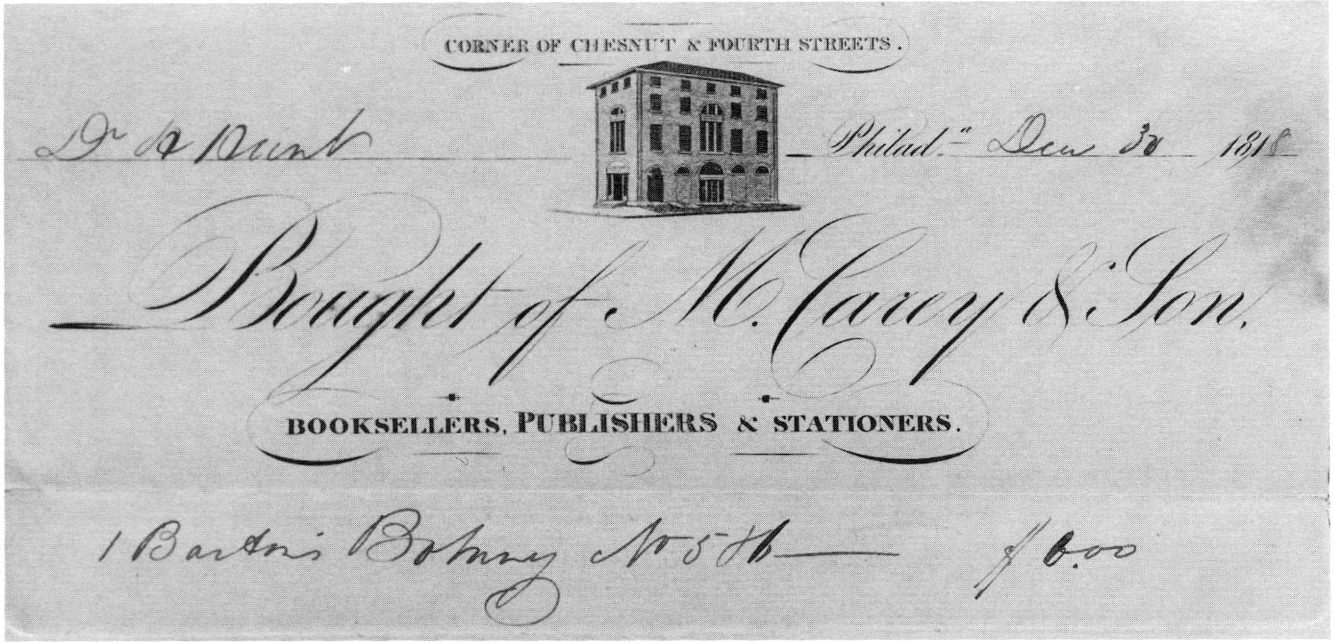

Figure 4. M. Carey & Son receipt, 1818. Photo courtesy of the Historical Society of Pennsylvania (Daniel Parker Papers).

Exchange

Early American publishers survived in the 1790s and the early nineteenth century largely because of a system of exchange. No American publisher could produce enough different titles (referred to by publishers as an "assortment") on his own to stock his bookstore. The exchange system worked in this way: When a publisher's book arrived in its finished state, unhampered by competing editions, the book became a medium of exchange. The more desired the particular title was, the better its chances of reaching other publishers' shelves. Publishers exchanged like for like: that is, they generally preferred to swap bound books for bound books, books in boards for other books in boards, and unbound books that were simply collated and stitched, or left in sheets, for their equivalent.[8] Exchange accounts were established much like regular cash and credit accounts, except very little money, if any, actually changed hands. The books were usually exchanged at retail prices in order to avoid confusion over trade discounts and commissions.

Once publishers had titles to exchange, they would often send neatly printed lists to colleagues, so they could mark off what they wished to acquire and exchange. Publishers often exchanged books they had obtained through earlier exchange. Exchanging allowed them to keep an assortment of "current" publications in stock. Thus when they advertised, they could list many titles that were not their own but which they knew they either could get or had already procured through exchange. In this way, there was a great deal of cohesion among American publishers, as they relied upon one another to make their businesses viable.

Over time, however, the widespread practice of exchange led to difficulties within the trade, and as the new century progressed, the problems began to outweigh the benefits. Publishers had grown used to producing the books they expected to use for exchange. This provided them with assortment and a ready distribution system through other publishers. Having an assortment meant greater wholesale and retail sales. In the most direct sense, then, the money they made through bookselling, as opposed to publishing, enabled them to amass enough capital to continue to publish. Ironically, however, as they scurried to publish a greater variety of books for exchange, and as the catalogues of their own imprints expanded, the need to exchange became less pressing. The function of exchanging had gradually shifted from one of providing assortment to one of creating wider wholesale distribution. For this reason, publishers grew increasingly uncomfortable with exchanges as they had been traditionally conducted. In their bookstores, books of their own publication vied for shelf space with books published by others. As more and more books were published by American publishers, this situation worsened.

Mathew Carey experienced all of the possible problems posed by exchange. In 1811 he joined with Thomas B. Wait of Boston and Samuel Pleasants of Richmond in publishing John Bigland's *Geographical and Historical View of the World*; he proceeded, as was his custom, to exchange the books with other publishers.[9] He soon discovered that the book sold more briskly than he had anticipated, and when two of his agents returned with long lists of subscribers, he was stuck without books to supply them. He had previously agreed with William Woodward to exchange a large number of the books for another work and had to ask Woodward to release him from the exchange. "It is out of my power to supply you with any more Bigland," he wrote Woodward, "unless I purchase them [from Wait and Pleasants] for the purpose of exchanging them and you are well enough acquainted with the disadvantageousness of this mode of doing business. I made a miserable miscalculation when I parted with the number originally exchanged." Woodward, however, refused; Carey had to borrow the books back from Woodward in order to supply his own customers, with a promise to resupply him, on exchange, when he could get the books from his co-publishers.[10] When Wait proposed a new edition of Bigland the following year, Carey declined taking part, referring to his "*faux pas* with the first [edition]." In fact, he was so traumatized that he promised to "throw open to [Wait] the whole [sales] of the middle and southern states" if he would supply him with enough copies of the first edition to satisfy his arrangement with the unyielding Woodward.[11] The process of exchange had made what would have been a very profitable publication into more trouble than it was worth for Carey.

Carey also experienced problems associated with the common practice of *re*-exchanging within the trade. He discovered that books he sent to Thomas and Andrews of Boston were then exchanged for books of Isaiah Thomas's (Worcester) imprint, making it impossible for Carey to exchange directly with Thomas. Carey complained that Thomas "was already supplied with as many as he wanted of my Books through you & therefore declined thus a very considerable channel of supply has been closed against me by your taking more of my Books than you wanted yourselves."[12] In this case, Carey was up against collusion by virtue of partnership connections, but such instances frequently occurred because of geographical circumstances as well. Booksellers in all of the cities routinely pooled the results of their exchanges with their neighbors, leaving "outsiders" fuming at the loss of exchange opportunities.

In general, publishers eschewed exchanges that promised to be lopsided. Writing to Abraham Blauvelt of New Brunswick, New Jersey, who had published only one book, Carey explained that he could not "consent to give an unlimited choice of my whole stock for a single Book, particularly when that book is little known & consequently not likely to meet a ready sale."[13] This was likeliest to happen with country printer-booksellers, or the occasionally publishing printer who printed a book in order to acquire through exchange an assortment to sell. Carey's own peripatetic brother operated from just such an outsider's position. After several unsuccessful attempts at publishing, James Carey confided to his brother that he wished he had listened more attentively when Mathew had tried to explain the exchange system to him. Deciding in New York to publish the proceedings of a sedition trial in Scotland, James wrote for advice: "I have now found out how remiss I was in not acquainting myself with the *minutiae* of the exchanging and other parts of the *American* bookselling. Any information on this head will be particularly grateful and acceptable. Who might I send them to in Boston, or elsewhere to the eastward, with an assurance of safety and a prospect of return?"[14] In an 1813 address to American booksellers, Carey enumerated the damaging effects of the practice of overproduction for the purpose of exchange. He noted that as edition sizes grew — partly through joint publishing schemes, such as his publication of Bigland — publishers were "impelled to exchange the work[s] too freely, and frequently for articles of equivocal value." The results of overly large editions and overzealous exchanging, according to Carey, were a glutted market and warehouses filled with unsalable books. These overstocks in turn tempted booksellers to "furnish auction stores with those superabundant supplies," which would again flood the market with the same books that had been overexchanged, at even lower prices.[15] The result of "the pernicious speculations in extravagantly large editions," according to Carey, was "the prostrate state of the bookselling business — the depreciation of the value of books — and the ruinous sacrifices of them at auctions."[16] In the realm of book wholesaling, a sort of Gresham's Law was at work, with exchange books driving out the "good" books.

Indeed, one Baltimore entrepreneur came up with the idea of taking on commission books that had *not* been exchanged in order to capitalize on this logjam:

The rage for exchanging Books, which has pervaded the United States for several years back, having been complained of by the most respectable of the profession, as having a tendency to prevent actual sales, and to keep back all those Books that the proprietors thought either too new or valuable, to throw into the Market . . . has given me an idea that it would have a good tendency, if one Book-Seller in each large Town, was to receive such works for sale, on account of the owners.[17]

Such clever schemes merely underscored the basic problem of exchange: exchanging books *within* the trade did not create actual sales of books *outside* the trade, and it inhibited new infusions of cash.

Despite the growing problems with the exchange system, most early publishers heavily relied on it. For Benjamin Warner, for instance, exchanging was primarily a form of distribution for the many children's books that he and his partner, Jacob Johnson, had published. Because he often dealt with smaller firms that could not offer him much in the way of exchange, he occasionally tendered pained explanations of the proper way in which fair exchanges should be conducted. To one complaining correspondent, he offered a hypothetical case to illustrate his point. Warner asked George Long "how the account [would] stand" if Warner were to exchange twenty-four copies of his massive Snowden's *America*, "bound and lettered," for the same number of another publisher's small format book in boards.[18] "Why it is almost too laughable to say," he continued, answering his own question, "for the binding *only* of Snowden will cost as much as [the other] book bound at $1." Warner concluded that to carry on such an uneven exchange would compel "my friends to send me to the asylum for lunaticks."[19] With larger publishers, however, Warner often found that the shoe was on the other foot. For example, Cushing and Appleton of New York controlled their exchanges with Warner, setting the terms and pressing Warner when he did not supply them fast enough.

Commission Sales

Selling and buying books on commission was another method for distributing books and keeping an assortment in one's shop. Initially, publishers acted as agents for one another, selling each other's books on commission. The books remained the property of the original publisher and could, if sales were slow, be returned to him. The agents received payment only after selling the books consigned in this manner, and the agent's profit came from the difference between the price charged the retail customer and the discount allowed by the original publisher.

By the beginning of the new century, commission sales were usually conducted between printer-booksellers who printed large numbers of works and had access through exchange to others and to lesser-known or less-established booksellers, shopkeepers, and printers who wished to have books on hand to sell. (This method, rather than exchange, is what Carey favored when dealing with country booksellers.) Books would be sent to be sold at commissions of anywhere from 5 to 25 percent. For small firms, printers, and country merchants, receiving books on commission made a great deal of sense. As with exchange, it provided them with assortment and relatively risk-free stock. For larger publishers, putting books out on commission offered an inexpensive method of distribution. As firms grew and their publications increased, the number of books they sent out, compared to the number they received, grew. As with the exchange system, small operators gained more dramatically by selling books on commission than did large firms. The larger publishing houses, however, were wedded to commission sales as long as the size and geographical distribution of the American book-reading population outstripped publishers' abilities to disseminate books with ease.

All things being equal, most printer-booksellers preferred exchanging books to selling and buying on commission because of the bookkeeping problems associated with commissions. Mathew Carey explained the differences between the two methods to a French bookseller who, newly relocated to Boston, wished to open a commission account with Carey. Carey clearly believed that the newcomer could be of use to him, perhaps by providing foreign credit, imported books, or even an assortment of Boston imprints, because he instead offered to establish an exchange with the Frenchman:

The sale of Books on commission is attended with great trouble to both parties and with very inadequate profit to the vender. I therefore think you had better turn your attention to the procuring a supply by Exch[ange] and although a general exch is disadvantageous to the person who has the largest assortment — or at least not nearly so advantageous as to him who has but a few kinds of Books; yet I am disposed to make a general Exch with you on the most liberal principles. You may have an assortment of such of my Books as I can spare; & I shall take payment in your Books, & in such of the Books of other Booksellers in Boston as you can procure.[20]

In 1795, Carey was convinced that few major booksellers sold books on commission. He wrote to John Bradford, that the "chief booksellers" of Philadelphia shied away from commission sales: "Mr. Young, a long time the most eminent Bookseller in this city, has never sent goods on commission anywhere," whereas "Mr. Dobson has almost altogether declined the wholesale business even on credit much more on commission & confines himself to a few select customers."[21] Other Philadelphia printer-booksellers occasionally relied on commission sales when it made the best sense to do so. For example, when Francis Bailey published a pamphlet-sized book by the English religious enthusiast Richard Brothers, he sold copies for cash or credit to most of the principal printer-booksellers in Philadelphia, Boston, and New York. To nineteen other, lesser-known printer-booksellers in areas outside the urban centers, he sold Brother's *Prophecy* on commission.[22]

Carey himself did a huge amount of commission business. He sent his publications and other books to hundreds of correspondents throughout the country. At the turn of the century, one of the aspects of Carey's business that set him apart from other Philadelphia booksellers who had been prominent throughout the 1780s and 1790s was the extent to which he actively moved into wholesaling, seeking out small merchants, shopkeepers, postmasters, and printer-booksellers to whom he could sell his books in quantities, on commission.

The distinction Carey made between wholesaling books on credit or by commission is worth clarifying, as the two methods of financing posed different levels of risk for the publishers. When a publisher offered books on credit, the risk was borne more directly by the buyer. The buyer would receive the books on his own account, meaning that he had simply bought them outright, with a promise to pay. This promise, of course, could be and often was broken, but the transaction represented more than anything else a credit contract and was, therefore, more legally enforceable. Taking books on commission, however, was riskier for the publisher, even as it offered distinct advantages. To begin with, the books were returnable. Robert Aitken's accounts reflect that of the fifty-five books he sent to William P. Young of Charleston beginning in March 1784, Young was only able to sell five; Young returned the remaining volumes to Aitken in September 1795, eleven years after their association began. Perhaps these works, the transactions of the American Philosophical Society, would not make ready sale in Charleston, but this protracted account was far from unusual. The reality was that most books routinely stayed on booksellers' shelves for extended periods of time.[23]

This time lag posed bookkeeping nightmares for publishers who could never really assume that the books they sold on commission would be out of their hands and off their accounts forever. Nevertheless, selling by commission increased significantly the publishers' ability to disseminate their publications. There were no computerized credit bureaus, and publishers, like all early American businessmen, relied on familiarity, character reports, and references to decide whether a customer was creditworthy. This clearly limited the publishers' distribution range, as they were unlikely to know well, if at all, their more far-flung correspondents. On the other side of the transaction, many wholesale buyers could not afford to take the books in any other way but by commission. It took little or no outlay of capital or exercise of credit to receive and sell books on commission, so it was often the only way young, unknown, or otherwise credit-poor agents could break into the business.

This may have been exactly why Carey was willing to take the risk with commission sales. He was able to exercise considerable power over his commission agents, determining commissions, choosing the books to send, and doling out advice and directives of all kinds. Carey even reserved the right to set up more than one commission store in an area, telling one disgruntled commission agent in Danville, Kentucky, who had heard rumors of competition that while he "had no intention at present to supply any other store than yours what I shall do at any future day shall be regulated by existing circumstances."[24] To another retailer in Knoxville, about whom Carey had had good reports, he took "the liberty to consign to you on commission a valuable collection of Books" and promised that "should I not be disappointed in these expectations I shall maintain in your store as extensive and valuable an assortment of books as are to be met with in any Country store in America." He went on to explain that he expected to be paid "the usual shop prices" — full retail price, minus a small commission — because of "the very obvious risque I run in sending them & the likelihood of some of them proving unsaleable." To recommend this way of doing business, he assured his new correspondent that "these are the terms in which I have hitherto sent the Books to Danville & Lexington."[25]

Sometimes consignment store keepers also bought books on their own accounts when they were specially ordered by customers. For example, one Virginia postmaster who kept a bookstore from which he vended Carey's books was careful not to let Carey forget that when he took the risk of buying the books outright (at higher discounts), he should have the right to demand what books he or his customers pleased, on the terms most acceptable to him. "I will thank you to endeavour to fulfill the orders I send for books," he wrote from Dumfries, " . . . as obliging particular people, depends principally on my sales."[26]

Quantity Sales to Retailers

Booksellers' surviving accounts indicate that after exchanges and commission sales "simple" wholesale transactions made up the next largest portion of their businesses. Publishers had always offered their books at a discount when they were purchased in quantity. Advertisements in newspapers, particularly those printed in rural areas, routinely offered "liberal allowances" to anyone wishing to buy numerous copies. Quantities of books could be bought at discounts of anywhere from 10 to 40 percent.

One publisher who sold large quantities of books to other booksellers and retailers was Michael Billmeyer, the major publisher and supplier of German language books in America.[27] His accounts show him sending German religious and school books by the dozens to the large and dispersed German communities across Pennsylvania and Ohio and in the backcountry settlements of Maryland and North Carolina. He kept wholesale accounts with other booksellers and with storekeepers and schoolteachers.[28] Because Billmeyer was the major source for German books, and because these books were needed to round out the assortment even in non-German bookstores, he was able to conduct a greater portion of his transactions on cash and credit terms rather than as exchanges or commission sales. Not all of the books he sold were his own publications, but he established himself as the wholesale supplier for the German-speaking nation. Billmeyer and his sons, who took over his business early in the nineteenth century, sat at the center of the German book network in Philadelphia, ordering from smaller German publishers, having books printed by German printers, and retailing and wholesaling to the rest of the community.

Because he specialized in German books and had a virtual monopoly on the German book market, Billmeyer did not need to be overly concerned with assortment, as no one expected to buy English-language books from him. He all but abandoned cumbersome exchanges, a practice still necessary for many others; instead, he could concentrate on being the country's most prominent publisher and supplier of German books. In these respects, Billmeyer resembled many mid-nineteenth-century publishers who had taken to specialized publishing and who spent their energies selling and distributing books through wholesale channels. It would be many years before his English-language colleagues would follow his lead.

There were occasions when publishers disagreed over whether a book should be transmitted through exchange, on commission, or on wholesale cash or credit terms. In part this was due to confusion over the differences between retail, wholesale, and various trade discounts. There was no set discount for books sold in quantity by any publisher to anyone else. Much depended on the quantity ordered, the demand for the book or books in question, the relationship between the two parties, and the terms of payment. Mathew Carey and James Rivington of New York squabbled over such issues when Rivington wanted to get a number of Carey's Bibles on exchange for novels he had imported from England. Carey stated that he never exchanged his Bibles — they were his main source of cash and credit in the trade — and that Rivington would have to take other titles on exchange. Carey knew that if his Bibles circulated through the exchange network, their value would plummet, so he kept them in a special state of reserve. His explanation to Rivington sheds light on the relative advantages of cash and credit wholesaling over exchanging, as well on the unwritten rules of discounting. It should be remembered that exchanges almost always were conducted at retail prices, to keep each transaction fair:

With respect to bibles, they . . . are sold at only 5 per cent discount on the wholesale price, and unless 100 or 200 be taken must be paid for in cash, on delivery. If the former number be taken, 45 days credit is allowed — if the latter, 60 days. If therefore any of these be put in exchange, they must be charged at the retail prices. . . . Indeed, we should rather except . . . bibles from the traffic altogether — but if they are to be brought in, it must be as we have said, at the retail rates.[29]

Publishing Combinations

Publishing combinations, which served many of the same purposes that exchanges and commission sales did, represented another of the publisher's attempts to participate on a national level. Combination was a method of financing and producing books that fit specifically the wholesale approach to publishing or the extension of publishing to a national market. These combinations resembled the late eighteenth-century English shareholding venture. As a partner in a combination publication, a publisher received his share of the books at cost or at a price lower than the cost to other members of the trade. This made him a true partner because his costs, profits, and losses were matched to those of the other partners. Combination publishing tended to be national in scope. Publishers from all urban areas, rather than publishers from the same city or region only, joined together to publish books. Inter-regional publishing combinations were inspired by the literary fairs begun in 1802. These gatherings allowed publishers to assign

faces to their numerous correspondents — people with whom they had conducted exchanges for years. Indeed, one of the chief benefits of these meetings, according to one attendee, was the network of "new connections,
leading to a more extensive and certain trade."[30]

Publishers from all of the major cities as well as numerous mid-sized
towns set to work forging myriad "partnerships" for publishing hundreds
of titles. The "first American edition" of Barthelemy's *Travels of Anacharsis
the Younger in Greece* was jointly published by Jacob Johnson & Company
of Philadelphia, along with Birch and Small (Philadelphia), W. P. and L.
Blake (Boston), Thomas and Whipple (Newburyport), James Oram (Trenton), James Wilson (Wilmington), Warner and Hanna (Baltimore), Samuel
Pleasants (Richmond), and John Hoff (Charleston) in 1804.[31] The printer,
whose name appeared in a separate printer's colophon, was William F.
M'Laughlin of Philadelphia. Each of the partners had a separate title page
printed to reflect the locations of their respective bookstores, from which
this large four-volume work could be purchased directly. The volume was
not likely to have been found for sale, however, at M'Laughlin's printing
shop, as his role was to print the book, not to publish or sell it.

Co-published books were primarily expensive, multi-volume editions.
Sometimes the printer and the place of printing were not even named in
the imprint, further emphasizing the national — indeed international — nature of the publication, as well as deemphasizing the role of the printer.
Joint publications tended to be works that previously had been considered
too expensive for one publisher alone to reprint. With nationally based,
shared risk, it became possible to undertake large publications; moreover,
although the books the publisher chose were classic British or European
texts, they lent themselves particularly well to American updating. The publishers were always looking for books that, once edited by an American —
and newly copyrighted — would take on a particular usefulness for American readers. World histories were thus emended to include discussions of
North America, Indians, and American development. Botanical works had
information on American plants and herbs added to them. Dictionaries
were given extra entries for American English words. In one example,
Jacques Henri Bernardin de Saint-Pierre's *Studies of Nature* contained "the
addition of numerous original notes and illustrations, by Benjamin Smith
Barton, M.D. President of the Philadelphia Linnean Society, and Professor
or Materia Medica, Natural History and Botany, in the University of Pennsylvania."[32] In light of Barton's attainments, the British translator of the

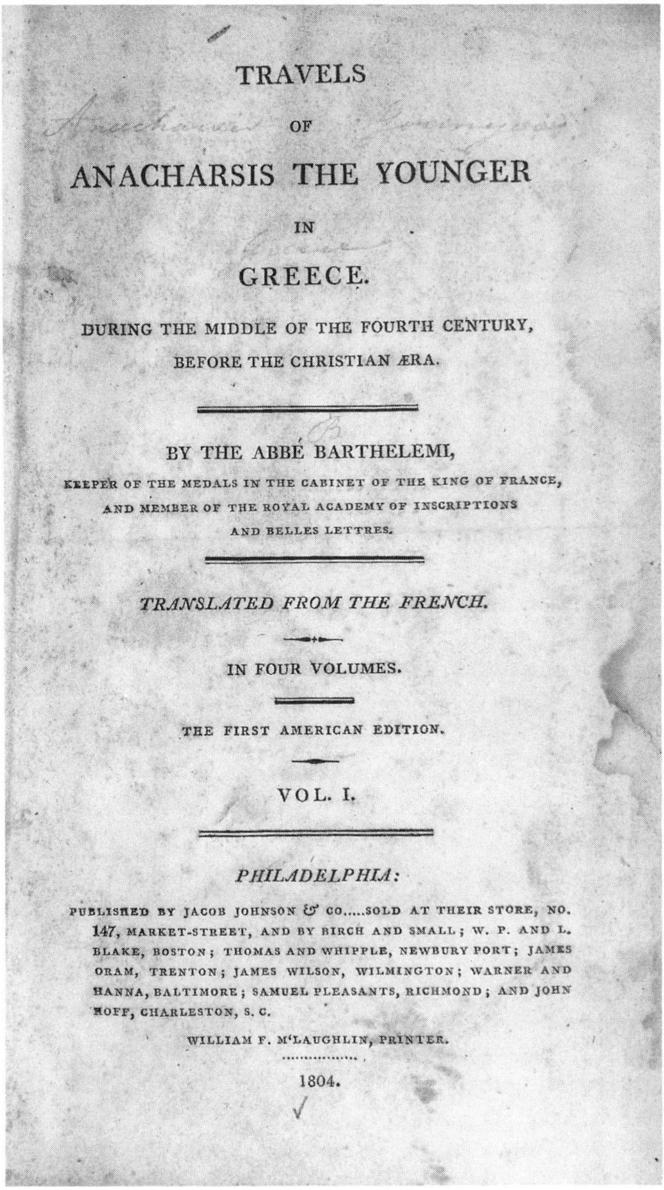

TRAVELS

OF

ANACHARSIS THE YOUNGER

IN

GREECE.

DURING THE MIDDLE OF THE FOURTH CENTURY,

BEFORE THE CHRISTIAN ÆRA.

BY THE ABBÉ BARTHELEMI,

KEEPER OF THE MEDALS IN THE CABINET OF THE KING OF FRANCE,
AND MEMBER OF THE ROYAL ACADEMY OF INSCRIPTIONS
AND BELLES LETTRES.

TRANSLATED FROM THE FRENCH.

IN FOUR VOLUMES.

THE FIRST AMERICAN EDITION.

VOL. I.

PHILADELPHIA:

PUBLISHED BY JACOB JOHNSON & CO.....SOLD AT THEIR STORE, NO. 147, MARKET-STREET, AND BY BIRCH AND SMALL; W. P. AND L. BLAKE, BOSTON; THOMAS AND WHIPPLE, NEWBURY PORT; JAMES ORAM, TRENTON; JAMES WILSON, WILMINGTON; WARNER AND HANNA, BALTIMORE; SAMUEL PLEASANTS, RICHMOND; AND JOHN HOFF, CHARLESTON, S. C.

WILLIAM F. M'LAUGHLIN, PRINTER.
....
1804.

Figure 5. Title page (v. 1), *Travels of Anacharsis the Younger in Greece*. Photo courtesy of the Library Company of Philadelphia.

work, Henry Hunter, received only small notice on the title page. As with so many reprints, the American edition was reduced in size and price, comprising three volumes rather than the five volumes of the British edition.

Reducing the size of books was a practice closely associated with both individual and combination publishing in America. By reducing book size, publishers could keep their costs down and offer their products at competitive prices. When enticing a fellow publisher to join in a venture, the initiator often mentioned shortening the text or making changes to the British or European editions that would make the book more cost-efficient. The decision to reduce a book's size, however, often brought with it a host of literary and textual decisions, such as those faced by Daniel Mallory of Boston when he published Sir Walter Scott's Waverly novels. Mallory hoped to tempt McCarty and Davis of Philadelphia into copublishing the book by explaining that the novels would be "condensed, [and] pruned of all the unnecessary digressions." Part of the story might be lost, but, he stressed, "You must be aware that there is a great deal of rubbish — such as the long introductions &c."[33] In a similarly economical vein, when McCarty and Davis planned to publish the complete dramatic works of Shakespeare, they shortened the edition by separating the plays' acts with dashes rather than copying the London edition in which "each act begins a page . . . swell[ing] the work unnecessarily."[34] Such decisions associated with combination publishing were often made by several publishers who argued back and forth about how best to reduce production costs.

Economic exigencies, trade relations, and inter-regional concerns all became intertwined with the finished literary product. This had always been the case with English novels republished in America. Throughout the eighteenth century, English novels reprinted in America were almost invariably reduced in bulk. They were issued in one volume if the English original had appeared in two, and if the original had been three volumes, the American version would usually be reduced to two. Often the American editions were abridged, although even "complete" versions used smaller type and reduced the texts' leading (space between lines) and margins.[35] The publishers were little concerned about the integrity of the texts they published; they simply wished to produce cheaper books in easy-to-sell formats. Reducing the size, adding explanatory footnotes to define archaic English words in Shakespeare, ridding books of tedious introductions — these were all decisions dictated by the balance sheets. Yet the enterprise of the cost-cutting publishers was supported by their belief that they understood American tastes and proclivities. Indeed, the democratization of print, combined with an increasingly literate but spread-out population, had decisive effects on texts and their presentation.

Some jointly published imprints were undertaken by groups of publishers who had family connections with one another. While national in scope, these publishing combinations may have mitigated any concerns about dealing with strangers. Thus, C. and A. Conrad of Philadelphia published a seventeen-volume edition of Shakespeare's plays with Conrad firms in Baltimore, Petersburg, and Norfolk.[36] As with many of the joint publications, no printer was named in the imprint. In forming this type of combination, the Conrads kept the fruits of their investment in the family while ensuring substantial southern distribution under the scrutiny of trusted family members and their respective partners.

At least one of William Woodward's joint publishing schemes represented a kind of "family" enterprise, as his copublishers of Thomas Scott's family Bible were evangelical publishers; like Woodward, they specialized in publishing and selling religious works. No doubt they were acquainted through church affairs and trusted one another. It is also likely that cooperation in publishing the Bible prevented competition among them even as it provided risk-sharing benefits.[37] It made sense to identify and work with one's competitors when it came to producing books for specific markets.

Combination publications are not always identifiable by their imprints, however. Publishers' business records reveal that risk-sharing took place in many more instances than title pages would indicate. Books published with combined resources and under the auspices of several publishers must be considered combination publications of a sort. For instance, David Longworth, a New York publisher, specialized in dramatic publishing. Yet according to his correspondence with Carey, there were few plays he considered publishing without offering substantial shares to Carey and other publishers. Carey's name would generally not appear on Longworth's title pages — although sometimes it did — but Carey was guaranteed a supply of the plays, an agreed-upon territory for distribution, and a part of the profits. As was the case for Woodward and his fellow religious publishers' monopoly on theological publishing, Longworth maintained a hold on dramatic publishing by including other major publishers throughout the country in his investments. In one instance, Carey, upset by a slow shipment of plays from Longworth, threatened to publish some plays himself. Longworth became frantic, saying that if Carey did so, he might retaliate by publishing Bibles, Carey's steadiest source of income. Carey dared him to try, and Longworth glumly conceded, "I perfectly understand [your] reply which naturally grows out of the high ground on which you stand; both as to capital and [your] vast stock on hand." But he felt it necessary to make his case absolutely clear:

The ground of complaint is simply this: if you print plays there are less left for me to print; if I print Bibles there are less for you to print and the natural consequence is our transactions must be lessened together and less cordial.[38]

Combinations then, served a variety of functions. They provided built-in distribution networks and wider assortments, just as exchanges and commission sales had always done. They kept publishers of like tendencies from reprinting the same titles and diminishing the market share. They allowed publishers to share risks on expensive books. With title pages listing publishers from all over the country, they created a greater sense of a national trade and a national market; the content of the works published in this manner was often subject to group decisions about production costs. At the same time, joint imprints had the effect of placing the printers in the background, often eliminating them from the public eye altogether. Printers' colophons, when they appeared at all, were miniscule when compared with the long lists of publishers' names gracing the title page. Joint publications made clear to consumers that printers were no longer likely to be a common source of supply for the books they wanted to buy.

Publishers as Capitalists

Throughout the colonial period in North America, printers were directly involved in other aspects of the trade. The Saurs of Germantown erected paper mills and set up type foundries that supplied them with paper and type for their German Bibles. Benjamin Franklin bought the contents of a French type foundry to set up his grandson Benjamin Franklin Bache in the business in Philadelphia. Francis Bailey bought a typefounding establishment from Jacob Bey and proceeded to supply mainly his own printing shops in Philadelphia and Lancaster with type. The Baines, Scottish typefounders, settled in Philadelphia at the behest of the printers Young and McCulloch. For the most part, when colonial printers branched out into other parts of the trade, either by engaging family members or by taking up the work themselves, they were assured of procuring better sources of supply than they might otherwise have had. In addition, they found employment for their families and friends, and remained flexible, largely through their expanded abilities. Christopher Saur was greatly admired because of his talents in all branches of the trade, something that earned him a reputation for "ingenuity" and flexibility. Isaiah Thomas remarked in his *History* that Saur "was adroit at sixteen different trades or avocations, by following either of which he could secure a maintenance."[39]

Publishers in early national Philadelphia not only looked to other publishers to pool resources and keep costs down, they also employed aggressive techniques to broaden their powers over the book trade as a whole. Publishers invested in and attempted to control other aspects of the trade, such as papermaking, inkmaking, and typefounding. It had long been the practice among printers to exercise control through vertical integration. Papermaking, in particular, was a vital trade connection, because paper represented the greatest expense to the printer. Relationships between printers and papermakers date to the earliest days of printing because, as Henri-Jean Martin has noted, "the prosperity of either trade depended upon that of the other."[40] Printers and booksellers throughout Europe would often buy shares in or rent local paper mills in order to guarantee access to this valuable commodity. The relationships often worked both ways, with papermakers acting as informal "bankers to the printers and booksellers," since books sold slowly and papermakers generally had to wait until the books were disposed of to collect their money.[41]

In some ways, Pennsylvania's first printer, more than his colonial contemporaries, resembled the publishers in the early national period who hoped to exercise as much control over ancillary trades as possible. William Bradford was a principal partner in America's first paper mill, located on the Wissahickon Creek near Philadelphia. For his investment he received an assured supply of printing paper and, for at least several years, obtained "[first] refusal of all the printing paper they made at ten shillings per ream."[42] Because he did not himself make the paper, and because one of his main interests was to shut out any potential competition, as well as to supply himself, his connections with the Rittenhouse Mill resembled the activities of the publishers of the early republic. Nevertheless, Bradford intended the paper to be for his own use, and in that respect he fit the model of the colonial artisan seeking out better sources of supply.

In the first few decades of the nineteenth century, publishers engaged in a flurry of investment in trades related to printing. In 1809, Carey instructed Bailey to concentrate more money and energy in his typefounding interests as new mines for antimony, a metallic element used in type, were being discovered. Carey wanted to prevent the local typefounders, Binny and Ronaldson, from securing a monopoly, as this would increase the price of type to the printers Carey employed.[43] In 1810, the Conrads invested in various aspects of papermaking with two main purposes in mind: First, they hoped to gain a better supply source for their many publishing projects, and second, they saw papermaking as a profitable venture, when coupled with their existing business of publishing and retail and wholesale bookselling.[44]

The printing and bookselling firm of McCarty and Davis investigated various ways to keep their publishing costs down through vertical integration. They gathered information about newfangled rag-bleaching and papermaking machines. They invested in a paper mill in New Jersey.[45] They toyed with the idea of opening stereotyping shops and with outfitting a new printing office with horse- or steam-powered presses. Each of these contemplated enterprises would be run by people who were already trained in the appropriate skills, at locations throughout New York, New Jersey, and Pennsylvania. The resulting paper, stereotype plates, and printing would supply McCarty and Davis's needs and would also be sold to other publishers; the profits from the enterprises would, of course, be McCarty and Davis's.[46]

Several factors then distinguish the later combinations from the colonial model: First, the later publishers did not restrict their interests in ancillary trades to their immediate geographic areas. They bought interests in paper mills and typefoundries (and antimony mines) all over the country. Second, they did not necessarily use the products of these trades for their own printing. As we have seen, many publishers gave up printing by the early nineteenth century. However, their interests as publishers more than ever lay in keeping printing costs low; being able to supply one's printer or printers with paper at cost was a distinct advantage.

The publishers sought to reduce costs by investing in technological improvements in printing and print-related trades.[47] Indeed, the early republic saw an astounding increase in invention and innovation in all trades.[48] One obvious explanation for this increase within the printing trade was the rise in demand for printed material, as described by historians who have explored readership and consumption.[49] Another way to explain the changes in printing technology is to refer, once again, to the division in the trade between publisher and printer. Mechanically minded printers could compete for publisher's business by offering the best, cheapest, and fastest printing. They could take on more jobs. The most innovative of the printer-inventors who knew how to market their inventions could become entrepreneurs themselves — which a number of them did, thereby leaving printing behind as their primary trade.[50]

Nevertheless, the impact of technological innovation remained somewhat limited. While printers and publishers sought ways to reduce costs, and investments in technology played a part in this, most of the effects of their efforts occurred later. Despite publishers' challenges to papermakers to develop new manufacturing techniques, most books before 1830 were still printed on handmade paper.[51] Mass-produced cloth case bindings for books were not used regularly until after 1825; before that time, every book still had to be bound by hand.[52] And while there was a move away from wooden presses, encouraged by the unveiling in 1814 of George Clymer's heavy iron press (the richly ornamented Columbian), few structural changes in presses were made that would affect the efficiency of printing.[53] It was also not until the late teens and early twenties that printers experimented with horse- and steam-powered presses. Yet it was no wonder the publishers were eager to encourage the development of power presses: the huge machines were often designed so that half-sheets could be printed on both sides. In addition, more than one press could be hitched to the source of power, thereby making for an exceptionally speedy printing process. One power press operated by three people could double the speed of the hand-press while lowering the cost of labor.[54]

Improvements in printing presses were obviously intended to meet the demand of publishers and other large customers. The various Bible and tract societies were advanced in their use of the latest technologies because of their urgent needs for huge amounts of printed matter.[55] The growth in newspaper and periodical publishing also pushed the limits of printing innovation.[56] Newspapers also made limited use of machine-made paper.[57] Book publishing was somewhat slower to capitalize on these improvements.

Still, stereotype plate printing, which printers experimented with in the late teens and twenties, was quickly embraced by book publishers. Indeed, they actively sought out printers who could master the technology.[58] The earliest known attempt to stereotype, or to "make type metal perfect facsimiles of the faces of pages of movable type," took place in China in the year 1041.[59] Since then, printers and typefounders tried numerous methods to make such plates, but it was not until the eighteenth century that a method practical for commercial printing was developed. The most significant innovation in the process came in 1800 when Charles Mahon, Earl of Stanhope, added his improvements to the existing methods.[60] Stanhope, a

nobleman with strong populist leanings who wanted to encourage the democratization of print, was eager for his innovations to be made available
to skilled craftsmen in England and in America; however, his methods
were adopted and understood only gradually in the United States. John
Watt, an Englishman familiar with Stanhope's methods and with those of
the Frenchman Firmin Didot, started a printing shop with stereotyping
facilities in New York in 1809. In 1813, a book was published bearing
the imprint "The Larger Catechism. The first book ever stereotyped in
America. New York: Stereotyped and printed by J. Watts & Co. for Whiting & Watson, June 1813."[61] In 1812, David Bruce, a New York printer, went
to London to attempt to learn the Stanhope process, while Mathew Carey
and other members of the American trade did what they could to find out
more about the technique.[62] Philadelphia's publishers were eager to have
their typefounders and printers learn the process as well, but they did not
succeed in luring an experienced stereotyper to Philadelphia until after New
York already boasted several.[63]

Stereotyping involved the casting of metal plates from molds taken
from set type. These plates could be used over and over again and then
easily stored; thus there was no longer any need to invest in large amounts
of type to keep a book standing. When a new edition was required, the
stereotype plates could be put on the presses to produce the printed material. This method also saved composition costs, as once the plates were
made, it would not be necessary to set the type again for subsequent editions. The original type could be distributed or sold. Stereotyping meant
that publishers could have small impressions printed frequently at little extra cost, without overproduction. Valuable capital would not be tied up in
paper that had been committed to print.[64] After all, little had changed from
fifteenth-century Europe, when papermakers acted as informal bankers to
printers and booksellers, waiting until books sold to collect payment on the
long credits they had given in exchange for their paper.

Because it could make the publishers' business more efficient, stereotyping had obvious attractions. The development of this technology, however, also carried greater significance: When a publisher went to the trouble
and expense of stereotyping a work, it was unlikely that another publisher
would be willing to "repeat" that effort; moreover, the publisher in possession of plates could go straight to press without the expense of repeated
composition, thus enabling him to reach a market quickly and cheaply. In
a sense, this created a form of copyright protection, giving the original stereotyping publisher a tremendous advantage. The plates' value did not end

there, however, as the original publisher could rent or sell them to other publishers who wished to bring out the book with their own imprint.[65]

Stereotyping was immediately regarded by publishers as invaluable for publishing steady-selling books. School books and Bibles were the most frequently stereotyped books, as their demand was assured and their texts underwent few changes.[66] Plates could, however, be altered to a limited degree, at a fraction of the cost of recomposition. Publishers also saw in stereotyping an opportunity to bring out enduring editions of books that had traditionally been imported from England. Books such as the complete works of Shakespeare required complicated composition and footnotes, and there already were good British editions available in the American market. American publishers had previously shied away from sinking money into such works, but McCarty and Davis's publication of Shakespeare's works demonstrates how this changed with the introduction of stereotyping into American publishing.

As early as 1820, McCarty and Davis decided to have the complete dramatic works of Shakespeare stereotyped. They commissioned the Philadelphia typefounder James Ronaldson to cast the necessary type. McCarty and Davis counted on being able to use their own workers to set the type and expected to find someone to make the stereotype plates from the set type. However, after they inquired around Philadelphia it became clear that no one there knew how to perform the process correctly. Ronaldson's partner, Binny, offered stereotype specimens so poor that McCarty exclaimed: "A pretty character indeed, to pretend to a capacity to do such a job as Shakspeare!"[67] Finally, McCarty and Davis had to resort to New York craftsmen, several of whom had mastered the technique. They settled on Jedediah Howe, a New York printer, and negotiated for months over price, who should set the type, how many sets of plates should be cast, and so on.

McCarty and Davis tried, without immediate success, to compel Howe to move to Philadelphia to set up a stereotyping shop, promising that no serious competition existed. Howe would not commit to such a move, however, expressing concerns about others who might try the same thing and about resettling his family in Philadelphia. He did not relocate until 1824, so the Shakespeare edition had to be produced in New York. To reduce composition costs, McCarty and Davis committed five "boys" (probably older apprentices) to Howe's care in New York, where they were to set the type for the stereotyper. In 1822, the production of the Shakespeare volume was underway, with the transplanted workers composing type under Howe's scrutiny. But it was not long before Howe began sending McCarty and Davis proof sheets that indicated that serious problems had arisen. "As is always the case with those not used to stereotype work," Howe wrote, "[the workers'] proofs have been *very troublesome*." Howe tried to convince the compositors that "good justification" was essential to setting type properly for stereotype platemaking. One frustrated lad, Howe reported, exclaimed that he "*did not care* [and] that if he could not do the work well enough I might inform Mr. Davis so, as he did not care to work on't any longer."[68] In addition, the boys began to grumble, insisting to their overseer that "as they are in N. York their work ought to be counted at the New York prices," something which McCarty and Davis had hoped to avoid. (In fact, McCarty and Davis had agreed to charge Howe New York wages for their workers' labor; they, in turn, paid the boys the lower Philadelphia wages.) Several quit and looked for work elsewhere in New York.

In 1823 the plates were finished and sent to McCarty and Davis, who had them printed from in their own shop in Philadelphia. The Shakespeare ordeal, however, proved to be profitable for McCarty and Davis. In 1823, at the height of the production problems, McCarty and Davis had struck a deal with Carey and Lea to copublish the work. This risk-sharing enabled the first edition to see the light of day; however subsequent printings — and there were many — belonged to McCarty and Davis alone. In addition, the firm sold or rented the plates to publishers in New York and Hartford, each of whom issued editions. Moreover, McCarty and Davis had learned from their experience with Shakespeare that while stereotyping was the most efficient and profitable way to publish, they needed closer control over the process as well as their craftsmen. Once they convinced Howe to move to Philadelphia to open his stereotyping shop, he stereotyped many of the books they subsequently published.[69] McCarty and Davis's edition of Shakespeare, with its two large octavo volumes, set the standard for how Shakespeare's plays would be published in America throughout most of the nineteenth century. As late as 1849, Thomas Davis, the surviving partner, was still producing the Shakespeare edition, and in 1851, at his death, the plates sold at a publisher's trade sale, on his estate's behalf, for $1400.[70] Competitors' editions bore marked resemblence to the first stereotyped Shakespeare, suggesting that capturing the Bard in a mold was a significant publishing feat indeed.[71]

During the first thirty years of the nineteenth century, the business activities of publishers diverged more and more from the daily work of printers. Publishers, concentrating increasingly on producing books for a national market, expanded their enterprises to include other publishers from around the country. They continued to rely upon the traditional methods of exchange and commission sales not so much to increase their assortments, as previously, but to establish wholesale bookselling networks. They turned to craftsmen from all over the country to produce their books, and they invested in and encouraged the development of new technologies, even if many of the fruits of innovation were not realized until later. The publishers' investment strategies and desire to tap new markets, as we shall see in the following chapters, led them to deal with unfamiliar people in distant places, but they had yet to fully allocate their resources to such goals. As long as the country lacked unified banking and monetary systems and a transportation network that would more easily allow for national distribution, publishers' business strategies, of necessity, remained regional rather than national.

5

Credit Networks and the
New Publishers

THE PUBLISHERS OF THE EARLY REPUBLIC acted, in every sense, as entrepreneurs. They manipulated a system of debt and credit, always looking
for ways to invest their capital in new publishing enterprises. They used
their profits and credit based on anticipated profits to publish more books.
Furthermore, these entrepreneurs of the book trade carefully estimated
production costs and overhead. By the process of estimating costs, the publishers attempted to impose some order and control over their enterprises
which, by their nature, were risky and speculative.

In 1794, Mathew Carey was able to boast to his father in Ireland that
his business had received a much-needed boost. "I have established credit
with the bank," he wrote, "by means of which I can employ in trade a thousand dollars beyond my capital." This extension, he added, "gives me great
advantages."[1] In the absence of adequate bank records, it is impossible to
tell just how many publishers would have made similar banking arrangements, but publishers' account books and correspondence suggest that
bank credit played a relatively minor role in their finances. Carey had a particular desire, as he later expressed in his autobiography, to gain bank favor.
It not only extended his capital, but made him feel that he had finally risen
above his artisanal station. Although he was as deeply mired in the credit
network of his trade as any other publisher, he hated the system that made
trade members rely on each other for credit. This system too often left them
clutching one another in an effort to stay afloat. Yet rely on each other they
did. The early republic lacked such financial amenities as a regulated banking system, a national bankruptcy law, and a standard currency, making the
amassing of credit through private means the key to publishers' operations.

Like many entrepreneurs of the early nineteenth century, publishers
spread their risks by extending and receiving large amounts of credit. Their
heavy reliance on credit to finance their publishing ventures made them

particularly eager to maintain strong credit standings and sterling business reputations. Nevertheless, publishers frequently faced insolvency or were connected with those who did, particularly during economic downturns. An analysis of the patterns of financial failure among members of the printing and publishing trades allows us to see how their credit networks provided publishers with the means to publish and distribute books while at the same time delaying their participation in a more national economy and market. This chapter explores the publishers' credit networks during the first thirty years of the nineteenth century by examining their surviving business records. In it, I argue that economic manipulation and financial instability defined the early national publishing trade. The transitional group of printers and publishers whose careers we have been following experimented with all sorts of financing, all the while expecting their peers to lend support when needed. This support usually came in the form of massive note endorsements, a form of credit extension that became obsolete within their lifetimes but which dictated the way they conducted their businesses. Future generations of publishers would enjoy the advantages of a more regulated banking system while exacting greater assurances of credit worthiness from individuals with whom they did business, whether they knew them or not.

Accounting Methods

The author of an 1826 guide to accounting entitled *The Mercantile Arithmetic* argued that "every one is bound by his duty to himself and others, to keep accounts."[2] The guide went on to demonstrate how a system of double-entry accounting would increase the efficiency and profitability of any tradesman's business. Indeed, it pointed out, keeping one's business profitable was the duty of every citizen. According to many economic historians, double-entry bookkeeping, which dates from fourteenth-century Italy, was essential to the development of modern capitalism because it allowed business owners to evaluate profits and losses by reference to their books; in turn, it had the effect of "rationalizing and methodizing business life."[3] Single-entry bookkeeping only allowed for a simple, linear evaluation of one's business, whereas double-entry provided a system to keep track of one's debts and credits by placing them side by side on opposing pages of a ledger. In addition, the new method required that separate books be kept in order to clearly record information in distinct ways. The waste book or daybook kept track, chronologically, of daily transactions. The journal broke the information down into debtor and creditor accounts, but kept them in chronological order. And the ledger recorded the final information, by account, usually alphabetically. According to one manual, the ideal to be "aimed at in Book-keeping," was as follows:

[H]e ought to know, by inspecting his Books, to whom he owes, and who owes him; what Goods he has purchased; what he has disposed of, with the Gain or Loss upon the Sale, and what he has yet on hand; what Goods or Money he has in the Hands of Factors; what ready Money he has by him; what his Stock was at first; what Alterations and Changes it has suffered since, and what it now amounts to.[4]

Very few full sets of account books survive for early American printing or publishing firms, but it is possible, from what is extant, to determine how business was transacted and recorded.

Despite the improvements in bookkeeping offered by the double-entry system, many Americans (with the notable exception of merchants), clung wholly or in part to single-entry systems well into the first half of the nineteenth century.[5] Perhaps they found, as one Philadelphian noted, that double-entry bookkeeping was "too diffuse, elaborate, and on the whole not well calculated for general and extensive business."[6] One accounting manual, first published in Edinburgh in 1736 and republished throughout Britain and America, noted that the double-entry method had only just caught on "in most Parts of *Europe*," suggesting that in Great Britain and in the colonies, such a system had yet to take root.[7]

Benjamin Franklin, always the innovator and systematizer, would have certainly been among the first to keep such records, yet he did so only in fits and starts, and never seemed to have developed a true double-entry system for his printing business. His cramped ledgers, sometimes kept by his wife, have always baffled historians who have tried to make sense of his business. Nevertheless, they are difficult not by virtue of any complicated system, but because they were kept linearly (in daybook fashion), with many accounts never finding their way into his ledgers. Double-entry bookkeeping was simply not as necessary to his kind of business—and to other colonial printing shops—as it would be for his nineteenth-century publishing successors. Franklin did resort to forms of double-entry and increasingly used a ledger when recording his larger, more complicated, and long-standing accounts—in other words, when he acted as "banker" or publisher. Interestingly, when Franklin went to London, he kept the best accounts yet, even recording profits and losses accounts, true to the form outlined in the up-to-date accounting manuals.[8] Other Philadelphia printers exhibited similarly idiosyncratic methods. Franklin's competitor, William Bradford, actually did a better job of incorporating the double-entry system into his books, yet his ledger was chronologically arranged (to correspond to the daybook) and he simply crossed out accounts when they were settled. This meant he still had to go through his books chronologically to find an old account.[9] In the last quarter of the eighteenth century, Robert Aitken's accounts show that the Italian method had made some inroads. He carefully stuck to the system of keeping a waste book (or daybook) and recorded regularly from it to double entries in a ledger, noting which accounts had been settled or lost.[10] It appears that for artisans (producers), double-entry bookeeping was less useful than it was for merchants (distributors).

The publishers of the early republic relied much more strictly on double-entry, multiple-book accounting. This reflected the requirements of their profession. They had a constant need to evaluate their profits and losses, as the nature of their business — investment in books — required such analysis. Without clear accounts, a publisher ran the risk of becoming insolvent without realizing it until it was too late.[11]

Keeping systematic accounts was necessary not only to be able to evaluate profits and losses, but to enable *others* to make sense of one's books. This was part of a tradesman's duty to his family, as upon his death, clear accounts would make settlement easier. A good accountant could protect his family after death as well as during his life. Keeping sloppy books carried the same kind of stigma as dying intestate. In addition, carefully kept books were often permissible in court as evidence, whereas poor records were usually tossed out. Thus one had a duty to protect his business and family in the eyes of the law by way of good bookkeeping.[12] From their accounts it seems likely that publishers realized the importance of good bookkeeping to the survival of their businesses and reputations. As publishers sat at the center of the book trade, they were involved in both wholesale and retail trade relationships. They also conducted complicated exchanges, which they meticulously recorded in their exchange books. These books invariably used a form of double entry, as it was necessary to see at a glance where an exchange account stood. Taking physical inventories was extremely difficult because of the constant reexchanging of books. Because publishers rarely used cash, and relied instead on notes, bank notes, books, paper, newspaper advertising space, rags, and a variety of goods and services, their account books had to make it easy to evaluate the relative worth of all these mediums of exchange. Daybooks alone would make such a feat impossible, particularly when it came to settling accounts. Therefore, aside from a daybook or waste book for recording daily activity, publishers often kept at least one formal ledger, as well as a less formal journal, an exchange book, letterbooks, and other types of logs recording such things as notes receivable and payable and bank transactions.[13] In this manner, every individual or firm with whom a publisher dealt was accorded a separate account to allow the publisher to evaluate the extent and profitability of his business with each customer and tradesman.

If a publisher needed to know the state of his business, he would take a full stock of his inventory and any printing work or other equipment in his shop or warehouse. He would also balance his books, something which required a great deal of cooperation from those with whom he did business. Publishers regularly requested accounts from one another, as well as from other tradesmen. This meant furnishing each other with copies of the account activity for the purpose of comparison. If one publisher found he was owed forty dollars by another, as well as one hundred dollars worth of exchange books, he could only hope that his correspondent had the same numbers recorded. The accounts were usually quite close, with most discrepancies due to differences over insurance and shipping costs. This indicates a degree of uniformity in how books were kept. The relatively low incidence of disagreement over accounts, however, was mainly due to the close written contact publishers maintained with their trading partners, constantly updating and reminding one another of payment or goods due to be received or shipped. Leaving little to chance, publishers kept careful tabs on their accounts.

Throughout the early decades of the nineteenth century, publishers maintained their regular local commercial ties while stretching the boundaries of their long-distance trade. Within their immediate community, publishers kept accounts with printers, bookbinders, papermakers, stationers, merchants, and other local tradesmen. In areas ranging from the hinterlands of Philadelphia to all other parts of the country, publishers transacted business with postmasters, schoolteachers, country storekeepers and printers, colleges, ministers, and other publishers. With individuals and firms who were familiar, publishers kept book accounts. With far-flung customers, book accounts were often combined with more formal, written credit instruments. There is no indication, however, that they took book accounts any less seriously than written contracts.[14] Publishers and the people with whom they did business entered into contracts, formal or informal, fully expecting to meet the terms of such contracts, whether as debtors or creditors.

Publishers extended and received vast amounts of credit based, in the final analysis, on their anticipated profits. They received credit from other publishers and from tradesmen whose work or products went toward the production of books. Printers, papermakers, binders, and engravers all took notes of hand, bank notes, cash or books in payment for services. Publishers extended credit by disseminating their books, whether on book accounts or by notes, payments promised at harvest time, or any number of other promissory-style arrangements.

The care with which publishers kept their accounts illustrates the depth of their involvement in, and the tight control they attempted to exert over, their credit networks. Their letters suggest a preoccupation with keeping in regular contact with creditors and debtors, for losing control could spell disaster in this delicate system of debt and credit. It was common to explain to a creditor that, because of late payment from one's debtors, it would be impossible to forward payment. To one's debtors a publisher might allude to the impossibility of further supply without payment. Hence the network of debtors and creditors was organically bound together.

The most obvious form of duty in the credit relationship was the obligation of debtors to pay creditors. But the relationship, however, is more reciprocal than this suggests. Creditors owed debtors a form of protection. It was in the creditors' best interests not to call in debts indiscriminately, partly because an insolvent debtor was likely to default and partly because that failure might cause others to default, or to call in their loans. The balance of power in credit relationships was, at best, ambiguous. This ambiguity prompted the publishers to further expand their credit networks, acting at once as creditors and debtors. At any given moment, Philadelphia publishers kept accounts with hundreds of individuals and firms. One of Michael Billmeyer's account books, for example, reveals that he kept accounts with 153 individuals and firms from 1809 to 1815. Most of his accounts were with country booksellers and shopkeepers to whom he supplied German-language books. In the early 1820s, Carey and Son had almost eight hundred accounts in their ledgers, and in 1824, McCarty and Davis's accounts numbered over four hundred.[15] Both Carey and Son and McCarty and Davis transacted business with other members of the trade, as well as with country merchants, traveling sales-men, auctioneers, schools, and libraries.

Credit Relationships Between Publishers and Allied Tradesmen

As publishers' influence grew, their business transactions began to include tradesmen in non-local areas, most notably country printers, with whom publishers negotiated for cheaper printing than could be had from their local, urban printers. We have seen how publishers exerted a degree of con-trol over printing, papermaking, and new technologies, and how this served to increase their centrality in the book trade. In a similar type of trade im-perialism, publishers held the upper hand in their credit relationships with printers and other tradesmen. When publishers were creditors in their re-lationships with printers, they acted as patrons who, in payment for the protection they offered, could demand prompt and often discounted ser-vices. And when publishers were printers' debtors, they could exact lenient terms of credit for the assurance of a steady source of job work. If a debtor were kept from working, for instance, he would be unable to discharge his debts. Publishers' accounts show that printers were often debtors to pub-lishers. Asher Miner, for example, a printer in Doylestown, Pennsylvania, was in debt to Mathew Carey for books, stationery, and cash Carey lent him. As he sank further into debt, he begged Carey to give him printing jobs to help him make his payments. As a result, Carey's continued patron-age of Miner enabled the printer to discharge his debt. Of course Carey was not Miner's only creditor, and when others pressed Miner for payments, he turned to one of his protector-creditors, Carey, for more cash loans. As an interested party, Carey complied. Failing to do so would have meant two things: Miner would probably have become a bad debt for Carey, and Carey would lose one source of cheap printing, that is, printing at prices set under duress.[16] This pattern was repeated over and over again.

The publishers' role in their credit relationships with printers often enabled them to pressure printers into lowering their prices. By the early years of the nineteenth century, having books and pamphlets printed out of the immediate area was fairly routine for urban publishers seeking lower production costs. The publishers would be able to get lower bids from out-of-town printers because expenses were generally higher in the city, and because urban journeymen printers had set prices below which they would not work.[17] Additionally, however, country printers were usually in debt to

Philadelphia publishers for books and other goods they bought to retail. They could pay their debts by printing. These transactions were increasingly possible because transportation between Philadelphia and most country towns in Pennsylvania and New Jersey had become easier and less expensive with the establishment of new turnpikes and the growth of regular stage and ferry services.[18]

Despite the fact that doing business as a printer in Philadelphia was more expensive, Mathew Carey regularly pressured Philadelphia master printers to lower their prices. This in turn meant they would make less profit on their journeymen's labor, but to capture printing jobs from the busy publisher, they would often underbid one another. If he was still not satisfied, Carey would solicit bids from printers elsewhere. For the printing of his pamphlet on the yellow fever epidemic of 1793, for example, Carey took bids from six major job printers in Philadelphia. They all quoted him a price of at least three shillings per token and thousand ems. (A token in Philadelphia was 250 sheets printed on one side. The price of presswork was given by token, thus one token was 250 impressions made on the printing press. Ems are the square of a body of type. They are used as a unit of measurement for composition.) Hoping to do better than this, he wrote to Jacob Bailey, a Lancaster printer, arguing that "if people can, in Philadelphia, work for 3/- they undoubtedly can in Lancaster, where expenses are so much lower."[19] In fact, Carey had a more persuasive if unspoken argument to convince Bailey to conform to his proposed terms. Jacob's brother, Francis, and his nephew, Robert, were deeply obligated to Carey. Carey not only lent money to Francis on an almost weekly basis, but also took in one of his daughters when Francis and his wife moved to the country, thereby allowing her to remain among her friends. Robert too, asked Carey for loans regularly and petitioned the publisher for printing jobs: "Have you any small work to do? I have some hands that I would gladly retain . . . but can't afford to pay them for standing idle." When Robert himself moved to Lancaster, he was always careful to assure Carey that any work he undertook for him would be "on as good terms as you can possibly have it done in the City."[20] Indeed, Jacob Bailey could hardly have refused Carey's terms under these circumstances. By obliging the publisher, the Lancaster printer could gain some credit as well as good will. Leaving little to doubt, Carey played his trump card, informing Jacob that "your brother . . . assured me . . . that he was satisfied, if you could afford the work for less, you would do it."[21]

In the 1820s, the firm of McCarty and Davis thought nothing of having books printed as far away from Philadelphia as Wheeling, Virginia, in order to get the cheapest printing. Thomas Davis and William McCarty each had younger brothers—both journeymen printers—whom they set up in a printing and bookselling partnership there. The western firm of Davis and McCarty relied on the Philadelphia house for books, loans, banking, and credit, and were thus bound to operate under McCarty and Davis's control. With their credit and resources emanating from Philadelphia, the younger partners were bound to print at journeymen's wages. Thus, despite their determination to seek their fortunes as western entrepreneurs, they remained in much the same position as when they set off from Philadelphia.[22] This arrangement was reminiscent of some of the family printing networks of the colonial period.

McCarty and Davis also exercised control over several local printers. Griggs and Dickinson leased the brick building in the back of McCarty and Davis's lot at 171 High (Market) Street in 1823. For the rental property and the assurance of steady printing jobs, Griggs and Dickinson bound themselves to pay the publishers four hundred dollars per year in printing, to be figured at forty cents per thousand ems for composition and forty cents per token for presswork. In order for any of the terms of this deal to be altered, either party had to "give three months previous notice in writing." Soon after striking this bargain, the landlord-publishers began to exact further tolls from the printers. When employing them to print Walker's *Dictionary*, they required Griggs and Dickinson to "bind themselves not to print any of the said Dictionary [for any one else] . . . under a penalty of Five Hundred Dollars." And a year later, Griggs and Dickinson agreed to print a law book for McCarty and Davis at the price of 37½ cents per thousand ems and per token, a reduced price for which the publishers were presumably required by the earlier agreement to give notice.[23]

Printers were not always prey to the controlling publishers, however, although direct defiance was more the exception than the rule. In a nineteenth-century trade journal, one printer reminisced about a very able journeyman named Jacob W. Adams who set type for the publishing firm of Clark and Raser in the years just following the War of 1812. Adams, according to this report, liked to "slack off" from work periodically and would spend several weeks at a time in the taverns. The effect of his absences, according to the writer, was to "nurse the market," creating greater demand for his typesetting services. When his employers became particularly busy, and when he was "so inclined," he would "step quietly in and resume work." At one point, during one of these sabbaticals, Adams heard that Clark and Raser desperately needed his services, so he "ventured to try a loan to prolong the spree." Both partners angrily refused to lend Adams the one dollar he asked of them, to which he was supposed to have replied: "Then I'll fix the pair of you; *I won't work for you; you may go and starve!*" The recounter of this story in the *Printer's Circular* observed that Adams's behavior proved the "only instance on record of a journeyman sending his employers away into beggary by refusing to earn wages from them."[24] As printers' folklore, the tale must have suggested to readers of the *Printer's Circular* a "golden age" of the autonomous printer.

Printers were not the only satellites in the publishers' credit networks. To the publishers' way of thinking, book binders played an irritatingly important role in the publication and distribution of books. For this reason, binders were not so easily controlled as printers. As binders were the last craftsmen to see a book through production, it was they whom publishers often blamed for delays. Until the second half of the 1820s, and the increasingly regular use of cloth-covered case bindings, there were no substantive technological developments in bookbinding to enable craftsmen to bind books more rapidly or efficiently than one at a time. Even with a large shop of employees, no single binder could keep up with the production of a book as it sped off the presses, particularly as edition sizes grew. So publishers usually employed several binders, often in different towns or parts of the country. More often than not, publishers became infuriated with the slow pace kept by binders to whom they had entrusted their books. Perhaps after all of the stages of waiting for their production to see the light of day, publishers reached the pinnnacle of their impatience.

Nevertheless, there was a more concrete reason for their anxiety, a reason that lay, once again, in credit relationships. When publishers sold unbound books to other publishers, they either offered many months' credit, or arranged for payment in exchange books, and little cash changed hands. When they sold books already bound to other publishers or to shopkeepers or nonpublishing booksellers throughout the country, their customers expected books delivered on time, neatly bound for their retail consumers, and payment was by note of hand or bank notes, both of which were convertible forms of payment. The sale of books already bound, then, provided essential infusions of cash into the publishers' credit networks. Without these infusions, the flow of credit would become sluggish and dangerously clogged.

Thus publishers begged, cajoled, and threatened binders to work more speedily and to deliver their books when promised. On one occasion, Carey and his son, Henry C. Carey, could not extract Mason Locke Weems's *Life of Franklin* from one of their binders until after they had already begun publishing a second edition of the work.[25] The binder, one James Lovegrove, not only took almost a year to complete the job but delivered at least fifty of the first edition bound "imperfectly."[26] Indeed, imperfectly bound books — usually those with pages out of order or missing — caused publishers a great deal of anguish, and the more they insisted that binders rush, the more mistakes were made. In one frantic but fairly typical letter to a binder, Carey resorted to insults to try to incite speed and quality from the workman: "Nothing can equal our astonishment & vexation, at finding the same shameful errors in the last parcel of Bibles that rendered [them] unsaleable. . . . Were the sheets put together by a child, and never examined afterwards, they could not be worse." Following this tongue-lashing, however, Carey ordered the binder to continue working on the Bibles, a sure sign that he could exercise little control over the situation.[27]

There was also a battle of wills between publishers and binders that was unlike anything that existed between publishers and printers. Perhaps this is because most publishers had a keener understanding of the printing process. As printers' colophons were getting smaller and less obtrusive in relation to the publishers' imprints, printers were seemingly willing to take a back seat to publishers. Binders, however, may have felt unacknowledged. In one instance, Carey and Son, after receiving a batch of their Bibles from a binder, challenged his signature on the inside front covers: "We think . . . that your name being placed in the front of the Book disfigures it very much. In future we sh[ould] prefer to have it in the back."[28] At about the same time, they sent to the same binder another small batch of Bibles, informing him that "it may probably lead to your having several hundred copies to do — if they are done as we wish them."[29] Meanwhile, to their increasingly impatient customers publishers wrote frantic explanations and apologies for delays and imperfections.

As publishers assumed the central role in the production and distribution of books, binding came ever more under their auspices. As publishers produced larger editions to meet a growing middle-class market, an ever-increasing proportion of their books were wholesaled already bound, ready for retail sale. In order to make their books competitive with the increasing numbers of books available, they gave greater attention to the outward pysical appearance and uniformity of their products. Indeed, the actual printing of a book was becoming subordinate to the external packaging. The publishers, significantly, were becoming mass marketers: They advertised books as being neatly and elegantly bound. Frequently, they advertised the same book as available in a variety of bindings and a range of prices. They promised that books published in series would have matching (edition) bindings, so that when shelved in a home library or parlor they would please the eye.

Consumers' expectations grew along with publishers' offerings. When dissatisfied with the appearance of a book, customers would complain or demand better or prettier bindings. When country booksellers ordered books from the publishers, they often mentioned that their customers wanted books bound in the fashion of an earlier imprint that had been issued by the same firm. Considering the numbers of binders publishers employed, this must have caused some consternation, as they may not have always remembered how an earlier book had been bound, or by whom. After all, McCarty and Davis, between the years of 1824 and 1830, employed thirty-six different binders to bind hundreds of titles.[30] There was no escaping the fact that so long as binding remained in the realm of the hand craftsman, publishers' efforts at mass production would often be thwarted.

The predicament of having books delayed at the binding stage or sent back for imperfections made publishers worry that they had lost control just at the moment when their investment could begin to pay off. This situation held far greater consquences than might initially appear. When a promised shipment of books was delayed, the flow of credit throughout the network was impeded. The entire credit network could be jeopardized by one transaction gone awry.

Calculating Risk

To gain a better understanding of the risks publishers took and how printers, binders, and any number of other individuals were involved in publishing investments, we must examine the kinds of cost analyses publishers performed with each prospective publication. Publishers carefully calculated each investment or publication they considered. Printers traditionally determined how much paper and type was needed to print a job. This process of calculation was known as "casting off," and experienced printers could be quite accurate, often predicting to a page or two the length of a book set in type. As we have seen, printers were not generally responsible for the success of a work; therefore, their calculations began and ended with the costs of production. Publishers, on the other hand, based their calculations not only on the costs of labor, equipment, and supplies, but also on their knowledge of the market, the existence of competing editions, and the general economy. Publishers' notations of these calculations offer a window into their decision-making processes.

Books kept solely for the purpose of estimating costs were common in the middle of the nineteenth century, by which time they had become a standard part of publishers' accounting systems. In these books, publishers recorded and calculated the anticipated costs of production and distribution.[31] The accounts kept by early national publishers, however, indicate that they operated in a less formal and regulated financial world. They engaged in the same types of cost estimates as their late-nineteenth-century successors did, but they simply scattered these calculations throughout memo books and daybooks and correspondence. A small memorandum book kept by Mathew Carey from 1800 to 1811 contained cost analyses, but this informal, pocket-sized book probably served Carey more as a notebook than as one of his official business account books.[32] Another early, more formally constructed, cost book was kept by the firm of Carey and Lea, run by Carey's son and his partner, Isaac Lea.[33]

The Carey and Lea cost book demonstrates some of the ways in which publishers' calculations went beyond printers' estimates of paper and type. Along with the basic costs of production such as paper, composition, and printing, publishers needed to plan for such "extra" expenses as the cost of registering the copyright, the price of the copyright if they were buying it from an author, the price of stereotype plates, and, in some cases, the labor of authors, editors, translators, and engravers. The cost book shows that, at different times, the firm published books that required anything from the most basic production cost analysis to the most elaborate calculations.

A fairly simple entry in Carey and Lea's cost book, for instance, was the calculation for Oliver Evans's guidebook for mill-wrights and millers.[34] Carey and Lea expected to pay 40 cents per page for 325 pages of Pica type; 83 cents per page for thirty pages of Brevier type; $1.66 per page for 26 pages of Rules and Figures; and 64 cents each for 2 pages of Long Primer type. The total cost of composition for the projected 384 pages would come to $208.95, including an estimated 35 hours of alterations. The presswork would cost $64.80 for 144 tokens. Forty-two reams of paper were needed, costing $3.80 each. Then the firm had to add $125.00 for the labor of the editor, a "professor of mechanics, in the Franklin institute of the state of Pennsylvania"; $80.00 for the right to publish from C. and O. Evans, the holders of the copyright; and $10.00 to cover miscellaneous expenses and the cost of registering the new copyright with the U.S. government.

All of these expenses, plus $132.50 for plate printing and plate paper, came to $781.19.

Now it was time for Carey and Lea to calculate their expected profits. The edition size was to be 750 copies, which, with the above calculations, would cost $1.04 in sheets to produce. The price Carey and Lea would offer the trade, with binding, was $2.70 per copy and $2.40 per copy unbound. At trade sales, where the book could be sold in large lots in sheets, they were willing to offer it at a sale price of $2.10 per copy. Their final calculation: selling all 750 copies "@ average of 2.25 will produce $1687.50." Shorter books, such as Karl Bernhard's *Travels through North America* posed different problems in production.[35] This book had to be translated from German into English, an expense that added about one-third to the book's total production costs for the first edition. In addition, calculations became more complicated when publishers had stereotype plates made. In such cases, calculations for the costs and probable profits of subsequent editions needed to be made.

When McCarty and Davis planned the publication of their stereotyped edition of Shakespeare, they experimented with different equations, changing the variables in a number of ways in order to determine the most profitable strategy. One of the variables was whether they would supply the compositors' and proofreader's labor, or whether Jedediah Howe, the stereotyper, would. Another concern was whether they could sell the five hundred pounds of improper type they had had made for the project. It was only after James Ronaldson, the Philadelphia typefounder, had cast the type that Howe informed McCarty and Davis that type for stereotyping required certain physical modifications in order to make clear impressions in the molds, and that he could supply the proper type. By the time McCarty and Davis began their calculations, Ronaldson demanded that they take delivery of his type, so they needed to include the "extra" type in their cost analysis. In negotiating with Howe, McCarty and Davis worked out a variety of scenarios. In one, they would supply the type and do the composition and proofreading. Another possibility was that Howe would take care of all of these things, but McCarty and Davis would send their own apprentices to Howe to undertake the composition under his watchful eye. The partners negotiated with Howe on all these points, as well as on the costs associated with making the stereotype plates, the boys' room and board, and the proofreader's fee. Finally, it was agreed that Howe would "find the type, proof reader, &c. allowing our 4 boys to do the composition at 30 cts per 1000 [ems]."[36]

Not long into the composition, however, problems began to arise, and the project extended well beyond the planned six months. Labor problems, the journeymen's inexperience with the stereotyping process, and an epidemic that drove Howe from the city for two months all conspired to stretch the production — composition, proofreading, and platemaking — to almost two years. Did McCarty and Davis wait patiently for the production to take its course? To some extent, there was little they could do, but about a year into the project, they coaxed Carey and Lea into the venture. It is interesting to note how the cooperation between McCarty and Davis and Carey and Lea unfolded. Undoubtedly, if they had been asked to invest directly in the Shakespeare edition, Carey and Lea would have refused, knowing that the uncertainties in production created a sort of financial bottomless pit. Carey and Lea did, however, want preferential access to the books when they were finished, so they exchanged $30,000 worth of their stock — a staggering amount — for futures in the Shakespeare project. According to the exchange recorded in McCarty and Davis's accounts, the books they received from Carey and Lea were old titles, most of which Carey and Lea had had in their warehouse for many years, dating back to Mathew Carey's days in the business.[37] McCarty and Davis knew they were not receiving premium books, but because so much of their wholesale business revolved around country distribution, they must have felt they could dispose of the books easily enough. McCarty and Davis would immediately send these newly gained books out to the country for wholesale and retail distribution and generate more income to continue to finance the Shakespeare edition.

The examples of Carey and Lea's cost books and McCarty and Davis's calculations for the Shakespeare edition demonstrate a number of important points about the publishers' investment strategies. For the most part, their estimates were derived from aspects of production over which they had some degree of control, or at least a very good idea of the expenses involved. Those who had been trained as printers knew how to cast off, and those who had not been, relied on their printers' advice on such matters. Moreover, before they calculated costs, they bargained with authors for copyrights, and with others who offered their services and therefore knew how much to factor in for copyrights and extra services.

Even production costs could vary substantially, however. Binding, for instance, was a particularly difficult expense to calculate. Binding was expensive, and prudent publishers would only have a portion of an edition bound at a time, not wishing to tie up their money in bindings for books that did not yet have buyers. Furthermore, a quantity of books was always sold to other publishers or used in exchange, and publishers preferred to conduct such wholesale transactions with books in sheets, as they were easier and cheaper to transport. Because of this uncertainty, binding did not always enter into a publishers' estimates for production, but the expense of binding nevertheless played a major role in the publishers' overall investment and expected profits.

While production costs could be ascertained with some degree of certainty, estimates of profits were an entirely different story. Profits depended on a countless variety of factors. For instance, knowing something about the production fiasco of the edition of Shakespeare, we can see some problems in McCarty and Davis's calculations. They did not know whether they would be able to sell Ronaldson's type. Right away, then, their Shakespeare project immediately took on "a dead expence" of five hundred dollars, the price they paid Ronaldson.[38] Similarly, they could not have planned for a close to three-fold increase in the length of production, nor could they have foreseen that an epidemic fever would strike New York. They could not have known that their transplanted workers would demand New York wages rather than the slightly lower pay they were receiving. Even with on-time production, many questions remained. With Oliver Evans's guidebook, Carey and Lea had no assurance that they could sell all 750 copies as they expected. Half of that edition might lie on the shelves of their warehouse, for one reason or another, a circumstance that would steadily eat away at their profits.

When all was said and done, publishers' estimates were just that — approximate calculations of the production, distribution, and sales of books. The vagaries of the economy were impossible to account for, as were the difficulties of distribution and the unpredictability of reading tastes. Publishers did what they could to ensure the success of their publications, but no publisher who wished to survive would stake all of his resources and hopes on one publication or one market. It was through a complicated system of debt and credit that publishers were able to undertake numerous publishing ventures at a time.

Credit Relationships Among Publishers

In the previous chapter we saw how publishers pooled resources through combination publishing, but even books published by a single person were, in a sense, underwritten by that individual's creditors and debtors. Nothing illustrates this point so well as an examination of the financial failures that plagued the publishing trade throughout the first thirty years of the century.[39] Publishing meant taking risks. Whenever possible, through their credit networks, publishers took on debt and offered credit in order to continue to publish and to spread out their risk. While this provided them with a degree of financial flexibility, it also meant that an individual's failure would affect almost everyone else in the trade. In addition, while publishers operated in a world of familiar names and faces, they could never ascertain with any certainty the level of indebtedness of their trading partners. They could see how accounts stood with one another, but they could not see into each other's account books to determine how all of the other accounts stood.

It should be noted that financial failures did not necessarily spell the end of an individual's or a firm's existence. Petitioning to be considered insolvent meant that enough of one's creditors agreed not to press their claims, thus allowing the debtor to take the time to resolve his difficulties. It represented a setback, to be sure, but how long a publishing concern managed to weather the ups and downs of business in the early republic said more about its level of success or failure than a few brushes with insolvency. A state of indebtedness was perfectly natural; it was how much credit a publisher could command that made the difference between a successful and unsuccessful publishing business.

In 1806, a Philadelphia printer named Richard Folwell wrote to Mathew Carey to ask for financial assistance. Folwell explained that he was unable to publish his newspaper "for the want of Credit." Folwell had not always labored under such difficulties, however. His financial woes had only recently begun "in consequence of Credit failing with the Paper-Maker."[40] Carey agreed to endorse some notes for Folwell, so that the printer could once again stand on good terms with his paper supplier. This meant that Carey signed onto notes that Folwell had previously given the papermaker, thus acting as a guarantor for Folwell's debt. In addition, when notes were endorsed, they took on new and later due dates. Carey's endorsements turned the business between the papermaker and the printer into a three-way transaction. In this fashion, Carey had taken on part of Folwell's burden of debt. If Folwell once again found himself unable to pay the papermaker, it might fall to Carey or another of Folwell's endorsers to supply the actual payment.

This scenario was repeated countless times in the everyday business of the early republic. It was just such transactions that, taken collectively, formed an extraordinarily delicate business structure. Risk-taking required infusions of credit, and most credit — or notes given — was short-term, usually not exceeding nine months or a year. Without six or nine months of credit protection from Carey, Folwell was unable to continue to take the risk of publishing his newspaper. Carey's endorsement of Folwell's notes, however, put Carey in a position of potentially increased risk. Carey did not consider endorsing a note the same thing as making a loan and thus did not record it as a debit against himself. Therefore, he had no real sense of how far he was extended. If Folwell defaulted when the note fell due, Carey would legally be required to pay.

In book publishing, note endorsement became a large-scale affair. Although it is impossible to calculate from surviving business records just how much of any one publisher's risk was "shared" in such a manner, not a working day went by that publishers did not request endorsement from fellow tradesmen or were not approached by others for the same purpose. McCarty and Davis kept books with lists of notes in their favor. These lists provide some indication of how much credit they extended. The firm sold books on a mostly wholesale basis and accepted notes of hand (bills of exchange) as payment. From 1824 to 1828, they took notes from 302 country merchants and other retailers, including a corps of traveling salesmen, for $44,135 worth of their books. The terms of these notes varied from ninety days to twelve months, with interest usually charged after six months. By the end of 1828, 219 of the accounts had been settled, either in payment of cash, goods, or by new notes. Of the remaining unsettled accounts, some proved to be bad debts, while others had yet to come due when the list was transferred to a new (and no longer extant) account book.

Debts were very often paid late. For instance, in March 1826, McCarty and Davis accepted seven notes for a total of $1373.96, with six of the accounts due in twelve months and the seventh due on July 15 of that year. While all of these accounts were settled, none was paid on time. The three-month account was paid fifteen months later, and the others were paid within two and three months of their due dates. As debts were often paid late, McCarty and Davis knew that they could not count on March 1826 notes until the following year. They could therefore invest their capital and become debtors to others with the "assurances" of this fairly consistent system in mind. In addition, when their debtors paid late, they were required by the terms of the notes to pay interest for the inconvenience. The credit networks then, had a built-in flexibility. Nevertheless, the potential for failure was always present, particularly if a variety of unusual circumstances combined to stop the flow of debt and credit.

Such circumstances often arose. When John Melish, a map and geography publisher, petitioned the Philadelphia Court of Common Pleas as an insolvent in 1821, he blamed unusual circumstances for his failure. In his petition, he stated that when Samuel Harrison, his partner, died in 1818, Melish was "overpowered . . . with labour, while . . . deprived of Mr. Harrison's valuable services as well as his capital and credit." Unfortunately for Melish, the following year brought many to their knees, with "the dreadful scarcity of money and almost total cessation of business." During this time, Melish explained to the court, "the Bank of the United States withdrew as far as possible all accommodation, while many of [my] friends were so seriously affected that they could render [me] no assistance." Melish's impassioned petition to become insolvent under law also referred the court to the side of his accounts that should have brought him much-needed relief: "[My] Debtors, one by one, suspended payments so that [I] could neither collect Debts nor sell property." Thus pressed to the limit by his creditors, his debtors, and an apparent contraction of bank notes, Melish concluded that had he not been in "a public business" which he conceived to "be of great importance to the community," he would have abandoned it "to its fate." Printers and papermakers made up a large proportion of Melish's creditors, as did publishers who had endorsed his notes.[41]

In a less elaborate statement, the printer-publisher John Bioren told the court that "Bad Debts and the depreciation of property are the cause of [my] insolvency." According to Bioren's petition, he had "property enough to pay the whole of his debts as well those he owes on his own account as on account of others, yet from the difficulty of the times" he could not convert these into money. His creditors included five banks, who together demanded about $13,000, as well as a long list of mechanics in the trade. His extensive property and even longer list of outstanding debts make it clear that the economic climate of 1819, the year he filed his petition, was indeed crippling. He had balances against almost every publisher in Philadelphia. If they had paid him, he would not have needed to file.[42] Under normal circumstances, Bioren's business would have been considered extremely healthy. An examination of his books, if his petition's accounts were accurate, would reveal that more money was owed him than he himself owed. Bioren knew every one of his debtors personally—they made up the cast of characters in the Philadelphia printing trade. Yet at any given time, he had no way of knowing how able they were to pay him.

The Conrads, one of the most prolific publishing concerns in Philadelphia, became insolvent when their creditors called in their debts and their endorsers began to balk. The Conrads began having financial difficulties during Jefferson's Embargo of 1807–8, which prohibited exports. Carey and a number of other publishers had endorsed notes for the firm of C. and A. Conrad for over $50,000 during the first decade of the century. By 1811, as Carey related, the "pressure" on the firm increased, much to his alarm, as "my responsibility for them had, by degrees, arisen to 13,000 dollars." John Conrad, the head of the failing firm, took out securities from his principal creditors, Carey, Gray and Taylor, and Bradford and Inskeep, but according to Carey, Conrad would not reveal the amount of security given by each creditor. In turn, Carey "resolved to cease lending, or indorsing notes for the house, till there was a full disclosure." Edward Gray, one of the other major creditors, visited Carey late one night in 1811 to persuade him to go along with the endorsements. In a thinly veiled threat, Gray demanded, "What do you mean, Mr. Carey? Do you mean to break up the house of Conrad and Co. by refusing your indorsements?"[43] Carey's desire to extract a disclosure from the Conrads, and indeed his public call for such a statement, reveals how anxious publishers could become when kept ignorant of the state of each other's affairs. His anxiety and pride led him to refuse the blackmail for increased endorsements, and this action apparently sealed the Conrads' fate.

The Conrad bankruptcy loomed large in Carey's mind for many years afterward. He had had much to do with making the case public with his published account of the events leading up to the collapse. Taking the high moral ground allowed him to assert rights to much of the firm's stock, which he did when he issued orders to the sheriff about how to divide up the books and supplies.[44] Even in this regard, however, he was somewhat disappointed. The sheriff divided the stock while Carey was on a short trip away from Philadelphia, and Carey wrote an accusatory note to the other endorsers: "You seized upon everything that was to be found in every direction here and there [and] you did not leave a single dollar's worth for me."[45] The bankruptcy, however, had shaken Carey deeply. In the years that followed, he often wrote to others that he still lay under obligation to "meet notes lent to the most execrable villain to the am[oun]t of 22,000 dollars."[46] It was many years before Carey recovered from the shock, and he often took the opportunity to mention it in letters, particularly when payment was required of him: "I hope you will believe I am as well disposed as I ever have been to conduct our business on liberal and fair principles," he explained to another publisher, " . . . but the cruel rapacity to which I have fallen a victim has so far straightened me as to require considerable circumspection in my disbursements."[47]

Isaac Riley, a prominent publisher and bookseller in New York, declared bankruptcy several times before beginning anew in Philadelphia, where he eventually declared bankruptcy twice, once in 1812 and again in 1820.[48] He never recovered from the first bout with his creditors, and in his second Philadelphia disaster a number of his creditors from the previous collapse were still unpaid. Riley's business, at its peak, was substantial, and it is possible that his love of creative financing had finally taken its toll. (In 1806, he had informed Carey that "we are now busy in delivering books to the amount of twenty two thousand dollars in exchange for turnpike stock in [New York] state, property guaranteed.")[49] The record of Riley's second failure is instructive because it provides a glimpse of how insolvents classified their creditors. Riley named thirteen publishers and booksellers as "Class 1" creditors, or those who should be paid first, based on the size of his debt to them. He also included in this first category "all mechanics which may have been omitted, to be paid in full." The eight mechanics listed were bookbinders. The unnamed mechanics were probably printers.[50] The last class of creditors (class 4) to be paid, according to Riley's instructions, were those who had filed suit against him, or those who otherwise pressed their demands. Riley stipulated that "should there be any other suits, I wish it expressly understood, that they all come under the class No. 4, unless withdrawn."[51] This reluctance to settle with anyone who had sought litigation against him was not at all unusual. To begin with, many insolvency laws provided that a debtor could seek protection under law if some proportion of his creditors—usually two-thirds—agreed to discontinue to press their claims. The cooperative creditors then, would be "rewarded" by gaining first consideration in the classification of creditors.

There was another bias against litigious creditors as well, and one which was more rooted in the overall framework of credit relationships. Debt litigation created havoc in the publishers' tightly knit credit networks. Lawsuits were expensive, unpleasant, time-consuming, and above all, inevitably involved almost every member of the publishing trade. When Carey sued Patrick Rice, a bookseller, reverberations were felt by publishers and booksellers all over the country who could no longer get the books or payment Rice owed them. Thomas and Thomas wrote Carey from their store in New Hampshire, asking if he could get Rice to send them books due in exchange. Carey replied that, as he was in the midst of a legal battle with Rice, he would not be the proper person to intervene.[52]

Lawsuits were so troublesome that the American Company of Booksellers provided for a "private" form of suit to be brought under the auspices of the organization. Before bringing a fellow member to court, an individual could sue in a "court" of his publishing peers. There is some evidence that the trade-regulated suit was used. Writing to Carey, Obadiah Penniman announced his intention of suing William Duane "under the 9th Article of the Bye-Laws."[53] Much as Thomas and Thomas had done, Penniman asked Carey to act as a witness at the proceedings, to which Carey was once again forced to reply that he too was wrangling with Duane over both exchange and cash accounts. Penniman acknowledged this, apologizing that "we did not know that your situation with him was peculiar, if we had, we should have made choice of some other person."[54]

It was equally troublesome to be sued, of course. Charles Peirce, a printer and bookseller in Portsmouth, told Carey that Joseph Dennie, the editor of the *Port Folio*, was "a careless negligent person about paying his debts, unless he is threatened pretty hard, and rather than be sued, he generally will exert himself and pay them."[55] Peirce requested that Carey "scare him to payment" and pointed out to Carey that the sooner this could be done the more quickly he would be able to settle his own outstanding accounts with Carey. As Peirce well understood, it was this financial consideration, if anything, that would spur Carey to pursue Peirce's claim against Dennie.

Publishers were accustomed to such threats, considering the number of dunning letters sent out and received by them. The threats probably kept many cases out of the courts: for the most part, the desire to maintain an honorable reputation kept the credit networks running smoothly. As common as failure seems to have been, news of a financial disaster always created a ripple of emotional responses. Publishers were eager to maintain untarnished reputations. They seemed to be almost superstitiously sensitive to the fact that failure could strike anywhere, at any time, and they therefore were quick to extend sympathy to those who had fallen prey to "unusual" circumstances. An agent of Carey's in Richmond, Virginia, sent Carey his condolences on hearing about the failure of another man who sold books for Carey, noting somberly that the unfortunate one "is said to be a very worthy and estimable man."[56]

The phrase most often used to describe a state of insolvency was "embarrassed circumstances," a genteel expression that calls to mind the inevitable shame and discomfort that financial failure brought, but which also invokes a certain blamelessness. A new bookselling firm in Salem, Massachusetts, solicited all of the major publishers in the nation wishing to open wholesale accounts. The two partners, Macanulty and Maxey, sent out a letter of introduction stating their purposes. They noted that "it may be proper here to observe, that Mr. Macanulty suffer'd some inconvenience or embarrassment some time since, by the villainy of two or three individuals." According to their letter, however, Mr. Macanulty was absolved of any guilt, and the "result was shameful to his enemies and honorable to himself."[57]

Indeed, when citing a faltering national economy, fire, or "a weak constitution" proved impossible, insolvents blamed others for their misfortunes in an effort to maintain credibility. Caleb Kimber stated that his weak constitution made him unfit to print, and he therefore was forced to become a schoolteacher, an occupation he "attempted at four different times but could not succeed." A papermaker named John Davis Jr. became insolvent when his mill caught fire "with the contents thereof . . . by which misfortune he is intirely ruined."[58] When the Philadelphia printer and publisher Eleazer Oswald became insolvent, he blamed the insolvency of one of his major debtors, George Helmbold, another printer and publisher.[59]

Insolvents placed the blame on others for two main reasons. Doing so made it clear that the insolvent had little or no control over the outcome of his affairs and thus made the failure more explicable. Further, assigning blame made it possible for creditors to continue to have faith in the insolvent, a condition necessary for recovery. In essence, blaming others did nothing more than identify a symptom, rather than a disease. The complicated system of debt and credit was simply part of the larger economic boom and bust cycles, a process over which individual actors had little control.

When debtors were forced to inform their creditors of impending failure, they invariably promised to make good on their debts even after they acquired protection under the law. As one young firm of booksellers put it: "[I]f our creditors deal gentle with us, it is our intention if it is even in our power to pay them every cent." To do this, Sage and Thompson promised to "arrange our business so that we may go to work and earn more."[60] One of Carey's printers fled to Baltimore when he became unable to pay his debts. Writing to Carey to request that he cooperate by releasing him from his debt, William Patton explained that he only sought release from debt and prosecution so that he could continue to work rather than be jailed. He was "determined," he wrote, "to pay when able."[61] Clearly, the choice to shoulder debts, even after their burden had been lifted by insolvency or bankruptcy protection, was a well-calculated one. Good intentions and a desire to work hard were often all it took to reestablish credit and the trust of important colleagues.

Publishers were so zealous to maintain a smooth flow of credit in this delicate system that they often went to enormous lengths to protect one another from disaster. When a publisher showed signs of insolvency, others would do what they could in order to prevent his failure. To David Longworth, the New York publisher who in 1812 suffered a loss by another publisher's insolvency, Carey offered sympathy and material support: "I sincerely regret your loss by Bird and to contribute toward lightening it you may charge me with 20 per cent of the bibles."[62] And when fire destroyed Charles Peirce's bookstore in Portsmouth, New Hampshire, the publishers and booksellers of Philadelphia, New York, and Boston all sent aid in the form of books to help him build up a new inventory. In 1806, when Cushing and Appleton of Salem suffered a similar fate, Thomas and Andrews wrote to New York and Philadelphia members of the trade to raise a subscription for the two unfortunate but "respectable Booksellers and worthy men." Thomas and Andrews instructed the booksellers to send "such books, bound or in sheets [giving] reference to their value in this part of the Union."[63]

These acts of trade solidarity cannot be wholly isolated from the urge to keep the lines of credit running smoothly. Peirce was a large bookseller who had accounts with almost all of the trade members who helped him, and it was in the interest of all to keep him on his feet. Cushing and Appleton were, if anything, more prominent in the trade, and Thomas and Andrews's rather pointed instructions to send books of some worth, rather than the dregs of their warehouses, alerted the subscribing publishers of the significance of this particular act of charity. If books of "value" were sent, the networks tying booksellers and publishers around the nation had a chance to run smoothly. If they failed to cooperate, they might soon find themselves sorting through the rubble of a fallen house of cards that had been built from thousands of endorsed notes.

The publishers' overriding concern with maintaining the delicate balance of the credit networks came directly from an instinct for self-preservation. But as they took on more numerous and larger risks, and as the people with whom they kept accounts lived in places ever more distant, the system of debt and credit became harder to control. No longer were most of their correspondents people with whom they had at least passing acquaintance. Furthermore, it was less and less likely that publishers even knew the identities of many of their co-endorsers. By the 1820s, for instance, it was no longer necessary to have a reference, as many individuals in the country, completely unknown to the publishers, wrote asking to buy books at wholesale prices, on long credits.

There was no denying that publishers needed to turn their attention to wider book distribution, but new problems accompanied such developments that threatened the systems of credit with which these early publishers were so familiar. To negotiate the unstable financial atmosphere of the first two decades of the century, and to lighten the load of growing urban competition, some of the more energetic publishers expanded their businesses into the country. Country markets, however, forced publishers to think about constructing new strategies of investment and finance. Some began to engage in more specialized publishing in order to find niches in an unfamiliar and highly competitive market. Thus they broadened their bases of distribution while narrowing their assortment of books, all in an effort to build sturdier bookselling empires.

6

"Forced Trade" and Distant Markets

IN 1805 MATHEW CAREY DESCRIBED the acute competition under which the Philadelphia publishing trade labored, noting that the "regular *unforced trade*" was no longer sufficient to support a bookseller. Instead, "a very large proportion of the business done consists in what may be fairly termed *forced trade*, viz. commission stores, subscriptions, &c."[1] The "regular unforced trade," if it ever existed, belonged to a past when a busy retail bookstore, attached to a printing shop and well situated for urban, walk-in business, could make for its owner a comfortable living. As early as 1800, however, many urban publishers were oversupplying their local markets and so began to pay greater attention to selling their books in distant locations. Carey had expected that the formation of the literary fairs in 1802 would have profound effects on booksellers' distribution efforts. If the annual fairs were successful, then "many a musty shopkeeper, [an old European moniker for a slow-selling book] which has long retained possession of the shelves of a store in Boston, New-York and Philadelphia, would find a ready market, when transported to the banks of the Susquehannah, the Potomack, or the Santee."[2]

Booksellers' ambitions to disseminate books throughout the country were stirred by both an entrepreneurial and a nationalistic spirit. The boundless optimism that characterized Jefferson's Louisiana Purchase fueled the publishers' perceptions of the backcountry as a beckoning, vast, and open market ready and willing to be incorporated into a national culture and economy. By selling books to the country, publishers hoped to relieve the financial pressures of overstocked shelves while acting to unify the growing nation through the distribution of the printed word.

These optimistic entrepreneurs of the early American book trade operated much as the British booksellers had during the colonial period. They relied on the underdeveloped nature of dependent rural economies and a favorable trade balance to create what they believed would be a captive market for their books. Inhabitants of frontier communities relied heavily on eastern financing, credit, goods, and information. After 1800, the population of the United States steadily shifted westward: less than 15 percent of the nation's inhabitants lived west of the Appalachians in 1810; by 1860 over 40 percent did.[3] Even with this rapid expansion, however, it would take years for settlers to establish stable, indigenous economic structures and cultural institutions, and eastern publishers continued to see western markets as critical to their success.[4]

Rural inhabitants, however, did not accept everything the urban East had to offer. Most books were not considered necessities in frontier societies, while in more developed western communities local printer-booksellers and shopkeepers established businesses before Philadelphia publishers could get a toehold in the market. Therefore, to sell their books in the country urban publishers needed to stimulate markets in areas that lay on a spectrum of development somewhere between newly settled frontiers and booming western cities. In short, the publishers needed to find locations that were experiencing the "formation of a market for cultural commodities in printed form."[5] Philadelphia publishers such as Mathew Carey looked mainly to the South and Southwest, to small towns along major trading routes. They sought markets in rural areas of western and northwestern Pennsylvania, Maryland, Virginia, Kentucky, parts of Indiana, Tennessee, and Alabama. Small market towns and county seats seemed to hold the greatest promise.

This chapter examines the methods of marketing and distributing books in the backcountry that were used by three Philadelphia publishing firms between 1800 and 1830. William W. Woodward, a prominent publisher of religious works, employed an ad hoc network of ministers to sell his religious books. To vend their assortment of schoolbooks, subscription works, and law books, the firm of McCarty and Davis dispatched a corps of professional traveling salesmen and later established branch stores in likely backcountry entrepôts. Two Quaker entrepreneurs, Jacob Johnson and Benjamin Warner, traveled extensively themselves, opening branch stores from which to sell their children's books and establishing large wholesale accounts with country storekeepers, printers, and booksellers. Of these three methods of distribution, the use of bookselling ministers and traveling salesmen was the most traditional, while the branch stores and the large wholesale accounts made perhaps the greatest inroads into nonurban markets. But these different methods could be useful to publishers at different times (and still are), so it is hard to compare them in terms of ultimate success. While Johnson and Warner were quite effective, for example, in their wholesale distribution efforts, McCarty and Davis, who succeeded them in the early 1820s, mainly used a combination of traveling salesmen and branch stores. Whatever the method, all of the firms encountered difficulties in serving country markets. Experience in mercantile trade and some knowledge of the communities to which they tried to sell their books may have counted most of all. These qualities were best exemplified by Johnson and Warner's business.

Employing peddlers and setting up branch stores represented the standard, time-honored approach to expanding businesses. During the colonial period, "hawkers and walkers" had supplied rural regions with manufactured goods, including books, and enterprising printers had sometimes set up family members or trusted employees in satellite printing establishments in other areas.[6] This trend continued well into the nineteenth century. The growing population in remote areas west and south of the Appalachians outstripped the communication and transportation systems available to eastern publishers and their agents. Until the advent of the railroad, the distribution of books was highly decentralized, making anything like a national literature and reading audience impossible.[7] Certainly the methods used by Philadelphia publishers discussed here did little to centralize the book trade. Also, inadequate currency and banking facilities made remittances cumbersome, leading to idiosyncratic bookkeeping and irregular methods of payment.

The differences between rural and urban culture also made the country market peculiarly elusive to Philadelphia publishers because they regarded rural inhabitants as less sophisticated than city dwellers. They saw the country communities as perfect sites for disposing of old, unsalable books, much as the British had regarded the colonies in the pre-Revolutionary period. In this, however, they were mistaken, for while the country consumers wanted cheap, practical books, they did not want products rejected by eastern consumers, and they seemed to know the difference, much as the American colonists had known. Finally, replicating urban retail bookselling techniques and establishments proved to be awkward and inefficient. Competition was anything but light in the rural areas, coming from country retailers and wholesalers as well as from the many eastern publishers who sent travelers throughout the country, and set up branch stores. In short, the publishers discovered after much trial and error that trade in the country necessitated as much "force" as their trade in the city. The eastern publishers who met with the most success in the country were those who were flexible and willing to adapt to the consumer needs of the frontier, the problems of unstable or inchoate market economies, and the simple fact of long-distance trade relationships.

Successfully selling books in the backcountry required a better understanding of developing societies and their markets. Publishers had to learn from their agents and peddlers what books were truly needed and desired in the South and Southwest and how best to supply such books. The publishers' agents met with different levels of literacy and cultural development than they were accustomed to in the East. They reported that credit often meant different things to people who lived on the shifting frontier. Finally, the enormous difficulty of sending books over hundreds of miles by wagon, stage, and riverboat taxed the publishers' ingenuity. Salesmen reported mishaps with dismaying regularity. The correspondence between Philadelphia publishers and their agents in the country enables us to see the disjunction between the publishers' desire to extend their markets and the realities of selling books to an expanding nation. Surviving letters from the agents to their employers are rich in material about developing rural societies, and they supply details about the difficulties of selling books on the road.

One of the most important lessons publishers learned from sending their agents into the country was that they needed to produce large editions of inexpensive books. Traditionally, booksellers had kept retail unit prices high and discounts to middlemen low by limiting the size of editions and avoiding remainders. While the price of individual books dropped with larger editions, the risk of unsold copies increased and the generous discounts required to clear inventories were seen as running contrary to trade interests. By the 1700s, London bookseller James Lackington had discovered that he could rely on volume sales to make up for small unit profits. His motto, "small profits do great things," would revolutionize the trade.[8]

Philadelphia publishers gradually arrived at similar conclusions for the American country markets. In 1801 Mason Locke Weems, who peddled books for Mathew Carey, lectured the publisher that heavy, expensive books would not sell in the country and would never constitute a mass market:

I deem it glory to circulate valuable books. I would circulate millions. This cannot be effected without the character of *cheapness*. Let but the public point to me and say *"there goes the little Parson that brings us so many clever books and so cheap,"* and I ask no more. But this building a high fortune on low priced books, appears to you strange as the fatn'ing a Calf by bleeding it. But the Scotch Merchants who are your best marksmen at a dollar on the wing, will tell you that there's nothing like the nimble ninepence.[9]

Twenty years later James F. McCarty, who operated a branch store for McCarty and Davis in Wheeling, Virginia, stressed the importance of this same formula. "It is not the large profits and small sales that makes the money," he proclaimed, "it is Large sales and small profits, for the man that is doing a large business is rich in mind at the prospect before him."[10] Thomas Davis echoed his employee's sentiment, writing to another publisher that "[q]uick returns with but small profits we have always found to be the most profitable part of our business."[11]

Putting the maxim of large sales and small profits to work meant producing books as cheaply as possible and doing so in large enough editions to bring down unit costs. It also meant publishing books that by their reputations as steady sellers provided a better guarantee of success than unproven works could offer. Schoolbooks, Bibles, and devotional works, along with books useful for home, health, and instruction fell into this category. Best-selling novels, books published in parts, and toy books also did well.[12] Some expensive books found buyers in the country, especially law books, deluxe Bibles, reference books, and imported scholarly works. But these expensive books were purchased by lawyers, judges, and wealthy elites or institutional libraries, and except for law books none of these had to be available in large numbers at all times. Generally, imported books sent to the country had been ordered from eastern wholesalers specifically by country buyers who may not have known whether such books had been published in any American city.

Schoolbooks made up the majority of the inexpensive books published for the country. Also popular were various self-help books and books designed for rural dwellers. William Woodward's edition of *Village Sermons* (1803), for example, a compilation of fifty-two sermons — one for each week of the year — was advertised as being perfect for "the use of families, Sunday schools, or companies assembled for religious instruction in country villages."[13] Another practical book was McCarty and Davis's *A Pocket Companion; or Every Man His Own Lawyer* (1818), a book of sample contracts printed to look like handwritten script so that the user could practice penmanship as well as law.[14] This handy manual directly appealed to the egalitarian sensitivities of the American "common man":

[c]ontaining a variety of Precedents, laid down in so plain a manner, that the Farmer, Mechanic, Apprentice, or School Boy can draw any Instrument of Writing without the assistance of an attorney . . . [p]refaced with twelve pages of Script, intended as a copy for those persons who wish to improve their handwriting at leisure hours at home, without the instructions of a teacher.[15]

Similarly, books of domestic medicine found a ready market in the country, as did other useful books like William Carver's *Practical Horse Farrier; or, the Traveller's Pocket Companion* (1818).[16] The need for and utility of such books is obvious: in areas where teachers, ministers, and lawyers were still relatively scarce, books like these were truly necessities. It is interesting to note that the books that appealed to rural and small-town readers were the same types—often even the same titles—that had been staples of the American book trade since at least 1700.[17]

After 1790, a new federal copyright law banning unauthorized reprinting of books by American authors conspired with the conservative requirements of the country market to inhibit the development of a backcountry publishing industry in the early years of the new republic. Established eastern publishers almost always owned the rights to basic American books. McCarty and Davis held copyrights for the schoolbooks they sent off with their salesmen, including Stephen Byerly's *New American Spelling Book* (1820), Zachariah Jess's *American Tutor's Assistant, improved* (1818), an arithmetic, and Stephen Pike's *The Teacher's Assistant or a System of Practical Arithmetic* (1822).[18] McCarty and Davis had negotiated directly with the authors for the copyrights to their books. Once they gained the rights, they could produce as many or as few of the books as they needed, pay the authors royalties, and keep the profits. Above all, they controlled the national distribution and sales of the books for which they owned copyrights. As long as few western or southern authors produced steady-selling books, country booksellers had few opportunities to obtain copyrights.

Preachers and Peddlers

Traveling salesmen sold and delivered subscription works and peddled the publishers' titles as well as those obtained through exchanges. Typically, these agents bought books on credit from their employers' stock. This meant that they assumed the risk for the books in their possession (although many had the option to return unsold books).[19] Peddlers received various discounts—usually 20 percent on most titles—and some were allowed margins as high as 33 percent. For subscription publications, publishers often granted their agents a certain number of free copies when they sold designated quantities.

Mathew Carey was among the first in the early national period to use a full-time book peddler; in fact, his peddler is better known than the publisher himself. Mason Locke Weems, an Anglican clergyman from tidewater Virginia, worked for the Philadelphia publisher for over twenty years, covering a swath of territory that included most of Virginia and Maryland.[20] He sold books by subscription and continually offered Carey advice on how to open country outlets that would feature Carey's imprints. Together they did a large business. The colorful parson pioneered many of the techniques that traveling booksellers would use to tempt country buyers. He put his extraordinary powers as a speaker to work to gather attention and manipulate a crowd; he arrived at court sessions to sell to captivate markets of judges and lawyers; he arranged for country postmasters and storekeepers

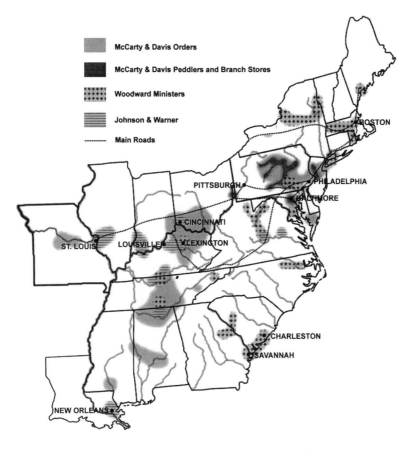

Map 1. Areas reached by traveling salesmen, ministers, branch stores, and wholesale accounts in the country trade, c. 1825.

to take books on commission, incorporating them into his and Carey's "army."[21]

Weems's role as a minister complemented his work as Carey's agent. He loved the idea of making a fortune and, at the same time, blanketing the nation with good, pious reading. He tried to instruct Carey on this point, making it clear that promoting one's own interests was wholly compatible with promoting virtue and cultural improvement. "This country is large, and numerous are its inhabitants," he wrote to Carey; "to cultivate among them a taste for reading, and by the reflection of proper books to throw far and wide the rays of useful arts and sciences, were at once the work of a true Philanthropist and prudent speculator."[22] Many clergymen shared this sentiment. Ministers were active book subscribers and readers and often collected subscriptions and distributed subscription books for publishers. With the founding of the Methodist Book Concern, in 1789, this fast-growing denomination institutionalized the long-established practice of itinerant ministers' selling Methodist books (with an admixture of general books) to supplement their meager incomes.[23] Still, bookselling remained an ancillary enterprise for most traveling clergymen.

Philadelphia publisher William Woodward formalized the use of preachers as peddlers by assembling a staff of ministers to sell his books throughout the nation. For Woodward, the frontier settlements represented a boundless market of souls in need of books and salvation. Between 1800 and 1825, he recruited at least forty-seven minister-salesmen. Denomination was not important: Woodward himself was a Presbyterian, and his sales force included seventeen Baptists, twelve Presbyterians, and four Congregationalists, along with two Methodists and one Episcopalian.[24] Letters from these clergymen to the publisher indicate how eager they were to supplement their fixed incomes by selling his books; and Woodward, because of his reputation for fine religious printing and personal piety, was just the sort of publisher with whom they felt comfortable dealing.[25]

The ministers were, for the most part, literate and cultured men, interested in having access to books for their own use and for the edification of their congregations and communities. Even "settled" clergymen with fixed parishes did a great deal of traveling while tending their widespread flocks. Some had charge of more than one congregation and still others were completely itinerant. At least one Baptist minister chose itinerancy in order to combine his calling with his retail avocation: "I refuse to settle in any place at present for I am desirous of spreading useful and religious publications among the churches."[26] Some of the ministers resided in or near urban sea-ports, but most lived in the pockets of settlement in the backcountry that stretched from Maine to Georgia and into Kentucky, Alabama, Tennessee, Ohio, and Indiana. They carried with them subscription papers for expen-sive works such as Charles Buck's *Theological Dictionary* (1807), John Gill's *Exposition of the Old and New Testaments* (1810), and the multivolume edition of the Bible with exhaustive notes and commentary by Thomas Scott, com-monly known as Scott's Family Bible (1811).[27]

In some measure, ministers succeeded at bookselling because they were influential figures in their communities, often taking charge of their congregants' moral and intellectual development. As one clergyman ex-plained, "my acquaintance in Kentucky gives me some advantage in circu-lating a subscription paper, & especially for Books — with which my *own* acquaintance gives me the opportunity to recommend."[28] Offering to serve as an agent for Woodward, the Congregational minister Samuel Osgood of Springfield, Massachusetts, boasted of his persuasive power as minister and book salesman.[29] Occasionally, preachers regretted their commercial inex-perience and felt out of their element dealing with commissions and pre-miums. Baptist preacher and historian David Benedict worried that he was "wholly unacquainted with the publishing business, especially that of a merchantile nature," and asked Woodward to inform him as to "what are the customary modes of preceeding [*sic*]."[30] Whether experienced in busi-ness or not, all but one of Woodward's forty-seven minister-salesmen con-tinued to sell until stopped by old age or death. Those who moved immediately continued their sales careers in new territories. Frequently, they commended Woodward for making his press useful to the nation and to the cause of religion. Like the publisher, the preachers saw selling the right books as essential to the fight against secularization. Jedediah Morse, for example, one of the most famous opponents of religious liberalism, sold subscription books for Woodward and exchanged his own writings and issues of the religious periodical the *Panoplist* for many of Woodward's publications.[31]

As enthusiastic as they were about putting good religious books in the hands of readers, the ministers were hampered by the scarcity of cash in volatile frontier markets. Most often the ministers complained of the prob-lems of collecting money from subscribers. Local bank notes seldom were accepted in Philadelphia (or only at prohibitive discounts). The Embargo of 1808, the War of 1812, and the depression of 1819–22 left the ministers deeply in debt to Woodward, as they found themselves unable to lighten their inventories and balance their accounts. "So scarce has the *Embargo* rendered Money," reported one, that he did not "expect that the Remainder will either be taken or sold untill [*sic*] the Policy of our Government puts on a different Feature from what it now does."[32] During the war, a Charleston minister complained about British attacks on coasting vessels and told Woodward to "suspend the shipment of books which I have ordered until there shall be reason to expect that the coast may be less infested by these depradators."[33] The 1819 depression induced Georgia planters "to hold back from selling their crops so that money is uncommonly scarce."[34] In 1823, Woodward proposed a monthly installment payment plan to make his large, expensive subscription works more affordable. The plan was ill-suited to a rural market, however, as his agent pointed out that "the time of receiving money here is annually, and they who could mostly pay once a month could all at a time as well."[35]

Woodward's ministers also claimed that country dwellers did not enjoy reading for its own sake and that this lack of interest, combined with economic hardship, made bookselling especially hard. Writing during the embargo, one Baptist minister reported that even in the best of times, "our citizens . . . have not been forward to encourage literature."[36] Another noted that most "are too poor to buy books & those who are able will not . . . many have no taste for reading of any kind."[37] From Virginia came minister James Black's observation that "where the state of society is rude, and the minds of the opulent sordid, it will require labor and time to affect a revolution of taste as to genuine refinement."[38] Country booksellers would have to cultivate these backcountry markets purposefully.

One of Woodward's pet projects was a book containing reports of the turn-of-the-century revivals from around the nation. Some of his early book-selling ministers provided descriptions of camp meetings and blossoming church membership. Once the book was published in 1803, however, sales reports were discouraging. At least one disappointed parson discovered that accounts of the revivals in magazines and cheaper books already had scooped Woodward's market. Many similar accounts circulated in the country; furthermore, readers where the revivals had taken place proved least interested in buying the book. As the Presbyterian minister Francis Cummins wrote from South Carolina, "the *Revivals* will not sell — the curiosity of the Public on that score is over — I mean having been Witness by ears and eyes to these things they will not buy books for information."[39]

Despite these and other efforts to publish lighter material, Woodward

continued to publish large, expensive, scholarly works that left him strag-
gling behind tract and Bible societies that had begun large-scale religious
publishing in the first decade of the nineteenth century. These societies
sponsored newspapers and magazines, distributed huge numbers of pamphlets and easy-to-read tracts, and supplied schools and Sunday schools
with religious reading material. By the early 1820s Woodward's ministers
began to inquire about religious tracts published by these societies and how
they could order large numbers of them to sell.[40] But Woodward did not
publish such tracts; he failed to see that tracts soon would make up the bulk
of religious reading in America and that the societies, with their intensive
production of inexpensive works and a massive wholesale distribution system, would become the largest disseminators of religious reading.

Woodward also faced competition from newspapers, pamphlets, and
other light, inexpensive works. At one point, he considered establishing a
press in Charleston, South Carolina, that would devote itself to publishing
a religious newspaper, but he decided against the project, fearing the lack
of steady patronage.[41] Woodward also considered other ways to increase
his sales in the country and sell a broader range of books. In 1821, University
of Georgia president (and Presbyterian clergyman) Moses Waddell urged
Woodward to open a branch store in Athens. Waddell himself had sold
books for Woodward, and he thought Athens would generate strong "demand for school-books, quills, stationary and every article in that line." He
even promised Woodward the university library's account.[42] But Woodward's son, who would have been given charge of the operation, chose to
move to Cincinnati, and the cautious publisher never made the leap from
peddling his books by ministers to opening branch stores.[43]

Beginning in the 1820s, competitive pressure from New York City
publishers increased. Woodward's ministers began to write of better prices
for New York books and supplies, reporting that financial transactions with
New York had become easier than with Philadelphia banks and merchants.
Moses Waddell warned Woodward about New York's growing influence as
a trading center, but clearly there was little the publisher could do short of
slashing prices or perhaps associating himself with the tract and Bible societies in Philadelphia.[44] As long as he offered good terms to his ministers,
they preferred to deal with him, but they were, after all, self-employed and
therefore tempted to seek better terms with other publishers or religious
publishing societies. Woodward may have recognized that the large sales of
light, inexpensive books represented a more successful formula for tapping
the country market than the small sales and large profits his heavy works

produced. But this publisher, firmly rooted in the "unforced" trade of an eighteenth-century bookseller, never copied the tract and Bible societies' innovative techniques.[45]

Peddlers

Secular publishers of the early republic experienced many of the same difficulties Woodward did in breaking into the country trade, but because they did not use ministers to sell their books, their distribution problems were often different. The firm of McCarty and Davis, formed in 1816, established a wide network of traveling salesmen who covered fairly populated areas that offered little in the way of economic organization. Unlike Woodward's ministers, the salesmen McCarty and Davis used were professional book peddlers who derived their whole living from selling books. A couple of the men dabbled in publishing themselves, hoping to profit more directly from the gaps they saw in the market; but mainly these travelers acted as the firm's employees. While possessed of more business savvy than some of the ministers, these secular peddlers' other idiosyncrasies and personal habits often defeated the purpose of making sales.

Salesmen for McCarty and Davis obtained subscribers for future publications, sold books on the spot, and exchanged titles with booksellers from other areas. While partner Thomas Davis minded the printing shop in Philadelphia, William McCarty and the firm's corps of salesmen journeyed through New Jersey, western Pennsylvania, and Virginia selling books, following the circuit courts, and endlessly complaining to Davis that they did not receive shipments of books from him fast enough to serve their customers. Davis supplied books to McCarty and the other salesmen in fits and starts, sometimes ignoring for several months their desperate pleas for almanacs, "anything in the novel way," schoolbooks, and Carey Bibles.[46]

McCarty and Davis published stereotyped editions of small, inexpensive books such as their copyrighted schoolbooks. Their imprints also included Carver's *Practical Horse Farrier* and *Every Man His Own Lawyer*, two self-help manuals popular with country consumers. For McCarty's court circuit sales, they published law books and the more expensive works that were indispensable to country lawyers and judges. Adding to the variety of books they published, McCarty and Davis spiced up their assortment by exchanging with other booksellers. Unlike Woodward and his ministers, McCarty and Davis and their salesmen were not committed by religious or moral convictions to selling certain kinds of books. As a result, they operated with greater flexibility. Still, while they may have better understood the requirements of a rural market, they nonetheless were beset with problems involving transportation, unreliable salesmen, bank notes, and competition.

Delivery problems plagued the traveling salesmen. William McCarty complained of hard weather and the difficulties posed by a river that was either too high or too low, by snow on the ground when the only transport at hand was a wagon, and by the lack of snow when the only transport at hand was a sled. On another occasion, McCarty's rounds were delayed when one of his horses expired suddenly, leaving him with "one horse dead, my family tumbled in the middle of the road, and the children all crying in concert."[47] This was one of McCarty's more cheerful moments — at least he had his family with him. On most other occasions, when his family stayed at home, he, like almost every salesman, complained bitterly of loneliness and lack of regular communication from Davis in Philadelphia.[48] In one instance sales were impeded because the dried codfish McCarty used as a premium for the lawyers at court did not arrive in time for a session, leaving the lawyers who had anticipated the treat in a less amiable mood for buying books.[49]

Unlike William Woodward, whose minister-salesmen seem to have been trustworthy, McCarty and Davis suffered losses at the hands of some of their agents. One of them, in a drunken fit, auctioned off the books he had in his possession, throwing in the firm's horse and wagon as well.[50] Another salesman, James Mulholland, reportedly spent "2 or 3 weeks in a state of partial or total intoxication, and cohabiting with lewd women, and of course squandering our money."[51] Not surprisingly, one of Mulholland's subscription lists proved to contain more than the usual number of fictitious names: "he seems to have raked up all the insolvents and blackguards of the country," McCarty grimly reported.[52] A third salesman, Ebenezer Hurd, tried to sell "a considerable number of fine editions of valuable books" for a mere five dollars in Mount Holly, New Jersey. His conduct was reported by a villager there who wrote to warn the publishers of Hurd's wanton disposal of their stock. Hurd, according to the report, "was perfectly gentlemanly and innocent in his manner, but evidently disordered in intellect."[53]

The traveling salesmen shared certain characteristics. They were generally young men, often single or with young families whom they seemed unconcerned about leaving for long periods of time. They seemed unusu-

ally restless, sometimes unwilling to stay in one place long enough to receive communications, always hoping to find the lucrative market just over
the horizon. Clearly they had a taste for adventure and in many ways did
not quite fit into more settled communities. From a satirical poem called
The Age of Print, written in 1830, it is clear that traveling book salesmen
developed a reputation not only for drunkenness and unreliability, but for
forcefulness as well:

> The Agent's here — whose visage is a bribe,
> Arm'd with each dear temptation to subscribe. Old or Young Rapid,
>   round the land he glides
> And talks as fast and headlong as he rides —
> Recites the same old tale in every village —
> Leaps walls, to tease grave farmers at their tillage;
> Debate octavos in the midst of hay,
> And whisper, with a nod, "No crops, no pay!"
> Be you in office drest, and wear the robes,
> Your weaker side still cunningly he probes —
> Talk you of times and stinted salary,
> The rogue still whispers — "leading men should buy;"
> Point to a family that must be fed,
> He'll prove his book should come before your bread! —
> He hunts you down as some devoted game,
> Nor gives the chase up till he gets your name.[54]

In opposing books to bread and octavos to hay, the Boston author of the
poem represented a distinctly urban view of rural America and the ways
in which it received and interpreted the antebellum version of the urban
carpetbagger. Nevertheless, it is not difficult to imagine that rural dwellers
felt wary of the wall-scaling peddlers, and that this wariness stemmed as
much from a distrust of their polished cunning as from their single-minded
persistence.

More tangible differences separated the urban setting from the less
well-defined country communities. The peddlers working for McCarty and
Davis often wrote to explain delays in disposing of books, gathering or
serving subscribers, and collecting money. The scarcity of cash reported by
Woodward's ministers hampered McCarty and Davis's expansion into the
country as well. In towns where William McCarty and his salesmen set up
temporary outlets, exchange accounts and credit made up the bulk of transactions with local tradesmen. But this system failed when the firm needed

Philadelphia notes. One way of coping with the problem of money exchange and prohibitive discounts on out-of-town notes was to bring in country goods such as beeswax, honey, rags for paper, and ginseng to sell in the city.

Branch Stores and Country Competition

In the country, McCarty and Davis and their salesmen competed with other urban publishers and their representatives, who proved to be as troublesome as their urban competitors. Publishers like Carey negotiated with McCarty and Davis for territorial distribution, but such collusions never seemed to last. McCarty and Davis's salesmen often complained about other salesmen in their areas. One noted incredulously that "Mr. Shryock sells *Peveril of the Peak* at *one dollar & seventy five cents*. How is this? It is in vain to attempt to sell your books unless the prices are lowered."[55]

Ultimately, the competition the salesmen simply could not overcome was from local shopkeepers who stocked books and from booksellers, printers, and newspaper owners who opened shops in the communities that lay along the salesmen's routes. Such businesses drove the travelers farther west in an attempt to stay ahead of established bookselling. William McCarty reported to Davis in 1825 that the schoolbook trade had slipped through his fingers because the local shopkeepers to whom he normally sold his assortment of schoolbooks had bypassed him by going to the city to make their purchases. Bad money may have hastened this change. McCarty reasoned that as urban merchants rejected the "depreciated paper" from the country, forcing storekeepers to pay their accounts in specie, the storekeepers decided to buy in the city, where cash would at least get them discounts or they could open book accounts.[56]

To counter such competition McCarty and Davis decided to establish branch stores in strategic locations. The firm boldly chose locations that they believed would become important to future country trade, as opposed to places where economic structures were well in place. Surprisingly, this spirited entrepreneurship did not serve them particularly well. They seemed not to have the interest and flexibility to allow their western businesses to develop in step with the country market. Their orientation remained awkwardly eastern, even as they expanded farther to the west.

One of McCarty and Davis's branch stores, for example, was planned for Chambersburg, Pennsylvania, a place considered convenient to Philadelphia and points west and south. There the road branched off to the south through the Shenandoah. Most of the salesmen traveled through Chambersburg on their way south or west, and it is likely that McCarty and Davis thought of the store as a distribution center as well. Their salesman, George Harper, arrived in Chambersburg in 1822 to set up shop for selling (on commission) McCarty and Davis's books. He was soon edged out by two other booksellers with the same idea. Harper complained that McCarty and Davis had not supplied him quickly enough to keep the competitors at bay. "The delay you suffered to take place," he wrote, "gave Mr. Blood & even Mr. Shryock the start of me; besides they both have larger & general assortments, which I have not. Could I have contemplated the establishment of two other bookstores, I certainly never should have thought of going into the business."[57]

Harper's experience in Chambersburg underscores the fact that in the country, even one or two competitors could prove fatal. These rivals were also getting their books from Philadelphia, but from other publishers. The competition that characterized the urban publishing environment was simply being reproduced and magnified in the country, where frontier economies supported fewer booksellers. Rather than escaping the competitiveness of the urban East, publishers found themselves equally vulnerable in the risky country trade.[58]

McCarty and Davis's other branch store in Wheeling, Virginia, fared only somewhat better than the Chambersburg establishment. According to a contemporary geography book, Wheeling was the first town on the Ohio River where goods could be loaded and unloaded even when the water was low. In addition, the great National Road from Baltimore led straight through Wheeling, meeting other roads connected to Pittsburgh. Wheeling's rapid development in the 1820s brought a courthouse, jail, bank, several churches, market place, library, school, and a number of stores and inns — including the bookstore and printing shop of Davis and McCarty, set up by the two younger brothers of the Philadelphia partners.[59] In contrast to Woodward's amateur sales force and McCarty and Davis's professional book salesmen, the younger McCarty and Davis were both trained as printers and, like their older brothers, were career booksellers. The branch was designed to address the problems of traveling sales, but it brought its own difficulties. The stock for Wheeling was supposed to have been delivered regularly from Philadelphia, but bad communication and poor planning made this impossible. Apparently, despite the relatively easy road and river access to Wheeling, shipping books still offered a significant challenge to the firm. The young James McCarty constantly wrote agitated missives to Davis in Philadelphia, imploring him to attend more punctually to their orders.

Despite Wheeling's rapid commercial development, Davis and Mc-Carty encountered the same apparent indifference to reading that William Woodward's ministers had described. When they arrived there, they felt as if they had been sent among savages. James McCarty referred sarcastically to Wheeling's cultural backwardness when writing to the Philadelphia firm. "To bring books among such rabble is like throwing Pearls before Swine," he remarked, "for I believe they know no more about books than a goose knows how to be a mathematician." He found it very frustrating to live in a society not oriented toward books:

Let me describe to you some of our customers (the people among whom you have sent us.) A man will come in the store and gaze with astonishment for perhaps ten minutes, and then he prefaces his observation with, "well, I guess (during this time he pauses about a minute and a half) you have got books enough to keep a man a lifetime to read." [A]nother comes in with "have you any raw cotton for sale, I want to buy a cents worth," while another will come in and look around with surprise and say, "well, I *thought* this was a *store*." [60]

McCarty sniffed that if the customers would not buy his books, "I can sit down and laugh at their folly and peruse them myself." [61]

Within five years, the younger brothers split up and went their separate ways, dismantling the Wheeling store and distributing the stock among McCarty and Davis's other salesmen. The venture had enjoyed only limited success. It is likely that the brothers in Wheeling lost credibility with local customers simply by being too oriented — economically and culturally — toward the urban east. They took their orders from Philadelphia, accepted the books sent them, converted their funds into eastern credit, and took no obvious enjoyment in their role as tenders of an "outpost." By the mid-1820s, some resistance to eastern influences, due in large measure to local boosterism and economic protectionism, had begun to surface, and the eastern, urban young men represented all that non-eastern citizens came to resent. [62]

Catering to the Country:
Flexibility and Wholesale Book Distribution

One early national Philadelphia publishing firm seems to have more effec-tively tackled the peculiarities of the country market. Two Quaker entrepreneurs, printer-publisher Jacob Johnson and his merchant partner, Benjamin Warner, joined forces in 1809 to publish children's books, schoolbooks, and a variety of other steady sellers. They kept a retail store in Philadelphia even though they concentrated most of their efforts on their wholesale country business. Johnson and Warner employed some agents but, more significantly, they traveled themselves to establish large wholesale accounts with country merchants, printers, and booksellers. It appears that whenever possible they dealt with fellow Quakers; their country sales network, including trusted agents, contained some Friends.[63] They adhered to the maxim of large sales and small profits, and they did not assume that country buyers would simply settle for old familiar titles. Their object was to provide their accounts with a "constant supply of every article in common demand — particularly schoolbooks and stationary articles and new works."[64]

Johnson and Warner took several trips to the West each year for the purpose of meeting people with whom they wished to do business. One would travel at a time, leaving the other partner to stay in Philadelphia to attend to the orders. On such trips the partners could evaluate the state of the market, the level of local competition, and the status and financial standing of the tradesmen they met. They also analyzed the local economies and calculated the best ways to demand and receive payment. After extensive travels in Kentucky and Tennessee, Warner decided how he wished to arrange monetary matters with his customers there and sent directives to his newly established contact in Louisville. It is clear that Warner paid close attention to the minutiae of frontier finances:

It was my intention to have my funds converted into Tenn. paper and invested in the purchase of cotton in Alabama, but the price of that article at the opening of the market was 12 cents . . . I wish thee to ascertain whether it can be bought at Huntsville for 9 or 10 cents, if so to convert all thy Kentucky money into Tenn. paper, excepting what thee can exchange for North or South Carolina or Georgia at a loss of not more than 5 per cent . . . The State Bank of North Carolina is generally 1 per cent better than the new Bank in Cape Town.[65]

Warner continued his detailed instructions, explaining that if cotton did not look profitable, then the agent should choose tobacco, and "after Tobacco I would select hemp and in fact would prefer it to tobacco only that it cannot find market earlier than Sept. or October at N. Orleans."[66] Here was one solution to the problem of money: accepting country produce — tobacco, cotton, honey, beeswax, rags, or ginseng — to sell in the city. Warner's understanding of local crop prices, banks, and markets throughout the country may not have been extraordinary for an early nineteenth-century merchant, but it was unusual for a publisher. His background as a merchant clearly gave him an edge in making a system of local economies work for him on a national level.

Johnson and Warner were not always successful in their country endeavors, but their personal understanding of the market allowed them greater flexibility than if they had relied solely on salesmen or agents they had never met. When Warner was in Louisville during one visit, he deemed it proper to close down a large wholesale account, which he thought to be unprofitable. Writing to his wife in Philadelphia, he reported that the merchant with whom he had been doing business, and to whom he was a major creditor, deeded his "bookstore and bindery, a house, sundry town lots and a small farm in Indiana some 15 to 20 miles distant from here."[67] While this was under negotiation, however, the industrious Warner chose to buy another bookstore and bindery in town "so that I became possessed of a monopoly of the Book Trade of this place." His plan was to "consolidate the two stocks & when a recruit is sent out, I think the prospect of a fair business is rather promising. I mean to give it a hard push & a fair trial."[68]

Warner made it his business to understand as much about country markets as possible before committing his firm's capital and books. He traveled to Huntsville, Alabama, in 1819 in order to assess the feasibility of opening a bookstore there. The following year he sent books and a printed catalogue for a store there, to be run by agents. Warner was something of a micro-manager. He sent those books "selected according to the best of my judgment as adapted for the demands of the quarter they are destined to," allowing that "there doubtless will still be a number of articles wanted which can best be ascertained when the store is opened." He instructed his agents to make "all transactions of the business . . . in my name," but that "if you think any benefit will arise to your business in having your name inserted in the card as having any agency in the establishment, you will know how to arrange it." Finally, Warner kept informed about local conditions in Huntsville, as well as general market conditions. In the depths of the depression following the panic of 1819, he was clearly exercising caution:

My opinion when out with you in the winter, was that the produce then on hand waiting a road to market, was sufficient to relieve . . . a great portion of the pressure that then existed. This I find has not been the case and by the rise of Exch[ange] and from the acts of y[ou]r legislature, I am inclined to think that even the crop of the present season will not yield that relief which I had contemplated would have resulted from the returns of sales of last years labour. Whether the consumption of Books will be reduced in the same ratio as forreign [*sic*] goods, is a point I cannot yet decide for myself, I am inclined it will not be [but] until some experience is to be had I think it will be much the safest to keep in very limited engagements in business. I have therefore made the selection of stock for my Huntsville store smaller than I would have done under a more settled state of things.[69]

While they traveled extensively, Johnson and Warner also used a few select agents to help collection throughout the country. But again, these agents were given little latitude by their employers. Warner sent John F. Drake a package with two account books to be used as he went about the business of collecting debts. One of the books recorded the accounts only, while the other contained Warner's "remarks on the different acc[ount]s." Warner designed "the former of these books . . . for thy pocket, but the latter containing my remarks, I think it will be better to carry in thy saddle bags — so that in case of a loss of either, my *free* remarks may not fall into improper hands." Familiar with the lay of the land, Warner had arranged the accounts "in the order of the towns, as thee will probably pass through them, though by this I do not mean to chalk out a route which circumstances or thy judgment may render it proper to alter."[70]

The firm of Johnson and Warner might well have become one of the largest national publishing houses had they been able to continue to supply the country in this manner. However, in 1819 Johnson died while on a trip to Kentucky, and in the fall of 1821, Warner died in Richmond, Virginia. Within two years, their stock and copyrights were sold to McCarty and Davis, boosting that firm's power in the trade considerably. Their records show that, after the purchase, they began to step up their wholesale activities by more aggressively seeking to establish large accounts in the country, indicating that they had inherited some of Johnson and Warner's techniques as well. Nevertheless, as we have seen, McCarty and Davis did not have the same acumen to guide them smoothly through the country trade, and they often did best when they allowed the country to come to them, as did many publishers who did not send out agents or travel through the country themselves.

Cultivating trade in the country may have been "forced," but it also led to increased direct business for the Philadelphia firms that undertook it. Despite the problems associated with traveling sales and distribution, the firms that made the efforts were rewarded with greater name recognition and could count on merchants and shopkeepers in politically and commercially developing backcountry towns of Alabama, Missouri, Tennessee, and Kentucky placing and picking up orders for the books they needed, just as they did for other manufactured goods. These orders might be made on a semi-annual buying trip to Philadelphia, by letter, or by a friend, wagon driver, or sea captain. It is clear from McCarty and Davis's daybook, for example, that one William Akin of Danville, Kentucky, must have come to their shop in Philadelphia and ordered $122.26 in books and stationery, as there is an additional debt against him in this entry for $30.00 "city cash," presumably a loan of negotiable currency to ease the rest of his transactions while he stayed in Philadelphia.[71] Other evidence of personal visits to Philadelphia is glimpsed in account entries where notes were issued on or near the same date the order was recorded. Thus it seems clear that when Thompson and Wardlaw of Shelbyville, Tennessee, ordered $347.50 in books and stationery on November 4, 1823, and gave a note at nine months for $349.31 on November 10, this business was transacted while they or their representatives were in Philadelphia.[72]

To boost their chances of receiving such unsolicited orders and to increase their name recognition for future orders, publishers issued and sent out catalogues listing their own books as well as those of others. It was not uncommon, upon receiving an order that included books not in stock, for McCarty and Davis to hurriedly exchange with other booksellers to fill the order. Since schoolbooks were a staple of backcountry general stores, and since McCarty and Davis were the publishers of three of the most popular school texts, more than their share of far backcountry book orders came into their Philadelphia store. They received orders from merchants in Mobile, Tuscaloosa, Huntsville, Florence, and Tuscumbia, Alabama; from Murfreesborough, Knoxville, and Memphis, as well as the smaller towns of Blountsville, Tazewell, Winchester, and Pulaski, Tennessee; from Lexington and Frankfort, Kentucky; and from towns along the Ohio River from Steubenville, Ohio, into Indiana and Kentucky. Far from unsettled, many of these sites were important to cotton exporting, and while not extremely populous, a number had academies (for which books were needed), and most had Presbyterian, Methodist, Baptist, and Catholic churches.[73]

Backcountry merchants, storekeepers, and their representatives made the arduous trip to the East because farmers sold their produce, especially such cash crops as cotton, to the representatives of wholesale merchants in seaboard cities. Country merchants received Philadelphia credit for the produce, with which they bought manufactured and imported goods for their stores, including books. Eastbound produce could generally be sent through the river systems to coastal ports, but westbound shipments of store goods often had to go overland at least part of the way.[74] This trade may have been "unforced" compared with efforts to sell books through the traveling salesman, but for the teamsters driving their wagons over Allegheny trails it was anything but easy. Until about 1830, Philadelphia was the main source for wholesale trade with southern and western merchants. While these merchants could supply themselves with manufactured goods from St. Louis or New Orleans, prices there were much higher than those in Philadelphia, making the trips east worthwhile, even with the extra transportation and insurance expenses.[75] Eastern publishers had a similar capital advantage, reinforced by the prevalent routes of wholesale trade and by their copyright monopoly on the basic books westerners wanted. As long as this pattern persisted, eastern publishers could benefit from their exertions to sell books to the west, whether they chose to "force" the market through agents and branch stores or to encourage sales more "gently" through wholesaling and individual orders.

As we have seen, the publishers' agents in the country often presented a picture of an all but impenetrable market, thick with illiteracy and indifference, inadequate financial amenities, and overbearing competition. As these areas developed, however, so did markets for books and, ultimately, local publishing endeavors. The West benefited from the American victory in the War of 1812, and reduced Indian and British threats accompanied economic optimism and expansion in commerce and industry, all of which did much to build the strength of the urban West.[76] Cincinnati rose to a prominent position in western publishing, and by the late 1840s it was the source for many of the staple books bought in the West.[77] Contemporary and scholarly historical descriptions of pre-railroad Pittsburgh, Cincinnati, Lexington, Louisville, and St. Louis portray developing urban societies with increasingly sophisticated cultural institutions and tastes. Lexington boasted established bookstores in the 1790s, and by the beginning of the new century, Zadock Cramer had opened his formidable book mart in Pittsburgh. In 1813 a newspaper writer in Pittsburgh could look back on the city's early days, noting that the "first exertions" of "colonists" in frontier areas are "the attainment of the necessaries of life and the struggle against wild nature," which must "for a long time retard the progress of the human mind, and the liberal culture of science and literature." Those formative years were over by the time the article appeared in the pages of the Pittsburgh *Mercury*.[78] Subscription libraries, academies, and schools of all kinds could be found in almost every western urban center by 1815. Despite the intensity of the depression that followed the postwar expansion, westerners felt increasingly encouraged to develop greater independence from the East, something which cannot have made the Philadelphia publishers and their agents any more hopeful. In short, Philadelphia publishers were caught between markets. By the time they were ready to reach out to the country, the urban West had developed too quickly for them to have achieved significant influence there. Yet less developed areas were simply not ready for large numbers of books.

*   *   *

According to one publishing historian, at mid-century "no special effort [to reach the country] on the part of publishers had been made since Parson Weems traveled as a salesman for Mathew Carey."[79] We can see, of course, that this was simply not the case, that early national publishers quite aggressively pursued rural and distant markets. Their success, however, was limited. Compared with mid-nineteenth-century railroad marketing, the distribution attempts of the early national publishers seem modest, disorganized, and decentralized.

Thomas Cochran has discussed the ways in which early national entrepreneurs evolved "an increasingly intensive intraregional network," and this is very much the pattern followed by the publishers in their efforts to distribute books to distant locations.[80] Nevertheless, their attempts to disseminate their products form an important link to a later, more nationally oriented system of distribution. Like eighteenth-century British merchants, Philadelphia publishers provided credit and merchandise to the "colonies," in this case, the American South and West. Like colonial American merchants, they bought and sold almost anything that they thought would bring profit. However, the ways in which the early publishers combined eighteenth-century business practices with the idea of a single nation and a national market, provide a glimpse of a larger transition in the American identity.

By the 1830s, publishers began to recognize that simply reaching the country was not enough. The next generation of publishers differed from their predecessors in several respects, enabling them better to serve a national market. Many produced and distributed books on a wholesale basis exclusively, something which none of the publishers in this study ever did.

Abandoning retailing also meant that publishers did not need to exchange, choosing instead to concentrate on their own titles. Many eliminated the extra middlemen — agents and the travelers — and in so doing saved costly commissions. The retailers to whom mid-century publishers sold their books did not necessarily have the luxury of returning unsold copies, as had always been possible in the early national trade. Railroads and improved communication would eventually make book shipments and payments more reliable and would link the American reading public through literature.[81] No longer would an overworked horse affect the sale of a book.

Conclusion

By the beginning of the fourth decade of the nineteenth century, the evolution from printer to publisher was almost complete, and Philadelphia's role as a major center of publishing had begun to diminish in relation to New York's and Boston's. In March 1836, a trade periodical published in New York saluted the accomplishments of the American publishing industry. Its editor, the young publisher George Palmer Putnam, reported that "our publishing trade appears to be flourishing, if we may judge from the number or the sale of new publications." He continued by praising technology and mechanization and their effects on entrepreneurial publishers:

[I]n this age of ballooning and railroading — printing by steam — where the machinery of book-making is such, that it is only necessary to put your rags in the mill and they come out Bibles — all ready printed — there is no telling what human invention will accomplish next. We like this go-ahead sort of spirit.[1]

Putnam believed that the "go-ahead sort of spirit" was able to thrive because of the healthy mixture of competition and cooperation in the trade, as evidenced by the "mutual confidence between booksellers throughout the country" and a singular lack of monopolies.

The *Booksellers' Advertiser* printed "Tables of American Publications" for each year, which in 1835 showed that new American publications numbered 268, as compared to 173 foreign republications. Only two years earlier, there were "one-third more foreign than original" works published in America; this clearly indicated that "we are rapidly forming our own literature — especially in the more useful and solid branches."[2] With the growth of American literature, publishing houses were becoming identified with particular American authors and specific areas of literature. Publishers began to issue catalogues that showed their increasing specialization — lists of novels, or religious works, or medical texts.

Putnam was one of a breed of "modern" American publishers who had begun their publishing careers as entrepreneurs, not as craftsmen. While many were trained in the realms of retailing, wholesaling, literature, and speculation, very few had any connections with printing, and fewer still had actually served as printers. While Putnam's comment about printing by steam was meant to be ironic, it also represented the genteel pose of someone so far removed from the mechanics of production that the process of printing seemed magical. As capable as Putnam was to comment on the current state of publishing, he did not have much experience or historical insight to bring to his editorials. He had only just joined the book trade, having been trained in the carpet business. His literary interests and ambition led him to pursue literary publishing after having served briefly as a clerk in a book and stationery store.[3]

Destined to become a major force in publishing, Putnam was joined by many other young entrepreneurs who in the 1830s and 1840s took up publishing as a profession. New York publishing was soon dominated by John Wiley, the Harper brothers, and Daniel Appleton, to name a few.[4] In Philadelphia, Henry Charles Carey, Grigg and Elliott, J. B. Lippincott, and the Blakiston Company led the industry, and Boston was represented by Ticknor and Fields, Houghton Mifflin, and Little, Brown & Company. With two important exceptions — the Harpers and Houghton Mifflin — none of these young businessmen had trained as printers. Wiley took over his father's publishing business and bookstore in 1826. Unlike his father, John Wiley never served as a printer. Appleton started out as a dry goods merchant and, upon finding the book section of his store was the busiest, gradually specialized in bookselling and then publishing.[5] In Philadelphia, Henry Charles Carey certainly had been bred to the trade, working at a very young age for his father and helping to run the store as well as various branch stores. There is no indication, however, that the elder Carey intended him to print, although he may have learned some of the skills. His partners over the years, Isaac Lea and Abraham Hart, were completely unconnected with printing or any other aspect of the book trade when they joined him.[6] John Grigg, a major medical publisher, began as a clerk in Jacob Johnson and Benjamin Warner's employ. His duties at the shop were to keep the operation running smoothly while the firm's principals were on the road. He was considered a clever book salesman with a sound mind for business, something his accomplished employers must have helped to cultivate. And, like Warner, Grigg had never worked in printing.[7] On Warner's death, the company's stock was sold to McCarty and Davis, and Grigg began his own publishing concern. Grigg later sold his business to Joshua Ballinger Lippincott in 1849 and went on to become a private banker and land speculator. Lippincott, who had never been a printer, had been a clerk for a Philadelphia bookseller before buying out Grigg.[8] William Davis

Ticknor of Boston was a farm boy who moved to the city to work in a brokerage house. His literary interests led him to publishing. His poet partner, James T. Fields, was equally inexperienced in the trade.[9] Charles Little also came from a New England farm and first worked in a shipping house before becoming a publisher.[10]

Meanwhile, the ranks of those who had been part of the transition from printer to publisher were rapidly thinning. While Mathew Carey was still around to read Putnam's analysis of the industry, he would live only a few years longer. Of his contemporaries, Francis Bailey, Patrick Byrne, Thomas Dobson, George Helmbold, David Hogan, John Inskeep, John Ormrod, Abraham Small, and William Young had all died before 1830. John Bioren, Thomas DeSilver, William Woodward, and many others died within the next five years.[11] Most of them, however, like Carey, had lived long enough to witness some dramatic changes in American publishing — changes they had done much to bring about.

In the course of this study we have traced the development of the differences between printing and publishing. Nevertheless, it is striking to see just how divorced from the craft of printing publishing had become by the early 1830s. Philadelphia's first publishers, the transitional figures of this study, had crossed an invisible line into a world of bourgeois solidity, leaving behind an eighteenth-century craft tradition for the new realm of the nineteenth-century entrepreneur. Nineteenth-century publishing seems to have provided a separate career track in the book trade for upwardly mobile, entrepreneurial individuals. Increasingly populated by clerks and booksellers at one end of the spectrum and investors and literary men at the other, it became increasingly exclusive and further removed from the craft of printing.

At the same time, many craftsmen saw opportunities appear that called upon their skills and training in printing, but which also were middle class in orientation. They too were imbued with a "go-ahead sort of spirit." Printers did not remain content simply to continue in the tradition of the eighteenth-century artisan. By mid-century, those master printers who had come to own large printing companies, and who employed hundreds of employees and machines, themselves moved steadily into the middle class. In printing trade journals of the mid-century, their portraits showed them in Victorian cravats and dress clothes rather than the traditional leather aprons.

The nineteenth-century printers' earliest employers have been the subjects of this study. Why did they not follow in the transitional publishers' footsteps? The transition from printer to publisher could be made only by one generation. Once publishing came into its own in America, it no longer "belonged" to printers who occasionally acted as booksellers and publishers. Even the sons of the transitional printer-publishers did not repeat the patterns of their fathers' careers. If they became publishers, they had not previously trained as printers. Indeed, few of Philadelphia's earliest publishers had sons who went into the book trade at all; generally, their sons became professionals in other fields. There was little continuity in the profession between the early national trade and mid-nineteenth-century publishing.

Publishing in early national Philadelphia mirrored developments within American society. The transition from printer to publisher occurred during the formative years of the new nation. Politically and commercially, it made sense for the leaders of Philadelphia's printing trade and a handful of non-printers to publish. While Philadelphia remained the nation's capital, its printer-publishers sat prominently in one of the busiest and most vital sites of the nation's book and printing trades. When the capital moved, and the nation began to expand its territories more rapidly and to more distant places than ever before, Philadelphia publishers worked to expand their operations to supply new and widespread markets. The country's chaotic domestic financial policies were reflected in the new publishers' accounts and credit networks; just as the nation's leaders tried to formulate economic policies to bind the regions of the country together, so the publishers undertook similar efforts to supply the nation with books.

As America's commercial center shifted to New York, so did the center of the book trade. Philadelphia still boasted some major publishing firms, but New York was indisputably the new capital of American publishing. As a rising industrial and manufacturing center, Philadelphia retained a large number of important printing companies and manufacturers of printing machinery and supplies.

If America's first publishers had remained "meer mechanics," their impact upon the new nation would have been limited; but the American book trade, developing according to its own internal logic, was linked to the entrepreneurial spirit of the early republic. As they entered the nineteenth century, America's first publishers continued to believe that the "black art" to which they were trained played a vital role in creating a national society and culture.

Appendix

PRINTERS WITH IMPRINTS, 1790

Robert Aitken
Benjamin Franklin Bache
Francis Bailey
Thomas Bradford
Andrew Brown
Mathew Carey
Charles Cist
David Claypoole
Theophilus Cossart
Joseph Crukshank
Thomas Dobson
John Dunlap
John Fenno
Parry Hall
William Hall
Daniel Humphreys
James Johnson
Andrew Kennedy
Thomas Lang
John McCulloch
Eleazer Oswald
Zachariah Poulson, Jr.
William Spotswood
Henry Taylor
Benjamin Towne
William Young

BOOKSELLERS, 1790

Robert Campbell
Philip Nicklin
Patrick Rice
William Poyntell
William Pritchard
Thomas Seddon
John Sparhawk
William Woodhouse

PRINTERS WITH IMPRINTS, 1795

Robert Aitken
Robert Aitken, Jr.

BOOKSELLERS, 1795

John Baker
Thomas Bradford

PRINTERS WITH IMPRINTS, 1795

Benjamin Franklin Bache
Francis Bailey
Archibald Bartram
Jacob Berriman
Charles Cist
Mathew Carey
Robert Cochran
Ephram Conrad
Peter Denham
Phillip Derrick
Thomas Dobson
William Hall
Daniel Humphreys
Joseph Johnson
James Johnson
Peter LeGrange
John McCulloch
Moreau de St. Mery
William Pechin
Eleazer Oswald
Zachariah Poulson, Jr.
William Ross
William Sellers
Samuel Harrison Smith
Melchior Steiner
Peter Stewart
John Thompson
John Turner
Zephaniah Webster
Archibald Woodruff
William W. Woodward
Francis Wrigley

BOOKSELLERS, 1795

Robert Campbell
James Crukshank
Joseph Crukshank
Benjamin Davies
John Dickens
Elizabeth Hall, widow
Henry Rice
Patrick Rice
Thomas Stephens

PRINTERS WITH IMPRINTS, 1799

Robert Aitken
Francis Bailey

BOOKSELLERS, 1799

Samuel F. Bradford
Daniel Brautigam

PRINTERS WITH IMPRINTS, 1799

Robert Bailey
Archibald Bartram
John Bioren
Andrew Brown, Jr.
James Carey
Mathew Carey
Joseph Charless
Charles Cist
David Claypoole
Robert Cochran
Samuel Finlay
Richard Folwell
Joseph Gales
Joseph Groff
William Hall
William Sellers
David Hogan
Daniel Humphreys
James Humphreys
Walter Hyer
Jacob Johnson
Heinrich Kammerer
John McCulloch
John Ormrod
George Pfaff
Zachariah Poulson, Jr.
Adam Ramage
James Robinson
Samuel Harrison Smith
Melchior Steiner
Peter Stewart
Henry Sweitzer
William Wands
———Way
William W. Woodward
Francis Wrigley
William Young

BOOKSELLERS, 1799

Robert Campbell
Joseph Crukshank
Benjamin Davies
Asbury Dickins
Robert Johnson
William Poyntell
Henry Rice
Patrick Rice
John Sparhawk
William Woodhouse

Printers with Imprints, 1805	Booksellers, 1805
John Adams	Samuel F. Bradford
Jane Aitken	Daniel Brautigam
Samuel Akerman	John Conrad & Co.
John William Allen	James Crukshank
John Bioren	Benjamin Davies
Thomas Bradford	George Davis, Law Bookstore
William Bradford	William P. Farrand
Mathew Carey	J. Johnson
Robert Carr	Emmor Kimber
Charles Cist	Isaac Pearson
Robert Cochran	Peter Snyder
Solomon Conrad	Sparhawk, widow of John
Peter Denham	William Woodhouse
John Dow	
Michael Duffie	
Silas Engles	
John Folwell	
Richard Folwell	
William Hall	
William Hancock	
John Hoff	
David Hogan	
Daniel Humphreys	
James Humphreys	
Richard Jennings	
Benjamin Johnson	
William Johnston	
John M'Culloch	
William M'Culloch	
William F. M'Laughlin	
Thomas Manning	
Hugh Maxwell	
John H. Oswald	
Thomas Palmer	
George Palmer	
Thomas Plowman	
Joseph Rakestraw	

PRINTERS WITH IMPRINTS, 1805

Adam Ramage
James Robinson
William Ross
John W. Scott
Abraham Small
William Spotswood
Peter Stewart
Thomas Stewart
Thomas T. Stiles
Henry Sweitzer
John Thompson
Thomas Town
Henry Tuckniss

Notes

Introduction

1. Mathew Carey to Thomas Carey, September 13, 1794. Carey Letterbook for 1794, Lea and Febiger Collection, Historical Society of Pennsylvania (LFC-HSP).

2. On Carey's political views and ambitions for the new nation, see Edward Carter II, "The Political Activities of Mathew Carey, Nationalist, 1760–1814" (Ph.D. diss., Bryn Mawr College, 1962), esp. 182–194.

3. These figures do not include printers who are listed in the city directories but for whom no imprints have survived. In 1790, the total number of printers listed was 34; there were 51 in 1795, 55 in 1799, and 74 in 1805. While some of those listed in city directories, but without imprints, could have been journeymen printers, those with imprints are less likely to have been. It is nearly impossible to determine how many journeymen there were, as they were often not heads of households and thus would not appear in the census or, routinely, in the city directories. The numbers here represent printers who, by virtue of their imprints, can be assumed to be masters, as journeymen would not appear in the imprints, nor would they have a colophon. See Edmund Hogan, ed., *The Prospect of Philadelphia* (Philadelphia, 1795), Evans 28845; William Cornelius Stafford, ed., *The Philadelphia Directory for 1799* (Philadelphia, 1799), Evans 36353; *The Philadelphia Directory for 1805* (Philadelphia, [1805]), Shaw and Shoemaker 9139; *Return of the Whole Number of Persons within the Several Districts of the United States* (Philadelphia, 1791), Evans 23916. Imprints were determined from Charles Evans, *American Bibliography* (Chicago: The Blakeley Press, 1903–1959). For the period after 1800, imprints were determined by consulting Ralph R. Shaw and Richard H. Shoemaker, eds., *American Bibliography: A Preliminary Checklist, 1801–1819*, 22 vols. (New York: Scarecrow Press, 1958–1966).

William McCulloch, a contemporary printer and close observer of the trade, determined that in 1803 there were 45 printing offices with a total of some 89 presses. "Of these printers," he wrote, "15 were also booksellers." C. S. Brigham, ed., "William McCulloch's Additions to Thomas's *History of Printing*," *Proceedings of the American Antiquarian Society*, 31 (April 1921): 89–247. Quote from p. 93.

4. The best description of the colonial printer's activities is found in Lawrence C. Wroth, *The Colonial Printer* (Portland, Maine: The Southworth-Anthoensen Press, 1938). These activities are also described for English provincial printers in John Feather, *The Provincial Book Trade in Eighteenth-Century England* (Cambridge: Cambridge University Press, 1985), 104–106.

5. For an excellent model and definition of the publisher, see Michael Winship, "Publishing in America: Needs and Opportunities for Research," in *Needs and Opportunities in the History of the Book: America, 1639–1876*, ed. David D. Hall and John B. Hench (Worcester, Mass.: American Antiquarian Society, 1987), 61–102.

6. See Thomas C. Cochran's discussion of the preconditions for innovation and entrepreneurship in early national industry in *Frontiers of Change: Early Industrialism in America* (New York: Oxford University Press, 1981).

7. See Alfred D. Chandler, "The Beginnings of 'Big Business' in American Industry," *Business History Review*, 33 (Spring 1959): 1–31.

8. Referring to the printing trade in English provincial towns, one historian of printing has argued somewhat provocatively that English provincial printers "were left with little more than the scraps from the London table." Feather, *The Provincial Book Trade*, 120. This applied to some extent to the British North American colonial printing trade in the early eighteenth century, but as the business of reprinting English books grew in American cities, Feather's formula becomes less useful. Richard B. Sher has shown through an analysis of the Eighteenth-Century Short Title Catalogue data base that Philadelphia, New York, and Boston can be counted among the growing publishing capitals, along with such cities as Aberdeen, Belfast, Edinburgh, and Glasgow. A problem inherent in counting imprints, however, will always be the difficulty of quantifying reprints versus original publications. The reprint trade flourished, at least in part, because of the reduced risk involved in reprinting works that had already shown signs of marketability. See Sher, "Commerce, Religion, and Enlightenment in Eighteenth-Century Glasgow," in *History of Glasgow*, 3 vols., ed. T. M. Devine and Gordon Jackson (Manchester: Manchester University Press), I: 312–359. On the Irish, see Richard Cargill Cole, *Irish Booksellers and English Writers, 1740–1800* (London: Mansell Pub.; Atlantic Highlands, N.J.: Humanities Press, 1986) and M. Pollard, *Dublin's Trade in Books, 1550–1800* (New York: Oxford University Press, 1989).

9. Edwin Wolf, *The Book Culture of a Colonial American City: Philadelphia Books, Bookmen, and Booksellers* (New York: Oxford University Press, 1988), 75–77.

10. On British republican activists see Richard J. Twomey, "Jacobins and Jeffersonians: Anglo-American Radical Ideology, 1790–1810," in *The Origins of Anglo-American Radicalism*, ed. Margaret Jacob and James Jacob (London: Allen and Unwin, 1984). Also see Roland M. Baumann, "The Democratic-Republicans of Philadelphia: The Origins, 1776–1797" (Ph.D. diss., Pennsylvania State University, 1970); Ray Boston, "The Impact of 'Foreign Liars' on the American Press," *Journalism Quarterly*, 50 (Winter 1983): 722–730; Joseph I. Shulim, "John Daly Burke: Irish Revolutionist and American Patriot," *Transactions of the American Philosophical Society*, 54 (1964).

11. Douglass C. North, *The Economic Growth of the United States, 1790–1860* (New York: W. W. Norton, 1966), 25–36. Writing about Philadelphia merchants and the impact of Federalist fiscal policy, Thomas M. Doerflinger has noted that the "upsurge in the Federalist period appears to have altered commerce substantially," and that while "[r]isks were as acute as ever for traders who now faced the constant threat of war, financial panic, and attacks by English, French, and Algerian

cruisers . . . the probability of making huge profits rapidly . . . undoubtedly improved decisively in the 1790s" (in *A Vigorous Spirit of Enterprise: Merchants and Economic Development in Revolutionary Philadelphia* [Chapel Hill: University of North Carolina Press, 1986], 286–287).

12. North, *The Economic Growth of the United States*, 35. Western Pennsylvania towns began to get printers and presses in the late 1780s and early 1790s. Lexington, Kentucky, had one printer in 1790; Knoxville, Tennessee, had one in 1792. By 1797, Kentucky had printers in Frankfort, Lexington, Paris, and Washington; Knoxville had two, and Nashville had one. By 1799 presses were set up throughout almost all of Pennsylvania. Evans, *American Bibliography*. On the spread of rural printing and rural print culture, see William J. Gilmore, *Reading Becomes a Necessity of Life: Material and Cultural Life in Rural New England, 1780–1835* (Knoxville: University of Tennessee Press, 1989), esp. chs. 5 and 6. Also see Allan Pred, *Urban Growth and the Circulation of Information: The United States System of Cities, 1790–1840* (Cambridge, Mass.: Harvard University Press, 1973) for an analysis of the movement of information and population.

13. The following are only a few of the recent thought-provoking works that explore issues related to book publishing. Cathy Davidson, *Revolution and the Word: The Rise of the Novel in America* (New York: Oxford University Press, 1986); Richard D. Brown, *Knowledge Is Power: The Diffusion of Information in Early America, 1700–1865* (New York: Oxford University Press, 1989); Gilmore, *Reading Becomes a Necessity of Life*; Nina Baym, *Novels, Readers, and Reviewers: Responses to Fiction in Antebellum America* (Ithaca, N.Y.: Cornell University Press, 1984); David Hall, "The Uses of Literacy in New England, 1600–1850," in *Printing and Society in Early America*, ed. William Joyce et al. (Worcester, Mass.: American Antiquarian Society, 1983), 1–47; idem, *Worlds of Wonder, Days of Judgment: Popular Religious Belief in Early New England* (New York: Knopf, 1989); and Michael Warner, *The Letters of the Republic: Publication and the Public Sphere in Eighteenth-Century America* (Cambridge, Mass.: Harvard University Press, 1990).

14. See David Hall, "The Uses of Literacy in New England, 1600–1850," and Nathan O. Hatch, "Elias Smith and the Rise of Religious Journalism in the Early Republic," in *Printing and Society in Early America*, 1–47 and 250–277; Richard D. Brown, *Knowledge Is Power*; William Gilmore, *Reading Becomes a Necessity of Life*; Michael Denning, "Cheap Stories: Notes on Popular Fiction and Working-Class Culture in Nineteenth-Century America," *History Workshop*, 22 (1986): 1–17; Nathan O. Hatch, *The Democratization of American Christianity* (New Haven, Conn.: Yale University Press, 1989); and the essays in Cathy N. Davidson, ed., *Reading in America: Literature and Social History* (Baltimore: Johns Hopkins University Press, 1989) by David Paul Nord, Ronald J. Zboray, Barbara Sicherman, and Cathy Davidson. In his *A Fictive People: Antebellum Economic Development and the American Reading Public* (New York: Oxford University Press, 1993), Zboray offers an interesting and convincing corrective to the pervasiveness of the "democratization" thesis, arguing that rising levels of literacy did less to spur development in the publishing trade than is usually supposed.

15. See R. Freeman Butts and Lawrence A. Cremin, *A History of Education in*

American Culture (New York: Holt, 1953), 191; *The First Report on the State of Education in Pennsylvania, Made to the Pennsylvania Society for the Promotion of Public Schools, to which is added the Constitution of the Society* (Philadelphia, 1828), Shoemaker 34709; and *The Annual Reports of the Controllers of the Public Schools of the First School District of the State of Pennsylvania; with their Accounts* (Philadelphia, 1819–1831), Shaw and Shoemaker 49042 for 1819. Duane and Carey were signers of the Board of Education's constitution.

16. Wroth's *The Colonial Printer* remains the standard for discussion of the printing trade itself. Wroth examined the trade, tools, machinery, methods, and output of printers. Wroth's second edition expanded his study to 1800, thereby allowing him to examine printing technology that had developed from the time of the Revolution to the turn of the century. Nevertheless, he focused on printing, not publishing. Other works on colonial and early national printing include Rollo G. Silver, *The American Printer, 1787–1825* (Charlottesville: University Press of Virginia, 1967); Milton Hamilton, *The Country Printer: New York State, 1785–1830*, 2d ed., with a new introduction by Ralph Adams Brown (Port Washington, N.Y.: I. J. Friedman, 1964); and Stephen Botein's influential article, "'Meer Mechanics' and an Open Press: The Business and Political Strategies of Colonial American Printers," *Perspectives in American History*, 9 (1975): 127–225.

Hellmut Lehmann-Haupt's *The Book in America: A History of the Making, the Selling, and the Collecting of Books in the United States*, 2d ed. (New York: R. R. Bowker, 1952) does concern itself with the growth of the book trade during the early national period. The section written by Lawrence Wroth gives a useful summary of the development of publishing, copyright laws, the literary produce of American publishing firms, and various bookselling methods. See pages 84–110.

17. See, for example, Eugene Exman, *The Brothers Harper: A Unique Publishing Partnership and Its Impact on the Cultural Life of America from 1817 to 1853* (New York: Harper and Row, 1965); William Charvat, "James T. Fields and the Beginning of Book Promotion, 1840–1855," *Huntington Library Quarterly*, 8 (1944): 75–94; Ellen Ballou, *The Building of the House: Houghton Mifflin's Formative Years* (Boston: Houghton Mifflin, 1970); Albert Johannsen, *The House of Beadle and Adams and Its Dime and Nickel Novels* (Norman, Okla.: University of Oklahoma Press, 1950); Madeleine B. Stern, "The Role of the Publisher in Mid-Nineteenth-Century American Literature," *Publishing History*, 10 (1981): 5–26. Ronald J. Zboray discusses the importance of the railroads in the development of a national publishing trade and a "truly national reading public," in *A Fictive People*, 55.

18. See Wroth in Lehmann-Haupt, *The Book in America*, 32–34.

19. Scholars are examining the trade in other cities, as well as establishing a national overview. Ronald Zboray is studying Boston publishing and James N. Green is completing a study of the national trade. In addition, the volumes resulting from the History of the Book in America project, administered by the American Antiquarian Society's Program in the History of the Book, will widen the scope on American publishing enormously.

20. Robert E. Cazden, *A Social History of the German Book Trade in America to the Civil War* (Columbia, S.C.: Camden House, 1984).

Chapter 1

1. Marjorie Plant, *The English Book Trade: An Economic History of the Making and Sale of Books* (London: George Allen and Unwin, 1965), 62–64.

2. Ibid., ch. 6.

3. On the Irish trade, see M. Pollard, *Dublin's Trade in Books, 1550–1800* (New York: Oxford University Press, 1989); Richard Cargill Cole, *Irish Booksellers and English Writers, 1740–1800* (London: Mansell Pub.; Atlantic Highlands, N.J.: Humanities Press, 1986): 74–109; and Plant, *The English Book Trade*, 120, 140. Currently, there is no comprehensive history of Scottish publishing, but for aspects of the Edinburgh trade and its connection to the American trade, see Warren McDougall, "Copyright Litigation in the Court of Session, 1738–1749, and the Rise of the Scottish Book Trade," *Edinburgh Bibliographical Society Transactions* 5 (Part 5, 1988): 2–31; and idem, "Scottish Books for America in the Mid-18th Century," in *Spreading the Word: The Distribution Networks of Print, 1550–1850*, ed. Robin Myers and Michael Harris (Winchester: St. Paul's Bibliographies, 1990), 21–46. For discussion of Glasgow's trade, see Richard B. Sher, "Commerce, Religion, and the Enlightenment in Eighteenth-Century Glasgow," in *History of Glasgow*, 3 vols., ed. T. M. Devine and Gordon Jackson (Manchester: Manchester University Press, 1995), I: 312–359.

4. On personal book buying among the colonial elite, see Edwin Wolf, *The Book Culture of a Colonial American City: Philadelphia Books, Bookmen, and Booksellers* (New York: Oxford University Press, 1988). With members of the colonial elite buying books directly from Britain, most colonial booksellers wanted to devote their businesses to importing cheap, steady-selling books.

5. Giles Barber, "Books from the Old World and for the New: The British International Trade in Books in the Eighteenth Century," *Studies on Voltaire and the Eighteenth Century*, 151 (1979): 185–224; Stephen Botein, "The Anglo-American Book Trade before 1776; Personnel and Strategies," in *Printing and Society in Early America*, ed. William L. Joyce et al. (Worcester, Mass.: American Antiquarian Society, 1983), 48–82; McDougall, "Scottish Books for America in the Mid-18th Century." For specific case studies, see Robert Harlan, "David Hall's Bookshop and Its British Sources of Supply," in *Books in America's Past: Essays Honoring Rudolph H. Gjelsness*, ed. David Kaser (Charlottesville, Va.: University Press of Virginia, 1966); and idem, "William Strahan's American Book Trade, 1744–76," *Library Quarterly*, 21 (1961): 235–244.

6. For a fuller exploration of the dynamics between the London and the colonial book trades, see Botein, "The Anglo-American Book Trade before 1776," 48–82. See 73–81 for discussion of rum books.

7. David Hall to Hamilton and Balfour, December 22, 1760, David Hall Letterbooks, 1750–1767, APS. On Hamilton and Balfour, see Warren McDougall, "Gavin Hamilton, John Balfour and Patrick Neill: A Study of Publishing in Edinburgh in the 18th Century" (Ph.D. diss., University of Edinburgh, 1974).

8. According to Hall, Rivington made these statements to another Philadelphia printer-bookseller, John Dunlap. See Hall to William Strahan, December 22,

1760, David Hall Letterbooks, 1750–1767, APS. On Rivington's career, see Leroy Hewlett, "James Rivington, Loyalist Printer, Publisher, Bookseller of the American Revolution, 1724–1802" (Ph.D. diss., University of Michigan, 1958).

9. See Lawrence C. Wroth, *The Colonial Printer* (Portland, Me.: Southworth-Anthoensen, 1938), 187–188; and Stephen Botein, "'Meer Mechanics' and an Open Press: The Business and Political Strategies of Colonial American Printers," *Perspectives in American History*, 9 (1975): 131–145.

10. Leonard W. Labaree et al., eds., *The Autobiography of Benjamin Franklin* (New Haven, Conn.: Yale University Press, 1964), 171.

11. This separate account book is bound in with David Hall's Account Current Book, 1748–1768, APS.

12. *Pennsylvania Gazette*, January 18, 1739. On printers' advertisements, see Wolf, *The Book Culture of a Colonial American City*, 75–77.

13. William Bradford's advertisement appeared at the back of his 1742 edition of John Robe's *Short Narrative* (as quoted in Wolf, *The Book Culture of a Colonial American City*, 76).

14. Account Book of Col. William Bradford of Philadelphia, 1742–1760, William Bradford Papers, HSP. In 1742, Franklin made several purchases of the mezzotints.

15. Plant, *The English Book Trade*, 95–97.

16. William Reese, "The Printers' First Fruits: An Exhibition of American Imprints, 1640–1742, from the Collections of the American Antiquarian Society," *Proceedings of the American Antiquarian Society*, 99 (1989): 412.

17. These numbers represent all recorded Philadelphia imprints from the first year of each decade. The source used for this and all imprint data is the North American Imprints Program data base at the American Antiquarian Society, a machine-readable catalogue of seventeenth-, eighteenth-, and nineteenth-century books, pamphlets, and broadsides held at the AAS and over 300 other libraries. For the seventeenth and eighteenth centuries, the data base contains nearly 1,000 and 40,000 records respectively. For the years 1801–1819, the records are based on imprints filmed as part of *Early American Imprints*, 2d ser. (Shaw & Shoemaker). The records were created at Stanford University, based on the microform set. For Philadelphia imprints, the search was narrowed to Philadelphia, Germantown, and Whitehall.

18. Isaiah Thomas discussed chapbooks in his *History of Printing in America*, ed. Marcus A. McCorison (Barre, Mass.: Imprint Society, 1970), 146.

19. On almanacs, see Chester Noyes Greenough, "New England Almanacs, 1766–1775, and the American Revolution," *Proceedings of the American Antiquarian Society*, 45 (1935): 288–316; Milton Drake, *Almanacs of the United States* (New York: Scarecrow Press, 1962); and Marion Barber Stowell, *Early American Almanacs: The Colonial Weekday Bible* (New York: B. Franklin, 1977).

20. Stowell, *Early American Almanacs*, x.

21. G. Thomas Tanselle, "Some Statistics on American Printing, 1764–1783," in *The Press and the American Revolution*, ed. Bernard Bailyn and John B. Hench (Boston, Mass.: Northeastern University Press, 1981), 344–345. New York printers produced a little over 15 percent of all American almanacs, and Massachusetts's output came to around 18 percent.

22. On early American peddling, see Richardson Wright, *Hawkers and Walkers in Early America* (Philadelphia: J. B. Lippincott Co., 1927), J. R. Dolan, *The Yankee Peddlers of Early America* (New York: Clarkson N. Potter Inc., 1964). Peddlers would often carry small books along with their other wares.

23. Pamphlets could be printed on single and half sheets, with up to as many as five sheets, containing anywhere from four to eighty pages, depending on how the sheets were folded. For a general description of pamphlets, see Bernard Bailyn, ed., *Pamphlets of the American Revolution, 1750–1776*, 2 vols. (Cambridge, Mass.: Belknap Press of Harvard University Press, 1965), I: 3–4.

John Feather discusses the "distributive" rather than productive nature of the British provincial trade, stressing that the primacy of the London booksellers made anything but newspaper and small book publishing nearly impossible. As with their colonial counterparts, however, the provincial printer-booksellers were able to publish books of local interest. *The Provincial Book Trade in Eighteenth-Century England* (Cambridge: Cambridge University Press, 1985), esp. ch. 6.

24. Bailyn noted that the pamphlet size suited Revolutionary era writers, as it "was spacious enough to allow for the full development of an argument," yet kept authors from ponderousness: "The best of the writing that appeared in this form . . . had a rare combination of spontaneity and solidity, of dash and detail, of casualness and care." *Pamphlets of the American Revolution*, I: 3–4.

25. As calculated from *North American Imprints Program Catalog (NAIP)* files, using imprints for the first year in every decade from 1690 to 1770. I have eliminated government imprints from the total, but broadsides are included. If broadsides were eliminated as well, the percentage of small publications would be slightly lower.

26. In his analysis of Franklin's publishing activities, James Green discussed "big books which entailed big risks." Such books consisted of more than ten full sheets of standard-size paper, a size that would require a significant investment in paper and labor. "Benjamin Franklin as Publisher and Bookseller," in *Reappraising Benjamin Franklin: A Bicentennial Perspective*, ed. J. A. Lemay (Newark, Del.: University of Delaware Press, 1993), 99–100.

27. The authority on American subscription publishing is Donald Farren, "Subscription: A Study of the Eighteenth-Century American Book Trade," (D.L.S. diss., Columbia University, 1982).

28. Plant, *The English Book Trade*, 227–234.

29. Quoted in Farren, "Subscription: A Study of the Eighteenth-Century American Book Trade," 7.

30. Ibid., 9.

31. Benjamin Franklin Bache to John Wolcott, February 26, 1793, Benjamin Franklin Bache Papers, Castle Collections, APS.

32. Plant, *The English Book Trade*, 227–237. On English trade sales and share books, see Terry Belanger, "Booksellers' Trade Sales," *The Library*, 5th ser., 30 (1975): 281–302.

33. Isaac Watts, *Psalms of David, imitated* (Philadelphia, 1729), Evans 3135; George Whitefield, *A Journal of a Voyage from Gibralter to Georgia, Vol. I; A Continuation of the Revered Mr. Whitefield's Journal, Vol. II* (Philadelphia, 1739–40), Evans 4453 and 4633.

34. On Franklin's publication of Whitefield's works, see Frank Lambert, "Subscribing for Profits and Piety: The Friendship of Benjamin Franklin and George Whitefield," *William and Mary Quarterly*, 3d. ser., L (1993): 529–554.

For a full discussion of Franklin's publishing strategies, see Green, "Benjamin Franklin as Publisher and Bookseller," 98–114.

35. On Franklin's printing networks see Ralph Frasca, "Benjamin Franklin's Printing Network," *American Journalism*, 5 (1988): 145–158, and Frasca's "From Apprentice to Journeyman to Partner: Benjamin Franklin's Workers and the Growth of the Early American Printing Trade," *Pennsylvania Magazine of History and Biography*, 114 (1990): 229–248. Also, on the printing network of the Green family, see Reese, "The First Hundred Years of Printing," 337–373.

36. James Green has explored the relationship between Franklin and Mathew Carey and has concluded that Carey's business practices were influenced by Franklin's example ("'I was always dispos'd to be serviceable to you': Benjamin Franklin's Relationship with Mathew Carey," paper delivered before Philobiblon, Philadelphia, November 10, 1987).

37. See Reese, "The First Hundred Years of Printing," and Botein, "'Meer Mechanics,' and an Open Press," 146–150, for the growth of newspapers and the accompanying prominence of their publishers in society.

38. Plant, *The English Book Trade*, 57, quote from p. 232.

39. Reese, "The First Hundred Years of Printing," 354.

40. *Pennsylvania Gazette*, November 21, December 4, and December 24, 1728.

41. Ibid., January 20, 1729.

42. Ibid., November 3–November 10, 1737.

43. James N. Green, "Book Publishing in Early America," A. S. W. Rosenbach Lectures in Bibliography, University of Pennsylvania, 1993. This argument is from the first of the three lectures, "Colonial Beginnings: Benjamin Franklin and Robert Bell."

44. The phrase was used by Botein in "'Meer Mechanics' and an Open Press," 127–225.

45. Ibid.

46. Labaree, *The Autobiography of Benjamin Franklin*, 165.

47. The year 1748 marks the beginning of Franklin's eighteen-year partnership with David Hall, his retirement from active participation in the printing business, and his first term in elective office (he was elected to the Philadelphia Common Council). Ibid., 305.

48. See Gary B. Nash, *The Urban Crucible: Social Change, Political Consciousness, and the Origins of the American Revolution* (Cambridge, Mass.: Harvard University Press, 1979), 58–63. Despite their attempts to maintain neutrality, colonial printers who published newspapers often became embroiled in factional disputes, particularly in colonies where there was early and strong opposition to imperial power. Various political struggles in mid-eighteenth-century Boston and New York led to the development of a "political press" in those cities, with newspapers deriving support from both the entrenched provincial leadership and its opponents.

49. On colonial newspapers, see Isaiah Thomas, *The History of Printing in America*, 8–19; Clarence S. Brigham, *History and Bibliography of American News-*

papers, 1690–1820, 2 vols. (Worcester, Mass.: American Antiquarian Society, 1947); Sidney Kobre, *The Development of the Colonial Newspaper* (Pittsburgh, Pa.: Colonial Press, 1944); William A. Dill, *Growth of Newspapers in the United States, 1704–1925* (Lawrence: University of Kansas Press, 1928); Arthur M. Schlesinger, *Prelude to Independence: The Newspaper War on Britain, 1764–1776* (New York: Knopf, 1958); Lauren Kessler, *The Dissident Press: Alternative Journalism in American History* (Beverly Hills, Calif.: Sage Publications, 1984); Michael Schudson, *Discovering the News: A Social History of American Newspapers* (New York: Basic Books, 1978); Jeffery A. Smith, *Printers and Press Freedom: The Ideology of Early American Journalism* (New York: Oxford University Press, 1987); David Paul Nord, "Newspapers and American Nationhood, 1776–1826," in *Proceedings of the American Antiquarian Society*, 100 (Part 2, 1990): 391–405.

Stephen Botein argues that the roots of the political press in America lay in the decade preceding the Revolution, and not before, as most of the other scholars cited here believe. See "Printers and the American Revolution," in *The Press and the American Revolution*, ed. Bailyn and Hench, 11–57.

50. For the increase in numbers of newspapers see Tanselle, "Some Statistics on American Printing, 1764–1783," 346–349.

51. Pauline Maier, *From Resistance to Revolution: Colonial Radicals and the Development of American Opposition to Britain, 1765–1776* (New York: Knopf, 1972), 91.

52. Botein, "Printers and the American Revolution," 13.

Chapter 2

1. For a discussion of public opinion, the press, and political ideology in the 1790s, see Richard Buel, Jr., *Securing the Revolution: Ideology in American Politics, 1789–1815* (Ithaca, N.Y.: Cornell University Press, 1972).

2. Increases also occurred in Boston (from 12 to 19, or 58 percent), New York City (from 21 to 34, or 62 percent), and Baltimore (from 4 to 16, or 300 percent). Charleston lost four of its eleven papers. Clarence S. Brigham, *History and Bibliography of American Newspapers, 1690–1820*, 2 vols. (Worcester, Mass.: American Antiquarian Society, 1947).

3. Sources for the politics and newspaper publishing of the 1780s include Jeffery A. Smith, *Franklin and Bache: Envisioning the Enlightened Republic* (New York: Oxford University Press, 1990); James Tagg, *Benjamin Franklin Bache and the Philadelphia Aurora* (Philadelphia: University of Pennsylvania Press, 1991); Donald H. Stewart, *The Opposition Press of the Federalist Period* (Albany, N.Y.: State University of New York Press, 1969); and David Paul Nord, "Newspapers and American Nationhood, 1776–1826," *Proceedings of the American Antiquarian Society*, 100 (Part 2, 1990): 391–405.

4. John W. Osborne, *William Cobbett: His Thought and His Times* (New Brunswick, N.J.: Rutgers University Press, 1966), 21.

5. For an excellent analysis of Jefferson's motives in offering patronage to Bache and Brown, see Smith, *Franklin and Bache*, 105–108.

6. Benjamin Franklin Bache, *Proposals for Publishing a News-paper, to be Entitled the Daily Advertiser* [Philadelphia, 1790], Bristol 7304.

7. Robert Morris to Benjamin Franklin Bache, July 28, 1790, Bache Papers, APS.

8. *[Authentic.] Treaty of amity, commerce, and navigation, between his Britannick Majesty, and the United States of America* (Philadelphia, [1795]), Evans 29744.

9. Benjamin Franklin Bache to Margaret Markoe Bache, July 3, 1795, Bache Papers, APS.

10. Mathew Carey, *Autobiography* (Brooklyn, N.Y.: Research Classics, 1942), 39.

11. Smith, *Franklin and Bache*, 94.

12. Bache's resolutions are dated 1789 and are in the Bache Papers, APS.

13. Bache to Richard Bache, September 1, 1791, Bache Papers, APS.

14. Bache to Charles Debrett, December 3, 1796, Bache Papers, APS. Emphasis added.

15. Ibid.

16. *A Pill for Porcupine: Being a specific for an obstinate itching, which that hireling has long contract for lying and calumny* (Philadelphia, 1796), Evans 30155.

17. William Spotswood to Robert Bailey, October 4, 1796, Robert Bailey Letterbook, 1796–1807, HSP.

18. Thomas Jefferson to Benjamin Franklin Bache, April 22, 1791, Bache Papers, APS.

19. By the end of the decade, Bache's paper, according to his widow, had "certainly not done more than support itself." Margaret Markoe Bache to the Pressmen and Compositors, [1799], Bache Papers, APS.

20. Thomas Paine, *The Age of Reason* (Philadelphia, 1795), Evans 29267.

21. Thomas Paine to Benjamin Franklin Bache, September 20, 1795, Bache Papers, APS.

22. James Moore, *A View of the Conduct of the Executive, in the Foreign Affairs of the United States, connected with the Mission to the French Republic* (Philadelphia, 1797), Evans 32491.

23. James Monroe to Benjamin Franklin Bache, October 9, 1797, Bache Papers, APS.

24. Edmund Hogan to John Nicholson, June 11, 1795 in *The Sequestered John Nicholson Papers, General Correspondence, 1772–1819*, in the Pennsylvania State Archives, Manuscript Group 96. Hereafter, Nicholson Papers.

25. Pierre Egron to John Nicholson, August 7, 1794; August 27, 1794; October 5, 1794. Ibid.

26. William W. Woodward to John Nicholson, June 7, 1795; July 29, 1795; quote from December 7, 1795; February 14, 1796; March 31, 1796; and April 1797, in which Woodward still talks of sixty-five dollars remaining to be paid. Ibid.

27. Francis Bailey to John Nicholson, February 15, 1790. Ibid.

28. Ibid., May 9, 1795.

29. Robert Bailey to John Nicholson, June 24, 26, July 4, 1800; quote from July 28, 1800. Ibid.

30. Thomas Dobson to John Nicholson, September 6, 1800. Ibid.

31. William W. Woodward to John Nicholson, June 23, 1800. Ibid.

32. The source for these numbers is the NAIP catalogue, American Antiquarian Society.

33. Robert Morris to Benjamin Franklin Bache, July 28, 1790, Bache Papers, APS.

34. Francis Bailey to Mathew Carey, April 15, 1802. Incoming Correspondence, LFC-HSP.

35. Carey, *Autobiography*, 32.

36. Worthington C. Ford, ed., "Letters of William Duane," *Massachusetts Historical Society Proceedings*, 2d ser., 20 (1906–1907): 257–394.

37. Ibid., 258.

38. William Duane to Albert Gallatin, March 15, 1802, Gallatin Papers, New York Historical Society. MacPherson's Blues was a city troop after the Revolution in Philadelphia, consisting of 1,500 men — artillery, grenadiers, and light infantry. The troops were apparently part of the government's policies of intimidation during the tense times of the Alien and Sedition Acts. J. Thomas Scharf and Thompson Westcott, *Philadelphia, 1609–1884*, 3 vols. (Philadelphia: L. H. Everts & Co., 1884), II: 1018.

39. Ford, "Letters of William Duane," 270.

40. The following summary of Carey's political publishing is drawn from Edward Carter II, "The Political Activities of Mathew Carey, Nationalist, 1760–1814" (Ph.D. diss., Bryn Mawr College, 1962).

41. Carey, *Autobiography*, 30.

42. *Detection of a Conspiracy formed by the United Irishmen* (Philadelphia, 1798), Bristol 10264; *A Plumb Pudding for . . . Peter Porcupine* (Philadelphia, 1799), Evans 35272. On Cobbett's ideas of conspiracy, see Edward Carter II, "A 'Wild Irishman' Under Every Federalist's Bed: Naturalization in Philadelphia, 1789–1806," *Pennsylvania Magazine of History and Biography*, 94 (1970): 331–346, and James N. Green, *Mathew Carey: Publisher and Patriot* (Philadelphia: Library Company of Philadelphia, 1985).

43. Carey, *Autobiography*, 30, 34.

44. On the libel suit, see George Spater, *William Cobbett: The Poor Man's Friend*, 2 vols. (Cambridge: Cambridge University Press, 1982), I: 99–104.

45. Carter, "The Political Activities of Mathew Carey," 289–298.

Chapter 3

1. A recent study examines the contracting opportunities for journeymen printers in this period. See Mark A. Lause, *Some Degree of Power: From Hired Hand to Union Craftsman in the Preindustrial American Printing Trades, 1778–1815* (Fayetteville: University of Arkansas Press, 1991).

2. See James Gilreath, ed., *Federal Copyright Records, 1790–1800* (Washington, D.C.: Library of Congress, 1987), Introduction.

3. Lause, *Some Degree of Power*, 36–39. A journeyman printer in Philadelphia observed to his father in Scotland that "there are no established regulations here as

at home in the printing business and it does not signify whether an apprentice serves 3, 4, 5 or 7 years to the business." Robert Simpson to his father, October 1, 1792, Robert Simpson Letterbook, HSP.

4. As quoted in Rollo G. Silver, *The American Printer, 1787–1825* (Charlottesville: University Press of Virginia, 1967), 10.

5. Edwin J. Perkins, "The Entrepreneurial Spirit in Colonial America: The Foundations of Modern Business History," *Business History Review* 63 (1989): 171, and W. J. Rorabaugh, *The Craft Apprentice: From Franklin to the Machine Age in America* (New York: Oxford University Press, 1986).

6. On the scarcity of journeymen in the colonial period, as well as the limited degree of trade organization, see Lawrence C. Wroth, *The Colonial Printer* (Portland, Me.: The Southworth-Anthoensen Press, 1938), 154–168. On the English Trade, see Cyprian Blagden, *The Stationers' Company: A History, 1403–1959* (Cambridge, Mass.: Harvard University Press, 1960), 229–233.

7. Carey to James H. Stewart, June 6, 1790, LFC-HSP. Itineracy had long characterized English journeymen. See D. F. McKenzie, *The Cambridge University Press, 1696–1712; A Bibliographical Study*, 2 vols. (Cambridge: Cambridge University Press, 1966), I: 54–71.

8. John Bioren's notes on journeymen printers are in the McCarty and Davis Papers, Rosenbach Museum and Library.

9. Lydia Bailey's employees from 1808–1855, extracted from the Bailey Journal, HSP.

10. Lause, *Some Degree of Power*; Ethelbert Stewart, "A Documentary History of Early Organizations of Printers," U.S. Department of Commerce and Labor *Bulletin*, 11 (November 1905): 857–1033.

11. Compositors and Pressmen in the Office of the *Aurora* to Margaret [Hartman] Bache, January 12, 1799; The Late Compositors and Pressmen of the *Aurora* to M[argaret] H[artman] Bache, January 15, 1799; and M[argaret] H[artman] Bache to the Compositors and Pressmen in the Office of the *Aurora*, [1799], Bache Papers, Castle Collection, American Philosophical Society. Also see Bernard Fay, "Benjamin Franklin Bache, A Democratic Leader of the Eighteenth Century," *Proceedings of the American Antiquarian Society*, 40 (1930): 300–302.

12. The Late Compositors and Pressmen of the *Aurora* to M[argaret] H[artman] Bache.

13. [Mrs. Bache to the Journeymen of the *Aurora*], January 15, 1799, Bache Papers, APS. Emphasis added.

14. As quoted in Silver, *The American Printer*, 19.

15. The list of journeymen's demands is copied out in Lydia Bailey's Memorandum Book, HSP.

16. C. S. Brigham, ed., "William McCulloch's Additions to Thomas's *History of Printing*," *Proceedings of the American Antiquarian Society*, 31 (April 1921): 135–136.

17. Robert Simpson to his father and mother, June 1, 1790, Simpson Letterbook, HSP.

18. Simpson was eighteen years old, well-educated, and had attended Scottish high school, unlike most apprentices who began their terms of indenture usually

between the ages of thirteen and fifteen. Their terms ran until they were twenty-one, and their masters were generally to provide some measure of protection, food, clothing, and lodging, and the rudiments of schooling. Simpson's age and education allowed him to negotiate a short apprenticeship with Brown. An account of Simpson's time in Philadelphia can be found in a journal that was published as the "Narrative of a Scottish Adventurer, 1788–1797" in the *Journal of the Presbyterian Historical Society*, 27 (March 1949): 41–67. On apprenticeship, see Rollo G. Silver, *The American Printer*, 2–4.

19. Simpson to Frank [no last name given], May 26, 1794, Simpson Letterbook, HSP.

20. Simpson to Andrew Brown, December 29, 1794. Simpson Letterbook, HSP. This is not the same Andrew Brown with whom Simpson served his apprenticeship. Simpson was not on good terms with Brown, the publisher: "I have been always in good employ, ever since I left Brown, which I did the moment I was free, & return thanks to God for preserving me in the midst of so much villainy, wickedness, and cruelty, as I labored under, whilst in the clutches of that vile Monster, whose name alone fills me with horror."

21. Simpson to his father, June 1, 1793, Simpson Letterbook, HSP.

22. Ibid.

23. Ibid.

24. Ibid.

25. Ibid.

26. Smart, Goldsmith, and Johnson, comp., *The World Displayed; or, A Curious Collection of Voyages and Travels* (Philadelphia, 1795), Evans 29926.

27. Their ads appeared in the summer of 1795 in Bache's *Aurora*, Fenno's *Gazette of the United States*, and Dunlap and Claypoole's *American Daily Advertiser*. The ads listed the terms of the proposal to publish, the price to subscribers, and information about where one could go to subscribe.

28. In the June 19, 1795 issue of the *Aurora*, the partners hoped to supply themselves with a plate they believed would enhance their book: "COLUMBUS: The publishers of the World Displayed, being desirous of ornamenting the first numbers of that work with a handsome Frontispiece, would be very thankful to any person in possession of a Portrait of COLUMBUS, if they would oblige them with it for a few days to copy from — The greatest care will be taken not to soil it."

29. Captain Jonathan Carver, *Three Years of Travels, through the Interior Parts of North America* (Philadelphia, 1796), Evans 30169. Three other Philadelphia editions of Carver existed by the time Simpson and Key took on the project. They were printed in 1784, 1789, and 1792. Simpson and Key's edition was, like *The World Displayed*, distinctive for its luxury and expense.

30. Simpson to his father, January 3, 1796, Simpson Letterbook, HSP.

31. Simpson to his father, May 24, 1796, Simpson Letterbook, HSP.

32. William Alexander, *The History of Women* (Philadelphia, 1796), Evans 29964. *The Holy Bible* (Philadelphia, 1798), Evans 33408. See James N. Green's discussion of the publication of Burkitt in "Variant Issues," the *Library Company of Philadelphia Annual Report* (Philadelphia, 1990), 18–27.

33. Simpson to his father, January 3, 1796, Letterbook, HSP.

34. James Carey to Mathew Carey, December 1, 1792, Incoming Correspondence, LFC-HSP.

35. Mathew Carey to James Carey, March 6, 1795, LFC-HSP.

36. James Carey to Mathew Carey, November 11, 1793, Incoming Correspondence, LFC-HSP.

37. Mathew Carey to James Carey, December 19, 1792, LFC-HSP.

38. Mathew Carey, *Autobiography* (Brooklyn, N.Y.: Research Classics, 1942), 25.

39. Mathew Carey to Rev. James Carey, [1792], LFC-HSP.

40. Mathew Carey to James Carey, June 6, 1794, LFC-HSP.

41. Mathew Carey to Christopher Carey, June 20, 1794, LFC-HSP.

42. Rivington to Mathew Carey, August 25, 1795. Camillus's "defence" was Alexander Hamilton's *A Defence of the Treaty of Amity, Commerce, and Navigation, entered into between the United States of America & Great Britain* (New York, 1795), Evans 28795. The "remembrancer" was Carey's short-lived periodical, *American Remembrancer; or, an impartial collection of essays, resolves, speeches, &c.* (Philadelphia, 1795–1796).

43. James T. Callender to Mathew Carey, February 13, 1795. The pamphlet is Callender's, *The Political Progress of Great Britain, or an impartial history of the abuses in the government of the British Empire* (Philadelphia, 1795), Evans 28381. It is likely that Rivington did publish the pamphlet, as his name appears as the primary bookseller in a 1795 New York edition.

44. Carey, *Autobiography*, 41.

45. In 1800 Carey had been "seized with the ambition to dominate the nation's Bible business," something he effected by publishing Bibles from standing type. After the success of his first bible, an elegant quarto family King James Bible, he bought the standing type for a duodecimo school Bible. Until 1820, Carey printed regular editions of these, offering them in his catalogues, which listed the Bibles by numbers so they could be identifiable according to their formats, bindings, and other "extras," such as psalms and Apocrypha. See James N. Green, *Mathew Carey, Publisher and Patriot* (Philadelphia: Library Company of Philadelphia, 1985), 18–19.

46. Mathew Carey to Jacob Bailey, February 1794, LFC-HSP.

47. Philadelphia newspapers surveyed were the *Aurora General Advertiser, Dunlap and Claypoole's American Daily Advertiser, Gazette of the United States*, and *Poulson's Daily American Advertiser*. Scanning the newspaper ads for books, translating the shortened "spine titles" listed in the ads into full, searchable titles, and determining the author—often not mentioned in the ad—and his or her nationality proved to be difficult and time-consuming tasks. The sample of half of the books listed in six months of ads reflects this difficulty. While the sample cannot be comprehensive, it is representative of the books advertised that year.

48. Mathew Carey to James Rivington, October 24, 1791, LFC-HSP. Rivington had suggested that Carey publish "Gibbon," in reference to Edward Gibbon's *History of the Decline and Fall of the Roman Empire*, which had only a year before been published in London in an abridged edition of two volumes. No such abridgment was published in America, however, until after 1800. Rivington's business

practices are discussed in Leroy Hewlett, "James Rivington, Loyalist Printer, Publisher, and Bookseller of the American Revolution, 1724–1802" (Ph.D. diss., University of Michigan, 1958).

49. Weems to Mathew Carey, Sept. 16, 1796 in Emily Ellsworth Ford Skeel, *Mason Locke Weems: His Work and His Ways*, 3 vols. (New York: [privately printed], 1929), II: 34.

50. Mathew Carey to Noah Webster, August 11, 1791, LFC-HSP.

51. See E. Jennifer Monaghan, *A Common Heritage: Noah Webster's Blue-Back Speller* (Hamden, Conn.: Archon Books, 1983), esp. 73–104.

52. On English shareholding, see Marjorie Plant, *The English Book Trade: An Economic History of the Making and Sale of Books* (London: George Allen and Unwin, Ltd., 1965), 224–225.

53. Mathew Carey to David West, October 14, 1795, LFC-HSP.

54. Mathew Carey to Jedediah Morse, January 23, 1795, LFC-HSP.

55. Mathew Carey to Thomas and Andrews, March 17, 1795, LFC-HSP.

56. *Proposals for establishing and conducting 'The Merchant's Advertiser'* (Philadelphia, December 3, 1796). In the Lea and Febiger Collection, HSP.

57. *The Constitution, Proceedings, &c. of the Philadelphia Company of Printers & Booksellers* (Philadelphia, 1793), Bristol 8449.

58. Campbell's reputation for selling cheap books was eloquently discussed by Mason Locke Weems, who tried to convince Carey to emulate Campbell's methods: "Every new beginner behind the counter writes 'Cheap Store' on his sign. He well knows that among our Christian Mammonites cheapness is everything. What made Lackington in Moorefields? Cheapness. What made Rob. Campbell Philadª? Cheapness . . . I *tell* you Cheapness is a great thing even to *one store*, what then must be its effect on 2 to 300 stores." The infamous English bookseller James Lackington built his career and bookselling empire on remaindering books. See Richard G. Landon, "'Small Profits Do Great Things': James Lackington and Eighteenth-Century Bookselling," *Studies in Eighteenth-Century Culture*, 5 (1976): 387–399. Weems's comparison of Campbell with Lackington suggests that Campbell's practices were not only to sell cheap books but to sell books cheap. In other words, he, like Lackington, cared little for the unwritten courtesies of the trade, selling at the lowest prices possible even when the books were hard to obtain and their editions almost exhausted. Weems to Carey, May 22, 1809 in Skeel, *Mason Locke Weems*, II, 406.

59. Brigham, "William McCulloch's Additions to Thomas's *History of Printing*," 135–136.

60. By 1801, William Young had become a merchant in Philadelphia and then in Whitehall, a suburb of Philadelphia.

61. *Constitution of the Philadelphia Company of Booksellers, Adopted February 18, 1802* (Philadelphia, 1802), Shaw and Shoemaker 2892.

62. Minutes of the Booksellers' Company of Philadelphia, American Miscellaneous Manuscripts, HSP.

63. *The Library*, February 25, 1804.

64. Ibid.

65. *The Library*, the periodical the company published, continued until 1809.

This is the only evidence that the company had not already completely folded, as no minutes survive after 1804.

66. Article VI of the Constitution of the American Company of Booksellers, as printed in the Philadelphia Company of Booksellers' periodical, *The Library; or, Philadelphia Literary Reporter*, no. 13, August 11, 1804.

67. *To the Booksellers of the United States* (New York, June 7, 1802). This broadside was probably written by Carey in a mood of self-congratulation. It was signed by the members of a committee, two each from New York (Isaac Collins and James Swords), Boston (John West and Ebenezer T. Andrews), and Philadelphia (Mathew Carey and John Conrad).

On the literary fairs, see Michael Winship, "Getting the Books Out: Trade Sales, Parcel Sales, and Book Fairs in the Nineteenth-Century United States," in *Getting the Books Out: Papers of the Chicago Conference on the Book in 19th-Century America*, ed. Michael Hackenberg (Washington, D.C.: The Center for the Book, 1987), 4–25.

68. *An Oration delivered before the Booksellers Convened in New-York, at their first Literary Fair, June 4th, 1802* (New York or Philadelphia, 1802); Charles L. Nichols, "The Literary Fair in the United States," in *Bibliographical Essays: A Tribute to Wilberforce Eames*, ed. George Parker Winship and Lawrence C. Wroth. [Cambridge, Mass.:] 1924.

69. *To the Booksellers of the United States* (New York, June 7, 1802).

70. Ibid.

71. Ibid.

72. Ibid.

73. *Office of the Classic Press* (Philadelphia, November 17, 1803), printed broadside. The Classic Press books were *Caesar, De bello quae extant* (Philadelphia, 1804), Shaw and Shoemaker 5971; *The Select Dialogues of Lucian* (Philadelphia, 1804), Shaw and Shoemaker 6675, and an 1806 edition, Shaw and Shoemaker 10754; *Sallust, Opera omnia* (Philadelphia, 1804), Shaw and Shoemaker 7227; Anna Seward, *Memoirs of the Life of Dr. Darwin* (Philadelphia, 1804), Shaw and Shoemaker 7246; Vergil, *Opera* (Philadelphia, 1804), Shaw and Shoemaker 7657; Horace, *Opera interpretatione* (Philadelphia, 1804), Shaw and Shoemaker 50443; Adam Ferguson, *The History of the Progress and Termination of the Roman Republic* (Philadelphia, 1805), Shaw and Shoemaker 8435; Ovid, *Metamorphoseon* (Philadelphia, 1805), Shaw and Shoemaker 9086.

74. Edwin Perkins defines maintainers: "These individuals can be described as petty traders, if shopkeepers and smaller merchants with limited inventories, or petty producers, if mainly artisans or family farmers. The primary aim of these individuals, and their households, was to maintain the status quo in their living standards rather than to enhance them." "The Entrepreneurial Spirit in Colonial America," 170.

75. Brigham, ed., "William McCulloch's Additions to Isaiah Thomas's *History of Printing*," 236.

76. Minutes of the Company of Booksellers of Philadelphia, HSP.

77. *Aurora*, July 27, 1804.

78. Ibid.

79. Ibid.

80. "A Journeyman" in the *Aurora*, August 4, 1804. This writer quotes from the master printer's resolution, noting that it was passed in recent years. I have not been able to find any record of this association or action. In response, "Cato" argued that "if the history of the resolution quoted by the journeyman was fairly investigated, it would be seen that there were faults on both sides [and that] it ought to be observed that it was never adopted by any permanent society of master printers; and was only brought forward to serve the particular purpose of a few." *Aurora*, August 2, 1804.

81. "Cato," in ibid., August 2, 1804.

82. "Cato," in ibid., July 27, 1804.

Chapter 4

1. The information about the careers and lives of the printers and publishers was gleaned from a wide variety of printed, manuscript, and bibliographical sources. The printed and bibliographical sources include Marcus A. McCorison's edition of the second edition of Isaiah Thomas, *The History of Printing in America* (Barre, Mass.: Imprint Society, 1970); C. S. Brigham's edition of "William McCulloch's Additions to Thomas's *History of Printing*," *Proceedings of the American Antiquarian Society*, 31 (April 1921): 89–247; and H. Glenn Brown and Maude O. Brown, *A Directory of the Book-Arts and Book Trade in Philadelphia to 1820* (New York: New York Public Library, 1950), a compilation of the information found in Philadelphia city directories.

In addition, I used a number of the directories themselves which, like present-day telephone directories, were published every year by one or more compilers: [Thomas Stephens], *Stephen's Philadelphia Directory, for 1796* (Philadelphia, [1796]) Evans 31235; Cornelius William Stafford, *The Philadelphia Directory for 1798* (Philadelphia, 1798), Evans 34593; Ibid. for 1800, Evans 38549; James Robinson, *The Philadelphia Directory for 1804* (Philadelphia, [1804]), Shaw and Shoemaker 7044; Ibid. for 1808, Shaw and Shoemaker 15911; *Census Directory for 1811* (Philadelphia, 1811), Shaw and Shoemaker 22497; *Kite's Philadelphia Directory for 1814* (Philadelphia, [1814]), Shaw and Shoemaker 31873; *Paxton's Annual Philadelphia Directory and Register — 1818* (Philadelphia, [1818]), Shaw and Shoemaker 45218; *Whitely's Philadelphia Directory for 1820* (Philadelphia, 1820), Shoemaker 2742; Thomas Wilson, *The Philadelphia Directory and Stranger's Guide, for 1825* (Philadelphia, 1825), Shoemaker 23350. I compared the data from the directories with the census data in the United States Census Bureau Returns for 1790, 1800, 1810, and 1820.

Obituaries for each individual whose date of death is known are in either *Poulson's American Daily Advertiser* or *The Public Ledger*, both daily papers published in Philadelphia. The American Antiquarian Society has an invaluable tool in their Printers' File Card Catalog. This file includes biographical information about printers and publishers as well as catalogue cards for all of their imprints held in the Society's collections.

2. Stuart Blumin, *The Emergence of the Middle Class: Social Experience in the*

American City, 1760–1900 (New York: Cambridge University Press, 1989), 153. For development of the city's neighborhoods, and a discussion of public space, architecture, and geographic mobility within Philadelphia, also see, Sam Bass Warner Jr., *The Private City: Philadelphia in Three Periods of Its Growth* (Philadelphia: University of Pennsylvania Press, 1968).

3. Blumin, *The Emergence of the Middle Class*, esp. chapters 2 and 5.

4. Obituary for Francis Wrigley, *Poulson's American Daily Advertiser*, September 30, 1829.

5. Blumin, *The Emergence of the Middle Class*, 150–155.

6. Mathew Carey to Thomas Carey, September 13, 1794, LFC-HSP.

7. Henry Wansey, *The Journal of an Excursion to the United States of North America, in the Summer of 1794* (Salisbury, 1796), 134.

8. Binder's boards, made of thin wood or, more typically for this period, of a type of thick, layered pasteboard, composed the most basic binding. Books in boards could be kept that way or rebound according to the taste and inclination of the book's owner.

9. John Bigland, *A Geographical and Historical View of the World* (Boston, 1811), Shaw and Shoemaker 22393.

10. Mathew Carey to William W. Woodward, January 14, 1812, LFC-HSP.

11. Mathew Carey to T. B. Wait & Co., February 4, 1812, LFC-HSP.

12. Mathew Carey to Thomas and Andrews, December 12, 1794, LFC-HSP.

13. Mathew Carey to Abraham Blauvelt, September 21, 1795, LFC-HSP. The book Blauvelt published was Benjamin Bennet, *Discourses on the Credibility of the Scriptures* (New Brunswick, 1795), Evans 28262.

14. James Carey to Mathew Carey, July 21, 1794, Incoming Correspondence, LFC-HSP. The book James published was William Ramsay, *The Trial of Maurice Margarot* (New York, [1794]), Evans 27594.

15. [Mathew Carey], *Address to the Booksellers of the United States, from the Booksellers' Company of Philadelphia* (Philadelphia, 1813), 4–5, Shaw and Shoemaker 27662.

16. Ibid., 4.

17. Untitled, printed broadside, signed, Samuel Butler, Baltimore, March 30, 1807.

18. Richard Snowden, *The American Revolution; Written in the Style of Ancient History. In Two Volumes* (Philadelphia, [1794]), Evans 27716.

19. Benjamin Warner to George Long, November 22, 1820, Benjamin Warner Letterbook "D," Bucks County Historical Society, Doylestown, Pa.

20. Mathew Carey to M. Nancrede, August 14, 1795, LFC-HSP. Carey was willing to open an exchange with Nancrede because he felt that Nancrede would afford extra access to the publications of Boston's printer-booksellers. He was less willing, as we have seen, to exchange with Abraham Blauvelt of New Brunswick, N.J., as there were fewer books produced there; Blauvelt would not have been able to participate in an exchange that would have benefited Carey.

21. Mathew Carey to John Bradford, November 13, 1795, LFC-HSP.

22. Francis and Robert Bailey's Day Book and Waste Book, HSP. Richard Brothers, *A Revealed Knowledge of the Prophecies and Times* (Philadelphia, [1795]), Evans 28355.

23. Robert Aitken's Account Books, belonging to the Library Company of Philadelphia, held at HSP. Aitlen would have sent Young *Transactions of the American Philosophical Society, held at Philadelphia, for Promoting Useful Knowledge. Vol. II.* (Philadelphia, [1786]), Evans 19465.

24. Mathew Carey to James Birney, July 6, 1795, LFC-HSP.

25. Mathew Carey to Charles McClung, July 6, 1795, LFC-HSP.

26. Timothy Brundige to Mathew Carey, April 13, 1795, Incoming Correspondence, LFC-HSP.

27. Germantown officially became part of Philadelphia in 1854. Billmeyer was the leading German printer, publisher, and bookseller in the Philadelphia area. For more on Billmeyer, and on the German book trade generally, see Robert E. Cazden, *A Social History of the German Book Trade in America to the Civil War* (Columbia, S.C.: Camden House, 1984).

28. Michael Billmeyer Ledger, 1809–1815, HSP; Michael Billmeyer Account Book, 1786–1804; Daniel L. Billmeyer Account Book, 1819–1822; G. D. Billmeyer, Bookstore Account Book, 1814–1819, Bucks County Historical Society, Doylestown, Pa.

29. Mathew Carey to James Rivington, October 7, 1791, LFC-HSP.

30. [Carey, Mathew], To the Booksellers of the United States . . . (New York, 1802), 2.

31. Jean Jacques Barthelemy, *Travels of Anacharsis the Younger in Greece* (Philadelphia, 1804), Shaw and Shoemaker 5807–5813.

32. Jacques Henri Bernardin de Saint-Pierre, *Studies of Nature* (Philadelphia: Printed by Abraham Small, for Birch and Small, M. Carey, C. & A. Conrad, W. W. Woodward, Jacob Johnson, and Kimber and Conrad in Philadelphia; Thomas and Andrews, Boston; Campbell and Mitchell, New York, and Backus and Whiting, Albany, 1808), Shaw and Shoemaker 16219.

33. [Daniel] Mallory to McCarty and Davis, [1824], MDP-AAS.

34. Thomas Davis to William McCarty, July 17, 1822, MDP-AAS.

35. See Robert B. Winans, "Bibliography and the Cultural Historian: Notes on the Eighteenth-Century Novel," in *Printing and Society in Early America*, ed. William L. Joyce et al. (Worcester, Mass.: American Antiquarian Society, 1983), 174–185.

36. *The Plays of William Shakespeare. In Seventeen Volumes* . . . (Philadelphia: Published by C. & A. Conrad & Co.; Conrad, Lucas, & Co. Baltimore; Somervell and Conrad, Petersburg; and Bonsal, Conrad, & Co. Norfolk, 1809), Shaw and Shoemaker 18593.

37. Thomas Scott, ed., *The Holy Bible, Containing the Old and New Testaments, with Original Notes, and Practical Observations, and Copious Marginal References* (Philadelphia, 1811–12), Shaw and Shoemaker 22356.

38. David Longworth to Mathew Carey, November 5, 1807 and November 25, 1807, Incoming Correspondence, LFC-HSP.

39. Thomas, *The History of Printing in America*, 408.

40. Lucien Febvre and Henri-Jean Martin, *The Coming of the Book: The Impact of Printing, 1450–1800* (New York: Verso, 1990), 41.

41. Ibid. Also see Judith A. McGaw, *Most Wonderful Machine: Mechanization and Social Change in Berkshire Paper Making, 1801–1885* (Princeton, N.J.: Princeton

University Press, 1987), 61–68, section entitled "New Markets," which analyzes paper sales, credit, and payments.

42. Alexander J. Wall Jr., "William Bradford, Colonial Printer: A Tercentenary Review," *Proceedings of the American Antiquarian Society*, 73 (1963): 365–366. On the Rittenhouse Mill, see James N. Green, *The Rittenhouse Mill and the Beginnings of Papermaking in America* (Philadelphia: Library Company of Philadelphia, 1990).

43. Mathew Carey to Francis Bailey, April 20, 1809, LFC-HSP.

44. "TO PAPER MAKERS!! C. & A. Conrad have received from the manufacturers, a few pieces of Felting of Superior Quality, which they offer for sale, and will receive orders for any quantity at short notice. Two or three journeymen papermakers wanted; apply as above," *Poulson's American Daily Advertiser*, January 11, 1810.

45. I am indebted to Mary Parke Johnson for providing me with references to McCarty and Davis's interests in the Wading River Paper Mill. They are [Accounts with the Wading River Manufacturing and Canal Company] in McCarty and Davis Account Books, Ledger [C], January 1822–1834, 187–190, and 372–373, HSP; Nathan and Coleman Sellers Papers, Order Book, 1834–36, September 6, 1835, APS. In the American Antiquarian Society Records, there are several letters and bills, some from "McCarty-ville," that indicate the firm's involvement in the mill: Box 1, Folder 6, Item 416; Box 2, Folder 4, Items 425 and 426; and Box 3, Folder 5, Item 471, AAS.

46. Entries in McCarty and Davis Memoranda and Misc. Bills, dated December 31, 1824; [1835]; McCarty and Davis, Letterbook, 1823–1844, entry dated June 1, 1827 and October 20, 1827, McCarty and Davis Papers, Rosenbach Museum and Library, Philadelphia.

47. Judith McGaw argues that mechanization in papermaking did not immediately transform the trade or techniques until after about 1830. Machines such as the cylinder and Fourdrinier still required "constant human intervention" to run smoothly and efficiently, and therefore true efficiency had yet to be achieved. She notes, however, that the Berkshire County, Massachusetts, paper mills were late to adopt the new technologies, and that when the machines were used efficiently, they created an enormous impact on the trade, the prices of paper, and the speed of production. *Most Wonderful Machine*, 94–95.

48. Kenneth L. Sokoloff, "Inventive Activity in Early Industrial America: Evidence from Patent Records, 1790–1846," *Journal of Economic History*, 48 (1988): 813–850.

49. For regional examples, see David Hall's discussion of intensive and extensive reading in "The Uses of Literacy in New England, 1600–1850," in *Printing and Society in Early America*, ed. William Joyce et al., 1–47; William J. Gilmore, *Reading Becomes a Necessity of Life: Material and Cultural Life in Rural New England, 1780–1835* (Knoxville: University of Tennessee Press, 1989); and John R. Pankratz, "New Englanders, the Written Word, and the Errand Into Ohio, 1788–1830" (Ph.D. diss., Cornell University, 1981), especially the chapter entitled "Reading," 160–239. There is as yet no study of reading habits, literacy, and consumption in the Middle Atlantic states or in the area's southern and western hinterland.

50. Kenneth L. Sokoloff and B. Zorin Khan argue that inventiveness, measured by the rise in patents, during the early years of American industrialization, was carried out "by ordinary citizens operating with relatively common skills and

knowledge rather than by an elite with rare technical expertise or extensive financial resources." See Sokoloff and Khan, "The Democratization of Invention During Early Industrialization: Evidence from the United States, 1790–1846," *Journal of Economic History*, 50 (1990): 363–378, quote from 364. This was generally the case with the printer-inventors, although they acted upon specific knowledge of the needs of the trade.

51. John Bidwell, "The Brandywine Paper Mill and the Anglo-American Book Trade, 1787–1837" (D. Phil. diss., University of Oxford, 1992), 41, 226–273.

52. For a discussion of the timing of the early use of cloth edition binding, see Joseph W. Rogers, "The Rise of American Edition Binding," in *Bookbinding in America: Three Essays*, ed. Hellmut Lehmann-Haupt and Hannah Dustin French (Portland, Maine: The Southworth-Anthoensen Press, 1941), 135.

53. Silver, *The American Printer*, 50–52.

54. Ibid., 55.

55. For the uses of printing technologies and distribution networks by Bible and tract societies, see Creighton Lacy, *The Word-Carrying Giant: The Growth of the American Bible Society (1816–1966)* (South Pasadena, Calif.: William Carey Library, 1977); Lawrence Thompson, "The Printing and Publishing Activities of the American Tract Society from 1825 to 1850," *Papers of the Bibliographical Society of America*, 35 (1941): 81–144; Edwin Bronner, "Distributing the Printed Word: The Association of Friends, 1816–1966," *Pennsylvania Magazine of History and Biography*, 91 (1967): 342–354; and David Paul Nord, "The Evangelical Origins of Mass Media in America, 1815–1835," *Journalism Monographs*, no. 88 (1984).

56. See Frank Luther Mott, *American Journalism: A History of Newspapers in the United States Through 260 Years: 1690–1950* (New York: Macmillan, 1962), 220–252, 303–306, 314–316.

57. Bidwell, "The Brandywine Paper Mill," 226.

58. For arguments connecting demand, economic growth, and invention, see Jacob Schmookler, *Invention and Economic Growth* (Cambridge, Mass.: Harvard University Press, 1966), and Kenneth L. Sokoloff, "Productivity Growth in Manufacturing During Early Industrialization: Evidence from the American Northeast, 1820–1860," in *Long-Term Factors in American Economic Growth*, ed. Stanley L. Engerman and Robert E. Gallman (Chicago: University of Chicago Press, 1986).

59. For the story of the invention and perfection of stereotyping, see George A. Kubler, *A New History of Stereotyping* (New York: J. J. Little and Ives Co., 1941), 23–74, quote from p. 23.

60. Michael L. Turner, "Andrew Wilson: Lord Stanhope's Stereotype Printer," *Journal of the Printing Historical Society*, 9 (1973–74): 22–65.

61. Westminster Assembly of Divines, *The Larger Catechism* (New York, 1813), Shaw and Shoemaker 30520.

62. Kubler, *A New History of Stereotyping*, 153–155. For other Americans' attempts to gain access to the secrets of the process, see John Bidwell, "Joshua Gilpin and Lord Stanhope's Improvements in Printing," *Papers of the Bibliographical Society of America*, 76 (1982): 143–159.

63. See, for example, notations in Mathew Carey's Memo Book, 1800–1811, LFC-HSP. Entry dated April 19, 1807. Carey copied out a letter written to John Watts from an English stereotyper, A[ndrew] Wilson, in which Wilson laid out the

terms by which he could be induced to move to America, or alternatively, to train American journeymen in England.

64. For a technical discussion of how stereotyping was performed in America, see Michael Winship, "Printing with Plates in the Nineteenth Century," *Printing History*, 5 (1983): 15–27.

65. For the best discussion of stereotyping and its effects on copyright and "courtesy of the trade," see Winship, "Printing with Plates."

66. Silver, *The American Printer*, 91.

67. William McCarty to Thomas Davis, July 11, 1822, McCarty and Davis Papers, AAS. McCarty and Davis's editions of Shakespeare, stereotyped, were: *The Plays of William Shakespeare*, 8 vols. (Philadelphia, 1823), Shoemaker 14095; and *The Dramatic Works of William Shakespeare*, 2 vols. (Philadelphia, 1824), Shoemaker 17946.

68. J. Howe to McCarty and Davis, February 9, 1823, McCarty and Davis Papers, AAS.

69. Howe did not apparently stay under McCarty and Davis's influence for many years. A description of Jedediah Howe and his business appeared in a printing trade journal in 1868, indicating that he eventually struck out on his own: "He was from New England, and in the prime of age. Not prepossessing in manners or person, with a crippled lower limb and sharp, discordant voice, he seemed just the one to need and yet the last to ask favors in life's race: yet he brought with him a spirit of healthy and hearty emulation second to none who ever entered our city [Philadelphia], which was then the center of the book-publishing business." According to the author of this piece, when Howe arrived in Philadelphia, he "determined to have the best type foundry, and to make the best stereotype plates in the world!" To do this, he enlarged the first quarters, found for him by McCarty and Davis, and put up "one of the finest business buildings of that day, and filled it with printers and bookbinders as tenants." Described in *Printers' Circular*, III (1868).

70. At the 1851 trade sale, stereotype plates, some remaining books, and the *de facto* copyrights for three major law books, two school arithmetic books, a popular speller, an edition of Franklin's works, Brown's *Commentaries*, and Hume's *History of England* were all disposed of by Davis's estate for a grand total of $26,472.70. Indeed, the plates and copyrights were more valuable than almost any number of the printed books themselves. During the firm's life, each of these titles served as a mainstay of their catalogue, with supply easily meeting, but not exceeding, demand. *Norton's Literary Advertiser*, I, no. VI (October 15, 1851).

71. Rosalind Remer, "Capturing the Bard: The American Publication of Shakespeare's Plays, 1822–1851" (paper presented at the Society for the History of the Early American Republic Conference, Gettysburg, Pennsylvania, July 1992).

Chapter 5

1. Mathew Carey to Thomas Carey, September 13, 1794, LFC-HSP.

2. Michael Walsh, *The Mercantile Arithmetic* (Boston, 1826), [iii.], Shoemaker 27542.

3. B. S. Yamey, "Scientific Bookkeeping and the Rise of Capitalism," *Economic History Review*, 2d. ser., I (1949): 99–113; quote from p. 100. Yamey's article offers an excellent historiographical overview of the relationship between bookkeeping and capitalism. For a specific monograph, see Frank J. Swetz, *Capitalism and Arithmetic: The New Math of the 15th Century* (LaSalle, Ill.: Open Court, 1987).

4. John Mair, a Scot, first published his manual in Scotland as *Book-keeping Methodiz'd: or, a Methodical Treatise of Merchant-Accompts, according to the Italian form* (Edinburgh, 1736). It was reprinted in Edinburgh and Dublin and repackaged many times. I have consulted a Dublin edition here: John Mair, *Book-keeping Methodiz'd: or, A Methodical Treatise of Merchant-Accompts, according to the Italian Form* (Dublin, 1750), 1–2.

5. B. S. Yamey, "Scientific Bookkeeping and the Rise of Capitalism"; James Don Edwards, "Early Bookkeeping and Its Development into Accounting," *Business History Review*, 34 (Winter 1960): 446–466; Patricia Cline Cohen, *A Calculating People: The Spread of Numeracy in Early America* (Chicago: University of Chicago Press, 1982).

6. William Mitchell, *A New and Complete System of Book-Keeping* (Philadelphia, 1796), [v], Evans 30802.

7. Mair, *Book-keeping Methodiz'd*, 3.

8. Franklin Accounts in the Franklin Papers, APS. For his London accounts, see Ledger, 1764–1776, "The Ledger of Benjamin Franklin containing Accounts of such Transactions only as have pass'd since his leaving Philadelphia Nov. 7, 1764 and during his residence in London."

9. Account Book of Col. William Bradford of Phila. 1742–1760, HSP.

10. Robert Aitken, Account Book, 1776–1806, Library Company of Philadelphia, held at HSP.

11. Yamey, "Scientific Bookkeeping and the Rise of Capitalism," 100–103.

12. Ibid.

13. For this survey of publishers' account books I have used Robert Aitken's Account Book, Library Company of Philadelphia, held at HSP; Francis and Robert Bailey Accounts, HSP; Lydia R. Bailey Ledger, HSP; account books for Mathew Carey, Carey and Son, and H. C. Carey and I. Lea, Lea and Febiger records, HSP; McCarty and Davis Accounts in McCarty and Davis Records, HSP; McCarty and Davis Business Records, Rosenbach Museum and Library; and Michael Billmeyer Ledgers, HSP and Bucks County Historical Society.

14. See Cornelia Hughes Dayton for an interesting discussion of written contracts versus book accounts, and of the nature of short and long distance credit relationships: "Women Before the Bar: Gender, Law and Society in Connecticut, 1710–1790" (Ph.D. diss., Princeton University, 1986), especially chapter 2, "The Litigated Economy." Also see Thomas L. Haskell, "Capitalism and the Origins of the Humanitarian Sensibility, Part Two," *American Historical Review*, 90 (1985): 547–566 for a discussion of the development of impersonal trade relationships, contracts, and obligations.

15. Michael Billmeyer, Ledger, "D," HSP; Carey and Son, Ledger, 1820–1824, LFC-HSP; and McCarty and Davis, Ledger, 1824, McCarty and Davis Records, HSP.

16. Ultimately, Miner offered Carey a new proposal to "cancel yr. demand" with a share in the Easton and Wilkesbarre Turnpike Road, "for which I paid fifty dollars." Asher Miner to Mathew Carey, May 4, 1807, Incoming Correspondence, LFC-HSP.

17. The Philadelphia Typographical Society was begun by journeymen printers in 1802 as the Asylum Company. The society set minimum wages for composition and presswork and acted as a beneficial association for needy printers. See "Historical Sketch of the Philadelphia Typographical Society," *Printers' Circular*, 2 (1867); and Ethelbert Stewart, "A Documentary History of the Early Organizations of Printers," U.S. Department of Commerce and Labor *Bulletin*, 11 (November 1905): 857–1033.

18. George Rogers Taylor, *The Transportation Revolution, 1815–1860* (New York: Rinehart, 1951).

19. Mathew Carey to Jacob Bailey, February 1794, LFC-HSP.

20. Robert Bailey to Mathew Carey, July 5, 1805, July 24, 1802, Incoming Correspondence, LFC-HSP. See also Robert Bailey to Mathew Carey in Robert Bailey Letterbook, HSP.

21. Ibid.

22. The story of McCarty and Davis's establishment in Wheeling is derived from McCarty and Davis in Account with Davis and McCarty, 1821–1825, Rosenbach Museum and Library; and from letters from James F. McCarty to McCarty and Davis, dated December 7, 1821 to November 26, 1825, in MDP-AAS.

23. McCarty and Davis Memoranda and Miscellaneous Bills, 1818–1823, Rosenbach Museum and Library. Several other editions of Walker's *Dictionary* were printed by Griggs and Dickinson, both before and after their agreement with McCarty and Davis; I have not located a McCarty and Davis imprint for this book.

24. *Printers' Circular*, 3 (1868): 327.

25. Mason Locke Weems, *Life of Benjamin Franklin* (Philadelphia, 1810), Shaw and Shoemaker 22001.

26. Carey and Son to James Lovegrove, March 19, April 9, April 20, August 9, 1821, LFC-HSP.

27. Mathew Carey to Fred. Craig, January 12, 1791, LFC-HSP.

28. Carey and Son to George Champley, April 18, 1821, LFC-HSP.

29. Ibid.

30. McCarty and Davis Binders' Accounts, 1824–1830, McCarty and Davis Papers, Rosenbach Museum and Library.

31. See, for example, Michael Winship, "Ticknor and Fields: A Study of Literary Publishing in Boston in the Mid-Nineteenth Century" (D. Phil. diss., Oxford University, 1989), chapter 2, "The Business Records of Ticknor and Fields."

32. Mathew Carey Memorandum Book, 1800–1811, LFC-HSP.

33. David Kaser, ed., *The Cost Book of Carey and Lea, 1825–1838* (Philadelphia: University of Pennsylvania Press, 1963). The original manuscript, as well as others for Carey and Hart and Lea and Blanchard (both successors to Carey's firms), are in the Lea and Febiger Records, HSP.

34. Kaser, *The Cost Book of Carey & Lea*, 30–31, entry 32. Oliver Evans, *The*

young mill-wright and miller's guide (Philadelphia, 1826), Shoemaker 24450. The final work contained 383 pages, one page short of the calculations.

35. Karl Bernhard, *Travels through North America, during the Years 1825 and 1826* (Philadelphia, 1828), Shoemaker 32277. Calculations are in Kaser, *The Cost Book of Carey & Lea*, 67, entry 145.

36. Thomas Davis to William McCarty, July 17, 1822, MDP-AAS.

37. McCarty and Davis Papers, AAS.

38. Thomas Davis to William McCarty, July 17, 1822, McCarty and Davis Papers, American Antiquarian Society.

39. The best overview of colonial, state, and national bankruptcy laws is Peter J. Coleman, *Debtors and Creditors in America: Insolvency, Imprisonment for Debt, and Bankruptcy, 1607–1900* (Madison: State Historical Society of Wisconsin, 1974), 7–8.

40. Richard Folwell to Mathew Carey, December 7, 1806, Incoming Correspondence, LFC-HSP.

41. Philadelphia Court of Common Pleas, Insolvency Records, September 25, 1821, Philadelphia City Archives.

42. Ibid., September 23, 1819.

43. [Mathew Carey], *Narrative of the Proceedings of Edward Gray, Samuel F. Bradford, and Robert Taylor, previous and subsequent to the Bankruptcy of C. & A. Conrad & Co.* (Philadelphia, 1813), Shaw and Shoemaker 29260.

44. Mathew Carey to Samuel F. Bradford, July 12, 14, 1812, LFC-HSP.

45. Mathew Carey to Bradford & Inskeep & Grey & Taylor, August 22, 1812, LFC-HSP.

46. Mathew Carey to Joseph Gales, August 31, 1812, LFC-HSP.

47. Mathew Carey to William W. Woodward, August 26, 1812, LFC-HSP.

48. [Isaac Riley], *Assignment. Isaac Riley to Joseph Greenleaf, William McKean, and Henry A. Riley* ([Philadelphia, 1820]), Shoemaker 3022.

49. Isaac Riley to Mathew Carey, July 16, 1806, Incoming Correspondence, LFC-HSP.

50. [Isaac Riley]. *Assignment*, 19.

51. Ibid., 18.

52. Thomas and Thomas to Mathew Carey, July 15, 1805, Incoming Correspondence, LFC-HSP.

53. There is no surviving copy of the bylaws of the company. There is a company constitution, but none of its articles discusses trade suits. The fifth article states that "the Board of Directors shall have the power of proposing such Bye-laws and Rules, as they shall from time to time deem advisable . . . " Constitution of the American Company of Booksellers, as printed in *The Library; or, Philadelphia Literary Reporter*, no. 13, August 11, 1804. This was the periodical publication of the Philadelphia Company of Booksellers. Obadiah Penniman and Co. to Mathew Carey, August 6, 1805, Incoming Correspondence, Lea and Febiger Records, HSP.

54. Obadiah Penniman and Co. to Mathew Carey, October 22, 1805, Incoming Correspondence, LFC-HSP.

55. Charles Peirce to Mathew Carey, March 28, 1805, Incoming Correspondence, LFC-HSP.

56. Samuel Pleasants to Mathew Carey, January 18, 1805, Incoming Correspondence, LFC-HSP.

57. Macanulty and Maxey to Mathew Carey, April 11, 1807, Incoming Correspondence, LFC-HSP.

58. Insolvency Petition of Caleb Kimber, Philadelphia Court of Common Pleas, Insolvency Records, September 18, 1816, Philadelphia City Archives. Davis's petition was posted the same day as Kimber's.

59. Ibid., September 20, 1821.

60. Sage and Thompson to Mathew Carey, December 8, 1806, Incoming Correspondence, LFC-HSP.

61. William Patton to Mathew Carey, December 29, 1807, Incoming Correspondence, LFC-HSP.

62. Mathew Carey to David Longworth, February 11, 1812, LFC-HSP.

63. Thomas and Andrews to Mathew Carey, May 8, 1806, Incoming Correspondence, LFC-HSP.

Chapter 6

1. Mathew Carey to John Carey, April 11, 1805, LFC-HSP.

2. Mathew Carey, *Address to the Printers and Booksellers throughout the United States* [Philadelphia, 1801], Shaw and Shoemaker 275.

3. Erik F. Haites et al., eds., *Western River Transportation: The Era of Early Internal Development, 1810–1860* (Baltimore, Md.: Johns Hopkins University Press, 1975), 111.

4. Ibid. Also see Francis S. Philbrick, *The Rise of the West, 1754–1830* (New York: Harper and Row, 1965), esp. 322–344; Robert D. Mitchell, *Commercialism and Frontier: Perspectives on the Early Shenandoah Valley* (Charlottesville: University Press of Virginia, 1977); and Lewis E. Atherton, *The Frontier Merchant in Mid-America* (Columbia: University of Missouri Press, 1971).

5. This process — the creation of a "Village Enlightenment" — is discussed in the context of New England publishing and country book distribution by David Jaffee in "The Village Enlightenment in New England, 1760–1820," *William and Mary Quarterly*, 47 (July 1990): 327–346; quote from p. 328. William J. Gilmore discusses the process of the formation of markets for printed commodities in *Reading Becomes a Necessity of Life: Material and Cultural Life in Rural New England, 1780–1835* (Knoxville: University of Tennessee Press, 1989).

6. On early American peddling, see Richardson Wright, *Hawkers and Walkers in Early America* (Philadelphia: J. B. Lippincott Co., 1927); J. R. Dolan, *The Yankee Peddlers of Early America* (New York: Clarkson N. Potter Inc., 1964); and Richard R. Beeman, "Trade and Travel in Post-Revolutionary Virginia: A Diary of an Itinerant Peddler, 1807–1808," *Virginia Magazine of History and Biography*, 84 (1976): 174–188. These works do not give particular attention to book peddling, primarily because early American peddlers sold a wide array of goods on their circuits.

On Franklin's practice of setting up former apprentices and family members, see Ralph Frasca, "Benjamin Franklin's Printing Network," *American Journalism*, 5 (1988): 145–158; and Frasca's "From Apprentice to Journeyman to Partner: Benjamin Franklin's Workers and the Growth of the Early American Printing Trade," *Pennsylvania Magazine of History and Biography*, 114 (1990): 229–248.

7. For an excellent discussion of book distribution both before and during the development of the railroad, see Ronald J. Zboray, *A Fictive People: Antebellum Economic Development and the American Reading Public* (New York: Oxford University Press, 1993), esp. chs. 3–5.

8. On Lackington, see Richard G. Landon's "'Small Profits Do Great Things': James Lackington and Eighteenth-Century Bookselling," *Studies in Eighteenth-Century Culture*, 5 (1976): 387–399.

9. Weems to Carey, February 1801, in Emily Ellsworth Ford Skeel, *Mason Locke Weems: His Work and His Ways*, 3 vols. (New York: [privately printed], 1929), II: 167.

10. James F. McCarty to Thomas Davis, February 6, 1824, MDP-AAS.

11. Thomas to Armstrong and Plaskett, May 16, 1826, McCarty and Davis Manuscripts (Rosenbach Library and Museum).

12. Books published in parts were sold serially, like magazines. Toy books were small-format children's books. Schoolbooks were readers, spellers, arithmetics, and geographies.

13. George Burder, *Village Sermons* (Philadelphia, 1803), Shaw and Shoemaker 3913; *Books published and sold by W. W. Woodward* (Philadelphia, 1810), Shaw and Shoemaker 22085. The latter is a broadside catalogue of books.

14. *A Pocket Companion; or Every Man His Own Lawyer* (Philadelphia, 1818), Shaw and Shoemaker 45357.

15. *The Carlisle Republican*, May 11, 1819.

16. William Carver, *Practical Horse Farrier; or, the Traveller's Pocket Companion* (Philadelphia, 1818), Shaw and Shoemaker 43547.

17. Edwin Wolf, *The Book Culture of a Colonial American City: Philadelphia Books, Bookmen, and Booksellers* (New York: Oxford University Press, 1988). Wolf notes that "the farmer and workman were satisfied with Bibles, prayer-books, schoolbooks, and—unbound cheaply produced, and miserably printed—almanacs, catchpenny pamphlets, chapbooks, and hack writers' compendiums" (2).

18. Stephen Byerly, *New American Spelling Book* (Philadelphia, 1820), Shoemaker 637; Zachariah Jess, *American Tutor's Assistant, improved* (Philadelphia, 1819), Shaw and Shoemaker 48375; Stephen Pike, *The Teacher's Assistant or a System of Practical Arithmetic* (Philadelphia, 1822), Shoemaker 9942.

19. The business records for the firm of McCarty and Davis best illustrate how the salesmen ordered books as they needed them, as well as the discounts they received, their standing accounts with the firm, and the rate of return for unsold books. McCarty and Davis kept clear records of notes receivable, from which it can be determined how much credit each salesman received, both in the form of stock and loans of money, and how much time he was allowed. Their business records and papers are held at the Historical Society of Pennsylvania (MDR-HSP), the Rosenbach Library and Museum, Philadelphia, and the American Antiquarian Society (MDP-AAS).

20. On Weems's relationship with Carey, see James N. Green, "From Printer to Publisher: Mathew Carey and the Origins of Nineteenth-Century Book Publishing," in *Getting the Books Out: Papers of the Chicago Conference on the Book in 19th-Century America*, ed. Michael Hackenberg (Washington, D.C.: Center for the Book, Library of Congress, 1987), 26–44; James Gilreath, "Mason Weems, Mathew Carey and the Southern Booktrade," *Publishing History*, 10 (1981): 27–49; Zboray, *A Fictive People*, ch. 3, "The Book Peddler and Literary Dissemination"; Lewis Leary, *The Book-Peddling Parson* (Chapel Hill, N.C.: Algonquin Books, 1984); Emily Ellsworth Skeel, *Mason Locke Weems: His Works and His Ways*.

21. Weems was fond of military metaphors to describe selling books in the country. He frequently referred to books as "ammunition" and the storekeepers with whom he set up accounts as his "aids de camp" or "co-adjutants." Skeel, *Mason Locke Weems*, II, III: passim.

22. Weems to Carey, October 15, 1796, in ibid., II: 47–48.

23. James Penn Pilkington, *The Methodist Publishing House: A History* (Nashville, Tenn.: Abingdon Press, 1968), ch. 1.

24. The ten remaining ministers could not be identified by denomination.

25. There are hundreds of letters from the ministers to Woodward in the Simon Gratz Collection, HSP, (SGC-HSP).

26. Joshua Bradley to Woodward, October 18, 1824, SGC-HSP.

27. Charles Buck, *Theological Dictionary* (Philadelphia, 1807), Shaw and Shoemaker 12228; John Gill, *Exposition of the Old and New Testaments* (Philadelphia, 1810), Shaw and Shoemaker 20217; Thomas Scott, ed. *Holy Bible, Containing the Old and New Testaments, with Original Notes, and Practical Observations, and Copious Marginal References* (Philadelphia, 1811–12), Shaw and Shoemaker 22356.

28. John Taylor to Woodward, March 21, 1813, SGC-HSP.

29. Samuel Osgood to Woodward, July 27, 1811, SGC-HSP.

30. David Benedict to Woodward, May 13, 1811, SGC-HSP.

31. Jedediah Morse to Woodward, June 20, 1805, SGC-HSP.

32. Francis Cummins to Woodward, May 17, 1808, SGC-HSP.

33. Isaac Stockton Keith to Woodward, October 15, 1812, in the Keith Papers, Firestone Library Manuscripts Department, Princeton University Library.

34. Moses Waddell to Woodward, February 23, 1819, SGC-HSP.

35. Jesse Mercer to Woodward, January 7, 1823, SGC-HSP.

36. Henry Holcombe to Woodward, February 1, 1808, SGC-HSP.

37. Samuel Osgood to Woodward, April 26, 1817, SGC-HSP.

38. Henry Holcombe to Woodward, June 20, 1805, SGC-HSP.

39. Francis Cummins to Woodward, Feb. 5, 1803, SGC-HSP.

40. On May 9, 1817, Waddell sent the following inquiry to Woodward: "I believe that a Mr. Bradford of Philadelphia is the gentleman who supplies the Tract Societies of the Presbyterian Church generally thro' the United States with Religious Tracts. If this be the case, will you have the goodness to inform him (or whoever is the person) that I wish he would forward me . . . the value of one hundred and thirty five dollars in religious tracts" (SGC-HSP).

41. Benjamin Morgan Palmer to Woodward, July 27, 1819, SGC-HSP. Charleston was long established in bookselling and printing, as well as in buying

books from eastern seaboard publishers. In 1796, the minister Isaac Stockton Keith, who sold books in Charleston for the Philadelphia bookseller William Young, wrote to warn him that booksellers there were advertising an edition of Newton's works; if Young hoped to publish an edition, he had better work fast, as "I am apprehensive that [customers] may supply themselves here with what they want if yours cannot be sent pretty soon." Isaac Stockton Keith to William Young, July 13, 1796, in General Manuscripts (Miscellaneous), Firestone Library Manuscripts Department, Princeton University Library.

42. Moses Waddell to Woodward, August 25, 1818; September 19, 1820; March 23, 1821, SGC-HSP.

43. Moses Waddell to Woodward, March 23, 1821, SGC-HSP; Walter Sutton, *The Western Book Trade: Cincinnati as a Nineteenth-Century Publishing Center* (Columbus: Ohio State University Press, 1961), 36–38.

44. Moses Waddell to Woodward, February 10, 1818; August 25, 1818; April 27, 1820, SGC-HSP.

45. For the uses of printing technologies and distribution networks by Bible and tract societies, see Creighton Lacy, *The Word-Carrying Giant: The Growth of the American Bible Society (1816–1966)* (South Pasadena, Calif.: William Carey Library, 1977); Lawrence Thompson, "The Printing and Publishing Activities of the American Tract Society from 1825 to 1850," *Papers of the Bibliographical Society of America*, 35 (1941): 81–144; Edwin Bronner,"Distributing the Printed Word: The Association of Friends, 1816–1966," *Pennsylvania Magazine of History and Biography*, 91 (1967): 342–354; David Paul Nord, "The Evangelical Origins of Mass Media in America, 1815–1835," *Journalism Monographs*, no. 88 (1984).

46. The expression is used in a letter from James F. McCarty to Thomas Davis, February 9, 1824, MDP-AAS. Throughout the 1820s the demands from salesmen for more novels increased dramatically.

47. Ibid., July 6, 1822.

48. Ibid., January 30, 1822.

49. William McCarty to Thomas Davis, February 21, 1822, and November 27, 1825, MDP-AAS.

50. Jonathan Ormsby to McCarty and Davis, July 2, 1821, MDP-AAS.

51. William McCarty to Thomas Davis, May 23, 1824, June 16, 1824; also George Morris to McCarty and Davis, August 16, 1824, MDP-AAS.

52. William McCarty to Thomas Davis, June 16, 1824, MDP-AAS.

53. B. R. Swain to McCarty and Davis, April 24, 1821, MDP-AAS.

54. Grenville Mellen, *The Age of Print: A Poem* (Boston, 1830), 36. Mellen was an author and minor poet. He delivered this scathing send-up of all aspects of the publishing industry at a meeting of the Phi Beta Kappa Society at Harvard in 1830.

55. George K. Harper to McCarty and David, March 10, 1823, MDP-AAS.

56. William McCarty to Thomas Davis, June 27, 1825, MDP-AAS. On the acceptance and depreciation of western moneys in the East, see Thomas Senior Berry, *Western Prices Before 1861: A Study of the Cincinnati Market* (Cambridge, Mass.: Harvard University Press, 1943), 403–404.

57. George K. Harper to McCarty and Davis, July 20, 1822, MDP-AAS.

58. On this "common frontier phenomenon," see Daniel B. Thorp, "Doing

Business in the Backcountry: Retail Trade in Colonial Rowan County, North Caro-
lina," *William and Mary Quarterly*, 3d ser., 48 (1991): 387–408, esp. 395–397; and
Winifred B. Rothenberg, "The Market and Massachusetts Farmers, 1750–1855,"
Journal of Economic History, 41 (1981): 283–414, esp. 291–292.

59. Timothy Flint, *A Condensed Geography and History of the Western States, or
the Mississippi Valley*, 2 vols. (Cincinnati, 1828), II: 410–411, Shoemaker 33201.

60. James F. McCarty to McCarty and Davis, March 1823, MDP-AAS.

61. Ibid., June 6, 1820.

62. Country businessmen eagerly sought connections with each other, hoping
to lessen eastern influence over their economy. See Ebenezer Smith Thomas, *Reminiscences of the Last Sixty-five Years* (Hartford, 1840), 93–100, in which he discusses
the advantages of developing trade between Charleston and Cincinnati, with Lexington as a middle point.

63. I am grateful to Neva Specht, whose work on Quaker migration to the
Midwest has enabled her to identify Friends among some of Johnson and Warner's
network. In his letters, Warner consistently used "thee" with Quaker correspondents and "you" with others, suggesting that he adjusted his form of address
accordingly.

64. Benjamin Warner to Philips and Spear, June 1821, Benjamin Warner Letterbook "D," Bucks County Historical Society, Doyestown, Pa.

65. Benjamin Warner to John F. Drake, December 11, 1820, Letterbook "C,"
Bucks County Historical Society.

66. Ibid.

67. Benjamin Warner to Lydia F. Warner, June 25, 1821, Fisher Family Papers,
Warner Section, Benjamin Warner Series, 1810–1821, HSP.

68. Ibid.

69. Benjamin Warner to Igram and Lloyd, August 25, 1820, Letterbook "C,"
Bucks County Historical Society.

70. Benjamin Warner to John F. Drake, December 4, 1820, Letterbook "C,"
Bucks County Historical Society.

71. McCarty and Davis Daybook, HSP.

72. McCarty and Davis Notes Receivable Book, AAS.

73. For contemporary descriptions of the towns mentioned here, see Flint, *A
Condensed Geography and History of the Western States*; John Melish, *Information and
Advice to Emigrants to the United States; and from the Eastern to the Western States*
(Philadelphia, 1819), Shaw and Shoemaker 48668; and David Thomas, *Travels
through the Western Country in the Summer of 1816* (Auburn, N.Y., 1819), Shaw and
Shoemaker 49585.

74. Lewis E. Atherton, *The Southern Country Store* (Baton Rouge: Louisiana
State University Press, 1946). Also see Thorp, "Doing Business in the Backcountry,"
399–402, for a discussion of backcountry supply tactics in the colonial period.
While not every shopkeeper needed to make the journey east, a number of them
would, acting as local sources of supply. Clearly there was a price to pay for not
going, just as there was in making the trip. An individual's decision to travel long
distances to a supply source would depend on how much time he had and his cash
flow. In addition, credit might be easier to obtain from local sources.

75. Atherton, *The Frontier Merchant in Mid-America*, 61–71; and Philbrick, *The Rise of the West*, 337–339.

76. On expansion after the War of 1812, as well as postwar contraction, see Richard C. Wade, *The Urban Frontier: Pioneer Life in Early Pittsburgh, Cincinnati, Lexington, Louisville, and St. Louis* (Chicago: University of Chicago Press, 1959), 161–190.

77. Sutton, *The Western Book Trade*. The book industry in Cincinnati became established as books published there began to go through multiple editions. Dr. Joseph Ray, a Cincinnatian, wrote arithmetic books published by Truman and Smith, the same firm later made famous by McGuffey's readers. The first edition of Ray's math book appeared in 1834, and thereafter editions were regularly issued every year or two. By 1846, a New York publisher bought the rights to publish this western work; however, no other local arithmetic book underwent multiple editions until well into the 1840s. Louis C. Karpinski, *Bibliography of Mathematical Works Printed in America Through 1850* (Ann Arbor: University of Michigan Press, 1940), 365–368; John H. Westerhoff, *McGuffey and His Readers: Piety, Morality, and Education in Nineteenth-Century America* (Nashville, Tenn.: Abingdon Press, 1978).

78. Pittsburgh *Mercury*, November 25, 1813, as quoted in Wade, *The Urban Frontier*, 40. For Wade's discussion of literary and cultural development in the other cities, see pp. 139–141.

79. John Tebbel, *A History of Publishing in the United States, Volume II: The Expansion of an Industry, 1865–1919* (New York: R. R. Bowker, 1975), 102.

80. Thomas C. Cochran, *Frontiers of Change: Early Industrialism in America* (New York: Oxford University Press, 1981), 22.

81. Zboray, *A Fictive People*, 55–68.

Conclusion

1. *The Booksellers' Advertiser and Monthly Register of New Publications American and Foreign*, Vol. II (New York, March 1, 1836), 1.

2. Ibid., 2.

3. For sketches of Putnam and the publishers discussed here, see John Tebbel, *A History of Book Publishing in the United States, Volume I: The Creation of an Industry* (New York: R. R. Bowker, 1972), I, 262–448, and George Haven Putnam, *A Memoir of George Palmer Putnam* (New York: G. P. Putnam's Sons, 1903). Also see Madeleine B. Stern, *Imprints on History: Book Publishers and American Frontiers* (Bloomington: Indiana University Press, 1956), and John Barnes Pratt, *A Century of Book Publishing, 1838–1938* (New York: A. S. Barnes & Co., 1938). Most of the works detailing nineteenth-century publishing companies are house histories. These are problematic for a number of reasons. Publishing houses often try to establish "genealogies" that reflect early American founding dates. They therefore suggest greater continuity between early printing and publishing establishments and later firms. Rarely do these credentials prove to be accurately drawn.

4. See John Wiley and Sons, *The First One Hundred and Fifty Years: A His-*

tory of John Wiley & Sons, Inc., 1807–1957 (New York: John Wiley & Sons, 1957); Eugene Exman, *The Brothers Harper: A Unique Publishing Partnership and Its Impact Upon the Cultural Life of America from 1817 to 1853* (New York: Harper and Row, 1965); and idem, *The House of Harper: One Hundred and Fifty Years of Publishing* (New York: Harper and Row, 1967).

5. D. Appleton-Century Company, *The House of Appleton-Century: I. D. Appleton and Company, 1825–1933* (New York: D. Appleton-Century Co., 1936). This is a house history pamphlet.

6. David Kaser, *Messrs. Carey & Lea of Philadelphia* (Philadelphia: University of Pennsylvania Press, 1957); Henry C. Carey, "Reminiscences of a Publisher," *American Publishers' Circular*, I (1863): 130.

7. "John Grigg, Esq., Philadelphia," *Ballou's Pictorial Drawing-Room Companion*, 10 (1856): 156.

8. J. Stuart Freeman, *Toward a Third Century of Excellence: An Informal History of the J. B. Lippincott Company, on the Occasion of Its Two-Hundredth Anniversary* (Philadelphia: The Company, 1992). This book is Lippincott's house history, in which the author seeks to establish the company's roots in the 1790s with the firm of Jacob and Benjamin Johnson. The connection cannot really be made, since Grigg, who eventually sold to Lippincott, had started his own business after Johnson and Warner's stock was liquidated. The only connection between Lippincott and the Johnsons' firm of the 1790s is that Grigg clerked for Johnson and Warner in the early 1820s before striking out on his own.

9. Howard Malcom Ticknor, *A Brief Biographical Sketch of William Davis Ticknor* (Cambridge, Mass.: John Wilson & Son, 1895); William S. Tryon, *Parnassus Corner: A Life of James T. Fields, Publisher to the Victorians* (Boston: Houghton Mifflin Co., 1963).

10. Little, Brown and Company, *One Hundred and Twenty-Five Years of Publishing, 1837–1962* (Boston: Little, Brown, and Co., 1962).

11. These are the members of the trade for whom I could find definitive death dates and obituaries.

Bibliography

Manuscript Collections

Permission to quote from the following manuscript collections is gratefully acknowledged: American Antiquarian Society (AAS), Worcester, Mass.; American Philosophical Society (APS), Philadelphia; Bucks County Historical Society (BCHS), Doylestown, Pa.; Historical Society of Pennsylvania (HSP), Philadelphia; and Princeton University Library, Princeton, N.J.

Robert Aitken's Account Books, Library Company of Philadelphia, held at HSP
Benjamin Franklin Bache Papers, Castle Collection, APS
Francis and Robert Bailey's Day Book and Waste Book, HSP
Lydia Bailey, Ledger, HSP
Daniel L. Billmeyer Account Book, 1819–1822, BCHS
G. D. Billmeyer, Bookstore Account Book, 1814–1819, BCHS
Michael Billmeyer Ledgers, 1809–1815, HSP
Michael Billmeyer Account Book, 1786–1804, BCHS
Bradford Family Papers, HSP
Mathew Carey Account Books, AAS
William Cobbett Account Book, AAS
Albert Gallatin Papers, New York Historical Society
Simon Gratz Collection, HSP
David Hall Letterbooks, 1750–1767, APS
David Hall's Account Book, 1748–68, APS
General Manuscripts (Miscellaneous), Princeton University Library
Lea and Febiger Collection, HSP
McCarty and Davis Papers, The Rosenbach Museum & Library, Philadelphia
McCarty and Davis Records, HSP
The sequestered John Nicholson Papers, General Correspondence, 1772–1819, in the Pennsylvania State Archives, Manuscript Group 96
Daniel Parker Papers, HSP
Philadelphia Court of Common Pleas, Insolvency Records, Philadelphia City Archives
Nathan and Coleman Sellers Papers, APS
Robert Simpson Letterbook, HSP
Society Collections, HSP
Stauffer Collection, HSP
Benjamin Warner Letterbooks "C" and "D," BCHS

NEWSPAPERS

Aurora
The Carlisle Republican
Claypoole's American Daily Advertiser
Dunlap's American Daily Advertiser
Federal Gazette
Gazette of the United States
Pennsylvania Gazette
Philadelphia Gazette
Porcupine's Gazette
Poulson's American Daily Advertiser
The Public Ledger
Relf's Philadelphia Gazette

PRIMARY AND SECONDARY PRINTED SOURCES

Alexander, John. *A Brief Narrative of the Case and Trial of John Peter Zenger, Printer of the New York Weekly Journal,* ed. Stanley Katz. Cambridge, Mass.: Harvard University Press, 1963.
American Philosophical Society. *Transactions of the American Philosophical Society, held at Philadelphia, for Promoting Useful Knowledge. Vol. II.* Philadelphia, [1786]. Evans 19465.
The Annual Reports of the Controllers of the Public Schools of the First School District of the State of Pennsylvania. Philadelphia, 1819–1831. Shaw and Shoemaker 49042 for 1819.
Arner, Robert. *Dobson's Encyclopedia: The Publisher, Text, and Publication of America's First Britannica, 1789–1803.* Philadelphia: University of Pennsylvania Press, 1991.
Atherton, Lewis E. *The Frontier Merchant in Mid-America.* Columbia: University of Missouri Press, 1971.
———. *The Southern Country Store.* Baton Rouge: Louisiana State University Press, 1946.
[Authentic.] Treaty of Amity, Commerce, and Navigation, between His Britannick Majesty, and the United States of America. Philadelphia, [1795]. Evans 29744.
Bache, Benjamin Franklin. *Proposals for Publishing a News-paper, to be Entitled The Daily Advertiser.* [Philadelphia, 1790]. Bristol 7304.
Bailyn, Bernard, ed. *Pamphlets of the American Revolution, 1750–1776.* 2 vols. Cambridge, Mass.: Belknap Press of Harvard University Press, 1965.
Ballou, Ellen. *The Building of the House: Houghton Mifflin's Formative Years.* Boston: Houghton Mifflin, 1970.
Barber, Giles. "Books from the Old World and for the New: The British International Trade in Books in the Eighteenth Century." *Studies on Voltaire and the Eighteenth Century,* 141 (1979): 185–224.

Barthelemy, Jean Jacques. *Travels of Anacharsis the Younger in Greece*. Philadelphia, 1804. Shaw and Shoemaker 5807–5813.

Baumann, Roland M. "The Democratic-Republicans of Philadelphia: The Origins, 1776–1797." Ph.D. diss., Pennsylvania State University, 1970.

Baym, Nina. *Novels, Readers, and Reviewers: Responses to Fiction in Antebellum America*. Ithaca, N.Y.: Cornell University Press, 1984.

Beeman, Richard R. "Trade and Travel in Post-Revolutionary Virginia: A Diary of an Itinerant Peddlar, 1807–1808." *Virginia Magazine of History and Bibliography*, 84 (1976): 174–188.

Belanger, Terry. "Booksellers' Trade Sales." *The Library*, 5th ser., 30 (1975): 281–302.

Bennet, Benjamin. *Discourses on the Credibility of the Scriptures*. New Brunswick, 1795. Evans 28262.

Bernardin de Saint-Pierre, Jacques Henri. *Studies of Nature*. Philadelphia, 1808. Shaw and Shoemaker 16219.

Bernhard, Karl. *Travels through North America, during the Years 1825 and 1826*. Philadelphia, 1828. Shoemaker 32277.

Berry, Thomas Senior. *Western Prices Before 1861: A Study of the Cincinnati Market*. Cambridge, Mass.: Harvard University Press, 1943.

Bidwell, John. "The Brandywine Paper Mill and the Anglo-American Book Trade, 1787–1837." D. Phil. diss., Oxford University, 1992.

———. "Joshua Gilpin and Lord Stanhope's Improvements in Printing." *Papers of the Bibliographic Society of America*, 76 (1982): 143–159.

Bigland, John. *A Geographical and Historical View of the World*. Boston, 1811. Shaw and Shoemaker 22393.

Blagden, Cyprian. *The Stationers' Company: A History, 1403–1959*. Cambridge, Mass.: Harvard University Press, 1960.

Blumin, Stuart. *The Emergence of the Middle Class: Social Experience in the American City, 1760–1900*. New York: Cambridge University Press, 1989.

Bonomi, Patricia U. "The Middle Colonies: Embryo of the New Political Order." In *Perspectives on Early American History: Essays in Honor of Richard B. Morris*, ed. Alden T. Vaughan and George Athan Billias. New York: Harper and Row, 1973.

The Booksellers' Advertiser and Monthly Register of New Publications, American and Foreign, Vol. II. New York: March 1, 1836, 1.

Boston, Ray. "The Impact of 'Foreign Liars' on the American Press." *Journalism Quarterly*, 50 (Winter 1983): 722–730.

Botein, Stephen. "The Anglo-American Book Trade before 1776: Personnel and Strategies." In *Printing and Society in Early America*, ed. William L. Joyce et al. Worcester, Mass.: American Antiquarian Society, 1983.

———. "'Meer Mechanics' and an Open Press: The Business and Political Strategies of Colonial American Printers." *Perspectives in American History*, 9 (1975): 127–225.

———. *"Mr. Zenger's Malice and Falsehood": Six Issues of the New-York Weekly Journal, 1733–34*. Worcester, Mass.: American Antiquarian Society, 1985.

———. "Printers and the American Revolution." In *The Press and the American*

Revolution, ed. Bernard Bailyn and John B. Hench. Boston: Northeastern University Press, 1981.

———. *Printers and Press Freedom: The Ideology of Early American Journalism*. New York: Oxford University Press, 1987.

Brigham, C. S., ed. "William McCulloch's Additions to Thomas's History of Printing." *Proceedings of the American Antiquarian Society*, 31 (April 1921): 89–247.

———. *History and Bibliography of American Newspapers, 1690–1820*. 2 vols. Worcester, Mass.: American Antiquarian Society, 1947.

Bristol, Roger Pattrell. *Supplement to Charles Evans' American Bibliography*. Charlottesville: University Press of Virginia, 1970.

Bronner, Edwin. "Distributing the Printed Word: The Association of Friends, 1816–1966." *Pennsylvania Magazine of History and Biography*, 91 (1967): 342–354.

Brothers, Richard. *A Revealed Knowledge of the Prophecies and Times*. Philadelphia, [1795]. Evans 28355.

Brown, H. Glenn, and Maude O. Brown. *A Directory of the Book-Arts and Book Trade in Philadelphia to 1820*. New York: New York Public Library, 1950.

Brown, Richard D. *Knowledge is Power: The Diffusion of Information in Early America, 1700–1865*. New York: Oxford University Press, 1989.

Buck, Charles. *Theological Dictionary*. Philadelphia, 1807. Shaw and Shoemaker 12228.

Buel, Richard, Jr. *Securing the Revolution: Ideology in American Politics, 1789–1815*. Ithaca, N.Y.: Cornell University Press, 1972.

Burder, George. *Village Sermons*. Philadelphia, 1803. Shaw and Shoemaker 3913.

Butts, R. Freeman, and Lawrence A. Cremin. *A History of Education in American Culture*. New York: Holt, 1953.

Byerly, Stephen. *New American Spelling Book*. Philadelphia, 1820. Shoemaker 637.

Callender, James T. *The Political Progress of Great Britain, or an Impartial History of the Abuses in the Government of the British Empire*. Philadelphia, 1795. Evans 28381.

Carey, Henry C. "Reminiscences of a Publisher." *American Publishers' Circular*, I (1863): 130.

[Carey, Mathew]. *Address to the Booksellers of the United States, from the Booksellers' Company of Philadelphia*. Philadelphia, 1813. Shaw and Shoemaker 27662.

———. *Address to the Printers and Booksellers throughout the United States*. [Philadelphia, 1801]. Shaw and Shoemaker 275.

———. *Autobiography*. Brooklyn, N.Y.: Research Classics, 1942.

[———]. *Narrative of the Proceedings of Edward Gray, Samuel F. Bradford, and Robert Taylor, previous and subsequent to the Bankruptcy of C. A. Conrad & Co.* Philadelphia 1813. Shaw and Shoemaker 29260.

[———]. *A Plumb Pudding for . . . Peter Porcupine*. Philadelphia, 1799. Evans 35272.

Carter, Edward II. "The Political Activities of Mathew Carey, Nationalist, 1760–1814." Ph.D. diss., Bryn Mawr College, 1962.

———. "A 'Wild Irishman' Under Every Federalist's Bed: Naturalization in Philadelphia, 1789–1806." *Pennsylvania Magazine of History and Biography*, 94 (1970): 331–346.

Carver, Jonathan. *Three Years of Travels, through the Interior Parts of North America.* Philadelphia, 1796. Evans 30169.

Carver, William. *Practical Horse Farrier; or, the Traveller's Pocket Companion.* Philadelphia, 1818. Shaw and Shoemaker 43547.

Cazden, Robert E. *A Social History of the German Book Trade in America to the Civil War.* Columbia, S.C.: Camden House, 1984.

Census Directory for 1811. Philadelphia, 1811. Shaw and Shoemaker 22497.

Chandler, Alfred D. "The Beginnings of a 'Big Business' in American Industry." *Business History Review,* 33 (Spring 1959): 1–31.

Charvat, William. "James T. Fields and the Beginning of Book Promotion, 1840–1855." *Huntington Library Quarterly,* 8 (1944): 75–94.

[Cobbett, William]. *Detection of a Conspiracy Formed by the United Irishmen.* Philadelphia, 1798. Bristol 10264.

Cochran, Thomas C. *Frontiers of Change: Early Industrialism in America.* New York: Oxford University Press, 1981.

Cohen, Patricia Cline. *A Calculating People: The Spread of Numeracy in Early America.* Chicago: University of Chicago Press, 1982.

Cole, Richard Cargill. *Irish Booksellers and English Writers, 1740–1800.* London: Mansell Pub.; Atlantic Highlands, N.J.: Humanities Press, 1986.

Coleman, Peter J. *Debtors and Creditors in America: Insolvency, Imprisonment for Debt, and Bankruptcy, 1607–1900.* Madison: State Historical Society of Wisconsin, 1974.

Constitution of the Philadelphia Company of Booksellers, Adopted February 18, 1802. [Philadelphia, 1802]. Shaw and Shoemaker 2892.

The Constitution, Proceedings &c. of the Philadelphia Company of Printers and Booksellers. [Philadelphia, 1793]. Bristol 8449.

Davidson, Cathy. *Revolution and the Word: the Rise of the Novel in America.* New York: Oxford University Press, 1986.

———, ed. *Reading in America: Literature and Social History.* Baltimore, Md.: Johns Hopkins University Press, 1989.

Dayton, Cornelia Hughes, "Women Before the Bar: Gender, Law and Society in Connecticut, 1710–1790." Ph.D. diss., Princeton University, 1986.

Denning, Michael. "Cheap Stories: Notes on Popular Fiction and Working-Class Culture in Nineteenth-Century America." *History Workshop,* 22 (1986): 1–17.

Dill, William A. *Growth of Newspapers in the United States, 1704–1925.* Lawrence: University of Kansas Press, 1928.

Doerflinger, Thomas M. *A Vigorous Spirit of Enterprise: Merchants and Economic Development in Revolutionary Philadelphia.* Chapel Hill: University of North Carolina Press, 1986.

Dolan, J. R. *The Yankee Peddlers of Early America.* New York: Clarkson N. Potter Inc., 1964.

Drake, Milton. *Almanacs of the United States.* New York: Scarecrow Press, 1962.

Edwards, James Don. "Early Bookkeeping and Its Development into Accounting." *Business History Review,* 34 (Winter 1960): 446–466.

Evans, Charles. *American Bibliography.* 12 vols. Chicago: The Blakely Press, 1903–1959.

Exman, Eugene. *The Brothers Harper: A Unique Publishing Partnership and Its Impact Upon the Cultural Life of America from 1817 to 1863*. New York: Harper and Row, 1965.

———. *The House of Harper: One Hundred and Fifty Years of Publishing*. New York: Harper and Row, 1967.

Farren, Donald. "Subscription: A Study of the Eighteenth-Century American Book Trade." D.L.S. thesis, Columbia University, 1982.

Feather, John. *The Provincial Book Trade in Eighteenth-Century England*. Cambridge: Cambridge University Press, 1985.

Febvre, Lucien, and Henri-Jean Martin. *The Coming of the Book: The Impact of Printing, 1450–1800*. New York: Verso, 1990.

Flint, Timothy. *A Condensed Geography and History of the Western States or the Mississippi Valley*. 2 vols. Cincinnati, 1828. Shoemaker 33201.

Frasca, Ralph. "Benjamin Franklin's Printing Network." *American Journalism*, 5 (1988): 145–158.

———. "From Apprentice to Journeyman to Partner: Benjamin Franklin's Workers and the Growth of the Early American Printing Trade." *Pennsylvania Magazine of History and Biography*, 114 (1990): 229–248.

Freeman, Stuart J. *Toward a Third Century of Excellence: An Informal History of the J. B. Lippincott Company, on the Occasion of its Two-Hundredth Anniversary*. Philadelphia: The Company, 1992.

Gill, John. *Exposition of the Old and New Testaments*. Philadelphia, 1810. Shaw and Shoemaker 20217.

Gilmore, William J. *Reading Becomes a Necessity of Life: Material and Cultural Life in Rural New England, 1780–1835*. Knoxville: University of Tennessee Press, 1989.

Gilreath, James, ed. *Federal Copyright Records, 1790–1800*. Washington: Library of Congress, 1987.

———. "Mason Weems, Mathew Carey and the Southern Booktrade." *Publishing History*, 10 (1981): 27–49.

Green, James N. "Benjamin Franklin as Publisher and Bookseller." In *Reappraising Benjamin Franklin: A Bicentennial Perspective*, ed. J. A. Lemay. Newark: University of Delaware Press, 1993.

———. "Book Publishing in Early America." A. S. W. Rosenbach Lectures in Bibliography, University of Pennsylvania, 1993.

———. "From Printer to Publisher: Mathew Carey and the Origins of Nineteenth-Century Book Publishing." In *Getting the Books Out: Papers of the Chicago Conference on the Book in 19th-Century America*, ed. Michael Hackenberg. Washington, D.C.: Center for the Book, Library of Congress, 1987.

———. "'I was always dispos'd to be serviceable to you': Benjamin Franklin's Relationship with Mathew Carey." Paper delivered before Philobiblon, Philadelphia, November 10, 1987.

———. *Mathew Carey: Publisher and Patriot*. Philadelphia: The Library Company of Philadelphia, 1985.

———. *The Rittenhouse Mill and the Beginnings of Papermaking in America*. Philadelphia: The Library Company of Philadelphia, 1990.

———. "Variant Issues." *The Annual Report of the Library Company of Philadelphia*, Philadelphia: The Library Company of Philadelphia, 1990, 18–27.

Greenough, Chester Noyes. "New England Almanacs, 1766–1775, and the American Revolution." *Proceedings of the American Antiquarian Society*, 45 (1935): 288–316.

Hackenberg, Michael, ed. *Getting the Books Out: Papers of the Chicago Conference on the Book in 19th-Century America*. Washington, D.C.: Center for the Book, Library of Congress, 1987.

Haites, Erik F., et. al., eds. *Western River Transportation: The Era of Early Internal Development, 1810–1860*. Baltimore, Md.: Johns Hopkins University Press, 1975.

Hall, David. "The Uses of Literacy in New England, 1600–1850." In *Printing and Society in Early America*, ed. William Joyce et al. Worcester, Mass.: American Antiquarian Society, 1983.

———. *Worlds of Wonder, Days of Judgment: Popular Religious Belief in Early New England*. New York: Knopf, 1989.

Hamilton, Milton. *The Country Printer: New York State, 1785–1830*. 2nd ed. Port Washington, N.Y.: I. J. Friedman, 1964.

Harlan, Robert. "David Hall's Bookshop and Its British Sources of Supply." In *Books in America's Past: Essays Honoring Rudolph H. Gjelsness*, ed. David Kaser. Charlottesville: University Press of Virginia, 1966.

———. "William Strahan's American Book Trade, 1744–76." *Library Quarterly*, 21 (1961): 235–244.

Haskell, Thomas L. "Capitalism and the Origins of the Humanitarian Sensibility, Part Two." *American Historical Review*, 90 (1985): 547–566.

Hatch, Nathan O. *The Democratization of American Christianity*. New Haven, Conn.: Yale University Press, 1989.

———. "Elias Smith and the Rise of Religious Journalism in the Early Republic." In *Printing and Society in Early America*, ed. William Joyce et al. Worcester, Mass.: American Antiquarian Society, 1983.

Hewlett, Leroy. "James Rivington, Loyalist Printer, Publisher, Bookseller of the American Revolution, 1724–1802." Ph.D. diss., University of Michigan, 1958.

Hogan, Edmund, ed. *The Prospect of Philadelphia*. Philadelphia, 1795. Evans 28845.

Jaffee, David. "The Village Enlightenment in New England, 1760–1820." *William and Mary Quarterly*, 3d ser., 47 (July 1990): 327–346.

Jess, Zachariah. *American Tutor's Assistant, Improved*. Philadelphia, 1819. Shaw and Shoemaker 48375.

Johannsen, Albert. *The House of Beadle and Adams and Its Dime and Nickel Novels*. Norman: University of Oklahoma Press, 1950.

Karpinski, Louis C. *Bibliography of Mathematical Works Printed in America Through 1850*. Ann Arbor: University of Michigan Press, 1940.

Kaser, David, ed. *The Cost Book of Carey & Lea, 1825–1838*. Philadelphia: University of Pennsylvania Press, 1963.

———. *Messrs. Carey & Lea of Philadelphia*. Philadelphia: University of Pennsylvania Press, 1957.

Kessler, Lauren. *The Dissident Press: Alternative Journalism in American History*. Beverly Hills, Calif.: Sage Publications, 1984.

Kite, Thomas, ed. *Kite's Philadelphia Directory for 1814*. Philadelphia, 1814. Shaw and Shoemaker 31873.

Klein, Philip S., and Ari Hoogenboom. *A History of Pennsylvania*. 2nd ed. University Park: Pennsylvania State University Press, 1980.

Kobre, Sidney. *The Development of the Colonial Newspaper*. Pittsburgh, Pa.: Colonial Press, 1944.

Krooss, Herman E. "Financial Institutions." In *The Growth of the Seaport Cities, 1790–1825*, ed. David T. Gilchrist. Charlottesville: University Press of Virginia, 1967.

Kubler, George A. *A New History of Stereotyping*. New York: J. J. Little and Ives Co., 1941.

Labaree, Leonard, et al. *The Autobiography of Benjamin Franklin*. New Haven, Conn.: Yale University Press, 1964.

Lacy, Creighton. *The Word-Carrying Giant: The Growth of the American Bible Society (1816–1966)*. South Pasadena, Calif.: William Carey Library, 1977.

Lambert, Frank. "Subscribing for Profits and Piety: The Friendship of Benjamin Franklin and George Whitefield." *William and Mary Quarterly*, 3d ser., L (1993): 529–554.

Landon, Richard G. "'Small Profits Do Great Things': James Lackington and Eighteenth-Century Bookselling." *Studies in Eighteenth-Century Culture*, 5 (1976): 387–399.

Lause, Mark A. *Some Degree of Power: From Hired Hand to Union Craftsman in the Preindustrial American Printing Trades, 1778–1815*. Fayetteville: University of Arkansas Press, 1991.

Leary, Lewis. *The Book-Peddling Parson*. Chapel Hill, N.C.: Algonquin Books, 1984.

Lehmann-Haupt, Hellmut. *The Book in America: A History of the Making, the Selling, and the Collecting of Books in the United States*. 2nd ed. New York: R. R. Bowker, 1952.

———, ed. *Bookbinding in America*. Portland, Maine: The Southworth-Anthoensen Press, 1941.

Levy, Leonard. *Emergence of a Free Press*. New York: Oxford University Press, 1985.

Little, Brown and Company. *One Hundred and Twenty-Five Years of Publishing, 1837–1962*. Boston: Little, Brown and Co., 1962.

Madison, Charles A. *Book Publishing in America*. New York: McGraw-Hill, 1966.

Maier, Pauline. *From Resistance to Revolution: Colonial Radicals and the Development of American Opposition to Britain, 1765–1776*. New York: Knopf, 1972.

Mair, John. *Book-keeping Methodiz'd: or, A Methodical Treatise of Merchant-Accompts, according to the Italian Form*. Dublin, 1750.

McDougall, Warren. "Copyright Litigation in the Court of Session, 1738–1749, and the Rise of the Scottish Book Trade." *Edinburgh Bibliographical Society Transactions*, 5, part 5 (1988): 2–31.

———. "Gavin Hamilton, John Balfour, and Patrick Neill: A Study of Publishing in Edinburgh in the 18th Century. Ph.D. diss., University of Edinburgh, 1974.

———. "Scottish Books for America in the Mid-18th Century." In *Spreading the Word: The Distribution Network of Print, 1550–1850*, ed. Robin Myers and Michael Harris. Winchester: St. Paul's Bibliographies, 1990, 21–24.

McGaw, Judith A. *Most Wonderful Machine: Mechanization and Social Change in Berkshire Paper Making, 1801–1885*. Princeton, N.J.: Princeton University Press, 1987.

McKenzie, D. F. *The Cambridge University Press, 1696–1712: A Bibliographical Study*. 2 vols. Cambridge: Cambridge University Press, 1966.

Melish, John. *Information and Advice to Emigrants to the United States; and from the Eastern to the Western States*. Philadelphia, 1819. Shaw and Shoemaker 48668.

Mellen, Grenville. *The Age of Print: A Poem*. Boston, 1830.

Miller, John. *The Federalist Era, 1789–1801*. New York: Harper, 1960.

Mitchell, Robert D. *Commercialism and Frontier: Perspectives on the Early Shenandoah Valley*. Charlottesville: University Press of Virginia, 1977.

Mitchell, William. *A New and Complete System of Book-Keeping*. Philadelphia, 1796. Evans 30802.

Monaghan, E. Jennifer. *A Common Heritage: Noah Webster's Blue-Back Speller*. Hamden, Conn.: Archon Books, 1983.

Monroe, James A. *A View of the Conduct of the Executive, in the Foreign Affairs of the United States, Connected with the Mission to the French Republic*. Philadelphia, 1797. Evans 32491.

Mott, Frank Luther. *American Journalism: A History of Newspapers in the United States Through 260 Years: 1690–1950*. New York: Macmillan, 1962.

Nash, Gary B. *The Urban Crucible: Social Change, Political Consciousness, and the Origins of the American Revolution*. Cambridge, Mass.: Harvard University Press, 1979.

Nelson, John R. *Liberty and Property: Political Economy and Policymaking in the New Nation, 1789–1812*. Baltimore, Md.: John Hopkins University Press, 1987.

Nichols, Charles L., "The Literary Fair in the United States." In *Bibliographical Essays: A Tribute to Wilberforce Eames*, ed. George Parker Winship and Lawrence C. Wroth. [Cambridge, Mass.], 1924.

Nord, David Paul. "The Evangelical Origins of Mass Media in America, 1815–1835." *Journalism Monographs*, no. 88 (1984).

———. "Newspapers and American Nationhood, 1776–1826." *Proceedings of the American Antiquarian Society*, 100, part 2 (1990): 391–405.

North, Douglass C. *The Economic Growth of the United States, 1790–1860*. New York: W. W. Norton, 1966.

Osborne, John W. *William Cobbett: His Thought and His Times*. New Brunswick, N.J.: Rutgers University Press, 1966.

Pankratz, John R. "New Englanders, the Written Word, and the Errand Into Ohio, 1788–1830." Ph.D. diss., Cornell University, 1981.

Paxton's Annual Philadelphia Directory and Register—1818. Philadelphia, [1818]. Shaw and Shoemaker 45218.

[Pennsylvania Society for Promotion of Public Schools]. *The First Report on the State of Education in Pennsylvania*. Philadelphia, 1828. Shoemaker 34709.

Perkins, Edwin J. "The Entrepreneurial Spirit in Colonial America: The Foundations of Modern Business History." *Business History Review*, 63 (1989): 160–186.

Philadelphia Company of Booksellers. *The Library; or, Philadelphia Literary Reporter*. Philadelphia, 1803–1809.

The Philadelphia Directory for 1805. Philadelphia, [1805]. Shaw and Shoemaker 9139.

Philbrick, Francis S. *The Rise of the West, 1754–1830*. New York: Harper and Row, 1965.

Pike, Stephen. *The Teacher's Assistant, or a System of Practical Arithmetic*. Philadelphia, 1822. Shoemaker 9942.

Pilkington, James Penn. *The Methodist Publishing House: A History*. Nashville, Tenn.: Abingdon Press, 1968.

Plant, Marjorie. *The English Book Trade: An Economic History of the Making and Sale of Books*. London: George Allen and Unwin, 1965.

A Pocket Companion; or Every Man His Own Lawyer. Philadelphia, 1818. Shaw and Shoemaker 45357.

Pollard, M. *Dublin's Trade in Books, 1550–1800*. Oxford: Oxford University Press, 1989.

Pratt, John Barnes. *A Century of Book Publishing, 1838–1938*. New York: A. S. Barnes & Co., 1938.

Pred, Allan. *Urban Growth and the Circulation of Information: The United States System of Cities, 1790–1840*. Cambridge, Mass.: Harvard University Press, 1973.

Putnam, George Haven. *A Memoir of George Palmer Putnam*. New York: G. P. Putnam's Sons, 1903.

Ramsay, William. *The Trial of Maurice Margarot*. New York, [1794]. Evans 27594.

Reese, William S. "The First Hundred Years of Printing in British North America: Printers and Collectors." *Proceedings of the American Antiquarian Society*, 99: 1 (1989): 337–373.

———. "The Printers' First Fruits: An Exhibition of American Imprints, 1640–1742, from the Collections of the American Antiquarian Society." *Proceedings of the American Antiquarian Society*, 99: 1 (1989): 41–88.

Remer, Rosalind. "Capturing the Bard: The American Publication of Shakespeare's Plays, 1822–1851." Paper presented at the Society for the History of the Early American Republic Conference, Gettysburg, Pennsylvania, July 1992.

Return of the Whole Number of Persons within the Several Districts of the United States. Philadelphia, 1791. Evans 23916.

[Riley, Isaac]. *Assignment. Isaac Riley to Joseph Greenleaf, William McKean, and Henry A. Riley*. [Philadelphia, 1820]. Shoemaker 3022.

Robinson, James, ed. *The Philadelphia Directory for 1804*. Philadelphia, [1804]. Shaw and Shoemaker 7044.

———, ed. *The Philadelphia Directory for 1808*. Philadelphia, 1808. Shaw and Shoemaker 15911.

Rogers, Joseph W. "The Rise of American Edition Binding." In *Bookbinding in America: Three Essays*, ed. Hellmut Lehmann-Haupt and Hannah Dustin French. Portland, Maine: The Southworth-Anthoensen Press, 1941.

Rorabaugh, W. J. *The Craft Apprentice: From Franklin to the Machine Age in America*. New York: Oxford University Press, 1986.

Rothenberg, Winifred B. "The Market and Massachusetts Farmers, 1750–1855." *Journal of Economic History*, 41 (1981): 283–414.

Scharf, Thomas J., and Thompson Westcott. *Philadelphia, 1609–1884.* 3 vols. Philadelphia: L. H. Everts and Company, 1884.

Schlesinger, Arthur M. *Prelude to Independence: The Newspaper War on Britain, 1764–1776.* New York: Knopf, 1958.

Schmookler, Jacob. *Invention and Economic Growth.* Cambridge, Mass.: Harvard University Press, 1966.

Schudson, Michael. *Discovering the News: A Social History of American Newspapers.* New York: Basic Books, 1978.

Scott, Thomas, ed. *The Holy Bible, Containing the Old and New Testaments, with Original Notes, and Practical Observations, and Copious Marginal References.* Philadelphia, 1811–12. Shaw and Shoemaker 22356.

Shakespeare, William. *The Dramatic Works of William Shakespeare.* 2 vols. Philadelphia, 1824. Shoemaker 17946.

———. *The Plays of William Shakespeare. In Seventeen Volumes.* Philadelphia, 1809. Shaw and Shoemaker 18593.

———. *The Plays of William Shakespeare.* 8 vols. Philadelphia, 1823. Shoemaker 14095.

Shaw, Ralph, and Richard H. Shoemaker, eds. *American Bibliography: A Preliminary Checklist, 1801–1819.* 22 vols. New York: Scarecrow Press, 1958–1966.

Sher, Richard B. "Commerce, Religion, and Enlightenment in Eighteenth-Century Glasgow." In *History of Glasgow.* 3 vols., ed. T. M. Devine and Gordon Jackson. Manchester: Manchester University Press, 1995, 312–359.

Shipton, Clifford K. *The American Bibliography of Charles Evans.* Worcester, Mass.: American Antiquarian Society, 1955.

Shoemaker, Richard H. *A Checklist of American Imprints.* 9 vols. New York: Scarecrow Press, 1964–1970.

Shulim, Joseph I. "John Daly Burke: Irish Revolutionist and American Patriot." *Transactions of the American Philosophical Society,* 54 (1964).

Silver, Rollo G. *The American Printer, 1787–1825.* Charlottesville: University Press of Virginia, 1967.

———. "The Book Trade and the Protective Tariff: 1800–1804." *Papers of the Bibliographical Society of America,* 46 (1952): 33–44.

Simpson, Robert. "Narrative of a Scottish Adventurer, 1788–1797." *Journal of the Presbyterian Historical Society,* 27 (March 1949): 41–67.

Skeel, Emily Ellsworth Ford. *Mason Locke Weems: His Work and His Ways.* 3 vols. New York: [privately printed], 1929.

Smith, Jeffrey A. *Franklin and Bache: Envisioning the Enlightened Republic.* New York: Oxford University Press, 1990.

Snowden, Richard. *The American Revolution: Written in the Style of Ancient History. In Two Volumes.* Philadelphia, [1794]. Evans 27716.

Sokoloff, Kenneth L. "Productivity Growth in Manufacturing During Early Industrialization: Evidence from the American Northeast, 1820–1860." In *Long-term Factors in American Economic Growth,* ed. Stanley L. Engerman and Robert E. Gallman. Chicago: University of Chicago Press, 1986.

———. "Inventive Activity in Early Industrial America: Evidence From Patent Records, 1790–1846." *Journal of Economic History,* 48 (1988): 813–850.

———, and B. Zorin Khan. "The Democratization of Invention During Early Industrialization: Evidence from the United States, 1790–1846." *Journal of Economic History*, 50 (1990): 363–378.

Spater, George. *William Cobbett: The Poor Man's Friend*. 2 vols. Cambridge: Cambridge University Press, 1982.

Stafford, William Cornelius, ed. *The Philadelphia Directory for 1798*. Philadelphia, 1798. Evans 34593.

———, ed. *The Philadelphia Directory for 1799*. Philadelphia. 1799. Evans 36353.

———, ed. *The Philadelphia Directory for 1800*. Philadelphia, 1800. Evans 38549.

[Stephens Thomas]. *Stephens's Philadelphia Directory, for 1796*. Philadelphia, [1796]. Evans 31235.

Stern, Madeleine B. "The Role of the Publisher in Mid-Nineteenth Century American Literature." *Publishing History*, 10 (1981): 5–26.

———. *Imprints on History: Book Publishers and American Frontiers*. Bloomington: Indiana University Press, 1956.

Stewart, Donald H. *The Opposition Press of the Federalist Period*. Albany: State University of New York Press, 1969.

Stewart, Ethelbert. "A Documentary History of the Early Organizations of Printers." U.S. Department of Commerce and Labor *Bulletin*, 11 (November 1905): 857–1033.

Stowell, Marion Barber. *Early American Almanacs: The Colonial Weekday Bible*. New York: B. Franklin, 1977.

Sutton, Walter. *The Western Book Trade: Cincinnati as a Nineteenth-Century Publishing Center*. Columbus: Ohio State University Press, 1961.

Swetz, Frank J. *Capitalism and Arithmetic: The New Math of the 15th Century*. Lasalle, Ill.: Open Court, 1987.

Tagg, James. *Benjamin Franklin Bache and the Philadelphia Aurora*. Philadelphia: University of Pennsylvania Press, 1991.

Tanselle, Thomas G. "Some Statistics on American Printing, 1764–1783." In *The Press and the American Revolution*, ed. Bernard Bailyn and John B. Hench. Boston, Mass.: Northeastern University Press, 1981.

Taylor, George Rogers. *The Transportation Revolution, 1815–1860*. New York: Rinehart, 1951.

Tebbel, John. *A History of Book Publishing in the United States, Volume I: The Creation of an Industry*. New York: R. R. Bowker, 1972.

———. *A History of Book Publishing in the United States, Volume II: The Expansion of an Industry, 1865–1919*. New York: R. R. Bowker, 1975.

Thomas, David. *Travels through the Western Country in the Summer of 1816*. Auburn, N.Y.: 1819. Shaw and Shoemaker 49583.

Thomas, Ebenezer Smith. *Reminiscences of the Last Sixty-Five Years*. Hartford, 1840.

Thomas, Isaiah. *The History of Printing in America*, ed. Marcus A. McCorison. Barre, Mass.: Imprint Society, 1970.

Thompson, Lawrence. "The Printing and Publishing Activities of the American Tract Society from 1825 to 1850." *Papers of the Bibliographical Society of America*, 35 (1941): 81–144.

Thorp, Daniel B. "Doing Business in the Backcountry: Retail Trade in Colonial

Rowan County, North Carolina." *William and Mary Quarterly*, 3d ser., 48 (1991): 387–408.

Ticknor, Howard Malcom. *A Brief Biographical Sketch of William David Ticknor*. Cambridge, Mass.: John Wilson & Son, 1895.

To the Booksellers of the United States. (New York, June 7, 1802). The only known surviving copy of this broadside is at AAS. It was probably written by Mathew Carey.

Tryon, William S. *Parnassus Corner: A Life of James T. Fields, Publisher to the Victorians*. Boston: Houghton Mifflin Co., 1963.

Turner, Michael L. "Andrew Wilson: Lord Stanhope's Stereotype Printer." *Journal of the Printing History Society*, 9 (1973–74): 22–65.

Twomey, Richard J. "Jacobins and Jeffersonians: Anglo-American Radical Ideology, 1790–1810." In *The Origins of Anglo-American Radicalism*, ed. Margaret Jacob and James Jacob. London: Allen and Unwin, 1984.

Wade, Richard C. *The Urban Frontier: Pioneer Life in Early Pittsburgh, Cincinnati, Lexington, Louisville and St. Louis*. Chicago: University of Chicago Press, 1959.

Wall, Alexander J., Jr. "William Bradford, Colonial Printer: A Tercentenary Review." *Proceedings of the American Antiquarian Society*, 73 (1963): 365.

Walsh, Michael. *The Mercantile Arithmetic*. Boston: 1826. Shoemaker 27542.

Wansey, Henry. *The Journal of an Excursion to the United States of North America, in the Summer of 1794*. Salisbury, 1796.

Warner, Michael. *The Letters of the Republic: Publication and the Public Sphere in Eighteenth-Century America*. Cambridge, Mass.: Harvard University Press, 1990.

Warner, Sam Bass, Jr. *The Private City: Philadelphia in Three Periods of Its Growth*. Philadelphia: University of Philadelphia Press, 1968.

Watts, Isaac. *Psalms of David, Imitated*. Philadelphia, 1729. Evans 3135.

Westerhoff, John H. *McGuffey and His Readers: Piety, Morality, and Education in Nineteenth-Century America*. Nashville, Tenn.: Abingdon Press, 1978.

Westminster Assembly of Divines. *The Larger Catechism*. New York, 1813. Shaw and Shoemaker 30520.

Whitefield, George. *A Journal of a Voyage from Gibralter to Georgia, Vol. I*. Philadelphia, 1739. Evans 4453.

———. *A Continuation of the Revered Mr. Whitefield's Journal, Vol. II*. Philadelphia, 1740. Evans 4633.

Whiteley, Edward, ed. *The Philadelphia Directory*. Philadelphia, 1820. Shoemaker 2742.

Wiley, John, and Sons. *The First One Hundred and Fifty Years: A History of John Wiley & Sons, Inc., 1807–1957*. New York: John Wiley & Sons, 1957.

Wilson, Thomas. *The Philadelphia Directory and Stranger's Guide, for 1825*. Philadelphia, 1825. Shoemaker 23350.

Winans, Robert B. "Bibliography and the Cultural Historian: Notes on the Eighteenth-Century Novel." In *Printing and Society in Early America*, ed. William L. Joyce et al. Worcester, Mass.: American Antiquarian Society, 1983.

Winship, Michael. "Getting the Books Out: Trade Sales, Parcel Sales, and Book Fairs in the Nineteenth-Century United States." In *Getting the Books Out: Papers of the Chicago Conference on the Book in 19th Century America*, ed. Michael

Hackenberg. Washington, D.C.: The Center for the Book, Library of Congress, 1987.

———. "Printing with Plates in the Nineteenth Century." *Printing History*, 5 (1983): 15–27.

———. "Publishing in America: Needs and Opportunities for Research." In *Needs and Opportunities in the History of the Book: America, 1639–1876*, ed. David Hall and John B. Hench. Worcester, Mass.: American Antiquarian Society, 1987.

———. "Ticknor and Fields: A Study of Literary Publishing in Boston in the Mid-Nineteenth Century." D. Phil. diss., Oxford University, 1989.

Wolf, Edwin. *The Book Culture of a Colonial American City: Philadelphia Books, Bookmen, and Booksellers*. New York: Oxford University Press, 1988.

———. *From Gothic Windows to Peacocks: American Embossed Leather Bindings, 1825–1855*. Philadelphia: The Library Company of Philadelphia, 1990.

[Woodward, William W.] *Books Published and sold by W. W. Woodward*. Philadelphia: 1810. Shaw and Shoemaker 22085.

Wright, Richardson. *Hawkers and Walkers in Early America*. Philadelphia: J. B. Lippincott Co., 1927.

Wroth, Lawrence C. *The Colonial Printer*. Portland, Maine: The Southworth-Anthoensen Press, 1938.

Yamey, B. S. "Scientific Bookeeping and the Rise of Capitalism." *Economic History Review*, 2nd ser., I (1949): 99–113.

Zboray, Ronald J. *A Fictive People: Antebellum Economic Development and the American Reading Public*. New York: Oxford University Press, 1993.

Index

A Pocket Companion; or Every Man His Own Lawyer, 129

Accounting methods and bookkeeping, 101–106

Adams, John, 25, 36

Adams, Jacob W., 108–109

Aitken, Robert, 33, 66, 84, 103

Akin, William, 145

Albany, N.Y., publishing and bookselling in, 7

Alexander, William (*The History of Women*), 48

Alien and Sedition Acts, 36, 169 n.38

Almanacs, 17–18

American Antiquarian Society, 164 n.17

American Company of Booksellers, 62, 67, 120, 183 n.53

American literature, 9, 39–40, 149

American Museum, 37, 50

American Philosophical Society, 84

Andrews, Ebenezer T., 41, 56, 174 n.67

Appleton, Daniel, 150

Asylum Company of Journeyman Printers, 43, 182 n.17

Aurora, 26–27, 30, 36, 42–43, 66–68, 168 n.19, 171 n. 28

Bache, Benjamin Franklin, 8, 19, 25–31, 34–36, 42, 92

Bache, Margaret (Margaret Hartman Markoe), 28, 36, 42–43

Bailey printing family, 8; Francis, 32–34, 38, 41, 70, 84, 92–93, 107, 151; Jacob, 107; Lydia R., 42–43, 72; Robert, 33, 72, 107

Baine (family) typefounders, 92

Baltimore: James Carey in, 48; and the Conrad printing family, 71, 91; an exchange scheme in, 81; location on the National Road, 140; publishing and bookselling in, 7, 40; and shared imprints, 88

Bank of Pennsylvania, 35, 38

Bank of the United States, 5, 38, 118

Bankruptcy, 117–124

Barthelemy, Jean Jacques (*Travels of Anacharsis the Younger*), 88

Barton, Benjamin Smith (*Studies of Nature*), 88

Benedict, David, 133

Bernardin de Saint-Pierre, Jacques Henri (*Studies of Nature*), 88

Bernhard, Karl (*Travels through North America*), 113

Berriman, Jacob, 72

Bey, Jacob, 92

Bible/tract societies, 6, 135, 186 n.40

Bigland, John (*Geographical and Historical View of the World*), 80

Billmeyer, Michael, 86, 105, 177 n.27. *See also* German books and German language printing

Binding and binders, 3, 109–111, 176 n.8

Binny (Archibald) and Ronaldson (James), 93–94, 97

Bioren, John, 34–35, 42, 60–61, 70, 118, 151

Birch (William Young) and Small (Abraham), 88

Black, James, 134

Blake, W. P. and L., 88

Blakiston Company, 150

Blauvelt, Abraham, 81, 176 n.20

Bookkeeping methods, 101–106

Bookseller's Advertiser, 149

Boston: bookselling in, 29, 36, 125; competition with Philadelphia publishers, 51, cooperation with Philadelphia publishers, 55–56, 80–84; and credit networks, 123; and literary fairs, 62; and the political press, 22; printing and publishing in, 7–8, 12, 40; prominence in the book trade, 149–151; and publishing combinations, 88–90

Botein, Stephen, 21–22, 167 n.49
Bradford printing family, 8; Samuel F., 70–71; Thomas, 56–57; William, 14, 18, 20–21 24, 93, 103, 164 n.13; Bradford and Inskeep, 119
Bradford, John, 83
Branch stores, 139–141
Britain: book exports to America, 12–13, 16–17; books reprinted in America, 7, 15–16; copyright law, 16; journeymen, 41; London trade copyrights, 12; newspaper publishing, 20; printers from, 8; provincial printing in, 11–12, 15, 17; radical émigrés from, 5; "rum books," 13; stereotype printing, 95–96
Broadsides, 16–17
Brothers, Richard (*A Revealed Knowledge of the Prophecies and Times*), 84
Brown, Andrew, 25, 26, 36, 44–45, 51
Bruce, David, 96
Buck, Charles (*Theological Dictionary*), 133
Burder, George (*Village Sermons*), 129
Burkitt, William (*Expository Notes . . . on the New Testament*), 48
Byerly, Stephen (*New American Spelling Book*), 130
Byrne, Patrick, 38, 50, 151

Callender, James T., 51, 172 n.43
Campbell, Robert, 43, 58, 173 n.58
Campbell, Samuel, 131
Carey (Henry Charles) and Lea (Isaac), 98, 112–115
Carey, Henry Charles, 70, 110, 150
Carey, James, 29, 48–49, 81
Carey (Mathew) and Son (Henry Charles), 105
Carey, Mathew: advice to brother, James, 48–49; on the American book trade, 1–2, 9; and Bible publishing, 172 n.45; on book distribution, 125–126, 128, 130–132, 139, 147; on commission sales, 82–85; and Conrad bankruptcy, 118–119; on cooperation and competition, 55–56; and credit, 100, 106–107, 109–110, 112, 116–117, 120–123; on exchange, 80–82, 87; importing books, 50; on journeymen and apprentices, 41; on overproduction, 52; and politics, 27, 29, 34–38; on public education, 6; as publisher, 50–52, 70, 73, 93; publishing decisions, 53; relationship with Benjamin

Franklin, 166 n.36; on shared imprints, 91–92; surviving records for, 8; and trade associations, 58–62
Carver, Jonathan (*Three Years of Travels*), 46–47
Carver, William (*Practical Horse Farrier*), 130, 136
Cazden, Robert E., 9
Chambersburg, Pa., bookselling in, 139–140
Chapbooks, 16–17
Charleston, S.C., publishing and bookselling in, 7
Childs (Francis) and Swaine (John), 34
Cincinnati, Ohio, publishing and bookselling in, 146, 189 n.77
Clark (John C.) and Raser (Matthias), 108–109
The Classic Press, 142, 143
Clymer, George, 95
Cobbett, William, 25–26, 29, 37, 71
Cochran, Thomas, 147
Collins, Isaac, 174 n.67
Collusion, 4, 54–55, 80. *See also* Competition and cooperation; Courtesy of the trade; Shareholding
Colonial period: book imports, 12–15; printing, publishing, and bookselling, 11–23; newspapers, 19–22
Commission sales, 82–87
Competition and cooperation, 55–65
Conrad, C. and A., and Co., 91–94, 178 n.44, 118–119
Conrad, John, 38, 70–71, 119, 174 n.67
Conrad, Solomon W., 71. *See also* Kimber and Conrad
Copyright: London trade, 12; U.S. Copyright Law (1790), 40, 53
Courtesy of the trade, 55, 173 n.58, 180 n.65
Cramer, Zadock, 146
Credit relationships among publishers, 115–124
Crukshank, Joseph, 58–60
Cummins, Francis, 134
Cushing and Appleton, 82, 123

David, John, Jr., 122
Davies, Benjamin, 71
Davis (William) and McCarty (James F.), Wheeling, Va., 108, 129, 139–141
Davis, Thomas. *See* McCarty and Davis
Davis, William. *See* Davis and McCarty

Debrett, Charles, 28–29
Dennie, Joseph, 121
DeSilver, Thomas, 151
Dickinson, Abel, 70, 72,
Didot, Firmin, 96
Dobelbower, J. H., 45–49
Dobson, Thomas, 29, 33, 38, 41, 50, 58–60, 70, 75, 84, 151
Doerflinger, Thomas M., 5, 160 n.11
Drake, John F., 144
Duane, William, 6, 25, 34–37, 43, 121
Duane, William, Jr., 36
Dunlap, John, 163 n.8

Edinburgh: printing and bookselling in, 11; books exported from, 13
Egron, Pierre, 32
Embargo of 1807–8, 119, 133–134
Evans, C. and O. (Oliver), 112–115
Exchange accounts, 79–82

Feather, John, 160 n.8
Federal Gazette, 44
Federalist era/Federalist Party, 25–26, 29, 34
Fenno, John, 25–26, 34–35, 44
Fenno, John Ward, 36
Fields, James T., 151
Folwell, Richard, 116–117
Franklin, Benjamin: *Autobiography*, 21; bookkeeping, 102–103; in competition with William Bradford and Samuel Keimer, 14–15, 20–21, 24; and government patronage, 14, 33; and politics, 22, 28; printing partnership with David Hall, 13, 166 n.47; as prototypical publisher, 19; relationship with Mathew Carey, 166 n.36; and typefounding, 92
Freneau, Philip, 25, 34, 36
Fry, William, 70

Gaine, Hugh, 62–63
Gazette of the United States, 26
General Advertiser, 67–68
German books and German language printing, 9, 86, 177 n.27. *See also* Billmeyer, Michael
Gill, John (*Exposition of the Old and New Testaments*), 133
Glasgow, printing and bookselling in, 11
Government printing contracts, 33–35
Gray (Edward) and Taylor, 119

Green, James N., 21
Grigg (John) and Elliott, 150
Griggs (Andrew) and Dickinson (Abel), 108

Hall, David: and government patronage, 14; as importer of British books, 13–14; partnership with Benjamin Franklin, 13, 166 n.47
Hamilton and Balfour, 32
Hamilton, Alexander, 34, 36
Harper Brothers, 150
Harper, George, 140
Harrison, Samuel, 118
Hart, Abraham, 150
Hartford, Conn., publishing and bookselling in, 7
Helmbold, George, 35, 122, 151
Hoff, John, 88
Hogan, David, 50, 70, 151
Hogan, Edmund, 31–32
Houghton Mifflin, 150
Howe, Jedediah, 97–98, 113–114, 180 n.69
Hunter, Henry (*Studies of Nature*), 88
Hurd, Ebenezer, 137

Independent Gazetteer, 37
Inskeep, John, 70–71, 151
Insolvency, 117–124
Ireland: dissidents, 5; reprint trade, 12
Italian method of bookkeeping, 101, 103. *See also* Accounting methods and bookkeeping

Jay's Treaty, 27
Jefferson, Thomas, 25, 30–31, 34–36
Jess, Zachariah (*American Tutor's Assistant*), 130
Job printing, 2–3, 15
Johnson (Jacob) and Warner (Benjamin): country book distribution, 126–127, 141–144, 150; engraving of bookstore, 74–75; and exchange, 82; shared imprints, 88; surviving records for, 8, 71
Johnson, Benjamin, 58, 190 n.8
Journeymen printers: as job printers, 40–44; organizations, 42–44; as publishers, 44–49

Kammerer, Joseph, 70
Keimer, Samuel, 19–20
Keith, Isaac Stockton, 187 n.41

Key, James, 45–49
Kimber (Emmor) and Conrad (Solomon, W.), 71
Kimber, Caleb, 122
Kite, Benjamin, 70

Lackington, James, 128, 173 n.58
Lea, Isaac, 112, 150
Leipzig book fairs, 62, 174 n.67. *See also* Literary fairs
Licensing Act of 1695, 29
Lippincott, J. B., 150, 190 n.8
Literacy and readership, 6–7, 134, 141
Literary fairs, 62–64, 174 n.67. *See also* American Company of Booksellers
Little, Charles, 151
Little, Brown, and Company, 150
Logan-Lloyd controversy, 22
London: as center of the British book trade, 40; publishers and booksellers, 2, 4, 11; trade specialization, 11; views of American trade, 18. *See also* Britain
Long, George, 82
Longworth, David, 91, 123
Louisiana Purchase, 125
Lovegrove, James, 110

M'Laughlin, William F., 88
Macanulty and Maxey, 121–122
Maier, Pauline, 22
Mallory, Daniel, 90
Manning, Thomas S., 70
Martin, Henri-Jean, 93
Maxwell, Hugh, 70
McCarty (William) and Davis (Thomas): and country book distribution, 126–127, 129–130, 136–141, 144–145, 185 n.19; and credit, 117; relationship to tradesmen, 107–108; and Shakespeare, 90, 97–99, 180 n.69; and technological innovations, 94
McCarty, James F. *See* Davis and McCarty
McCulloch, William, 44, 58–59, 159 n.3
McGaw, Judith, 178 n. 47
McGuffey's readers, 189 n.77
Melish, John, 117–118
Mellen, Grenville (*The Age of Print*), 138
Mercantilism, 4, 12, 17
Merchant's Advertiser, 56–57
Methodist Book Concern, 132
Miner, Asher, 106
Monroe, James, 30–31

Morris, Robert, 27, 30, 32, 34–35
Morse, Jedediah, 56, 133
Mulholland, James, 137

Nancrede, M., 176 n.20
National Road, 140
National Gazette, 26
New York: almanacs, 17; newspapers, 22, 25; publishers, 40; publishing and bookselling in, 7–8
Newcastle, England, printing and bookselling, 11
Newspapers: colonial, 19–22; in England, 20; Federalist era, 25–27, 35–36, 38; growth in American newspapers, 25; in Philadelphia versus Boston and New York, 22
Nicholson, John, 31–33
Note endorsement, 106–108, 115–124

Oram, James, 88
Ormrod, John, 50, 70, 151
Osgood, Samuel, 133
Oswald, Eleazer, 37, 122

Paine, Thomas (*Age of Reason*), 30–31
Pamphlets, 4, 16–17, 165 nn.23–24
Panic of 1819, 133–134, 147, 189 n.76
Panoplist, 133
Paper and papermaking, 3, 94, 178 n.47
Patton, William, 122
Peddlers, 17, 126–139
Peirce, Charles, 121, 123
Penniman, Obadiah, 121
Pennsylvania Gazette, 20
Pennsylvania General Assembly, 14
Pennsylvania Herald, 37
Pennsylvania State House of Representatives, 35
Philadelphia: almanacs, 17; as case study, 7; declining importance in publishing trade, 149, 152; imprints, 15, 40; newspapers, 22, 25–27, 35–36, 38; publishing history sources, 8; publishing output, 17
Philadelphia Company of Booksellers, 60–62
Philadelphia Company of Printers and Booksellers, 57–60
Philadelphia Linnean Society, 88
Philadelphia Typographical Society, 43, 182 n.17

Pike, Stephen (*The Teacher's Assistant*), 130
Pittsburgh, 146–147
(Pittsburgh) *Mercury*, 146
Pleasants, Samuel, 80, 88
Porcupine's Gazette, 26
Port Folio, 121
Poyntell, William, 64–66. *See also* The Classic Press
Preachers as peddlers, 130–136
Prentiss, William, 54
Printer's Circular, 109
Printers: colonial, 11–23; credit relationships with publishers, 106–109; distinguished from publishers, 2–3; early national, 69–73; in conflict with publishers, 65–68; journeymen, 39–49; mid-19th century, 152; organizations, 57–60, 67; and politics, 21–23, 166 n.48; as publishers, 16–22, 49–52
Public education and schools, 6–7
Publishers: as capitalists, 92–99; colonial, 16–19; competition and cooperation, 55–65; distinguished from printers, 2–3; in conflict with printers, 65–68; credit relationships, 106–109; organizations, 57–65; and politics, 24–38
Publishing: combinations, 87–92; decisions, 52–55; shareholding, 55–57; distinguished from printing, 2–3
Putnam, George Palmer, 149–151

Quantity sales to retailers, 86–87

Ray, Joseph, 189 n.77
Republican(s) and Republican Party, 25–27, 36
Revolution, American, and the political press, 5, 22
Rice, Henry and Patrick, 58–60, 120
Riley, Isaac, 120
Risk, calculations of, 111–115
Rittenhouse Paper Mill, 93
Rivington, James, 13, 51, 53–54, 87, 163 n.8
Ronaldson, James, 97, 113, 115
Rush, Benjamin, 37

Sage and Thompson, 122
Saur, Christopher, 92–93
Schoolbooks, 7, 16–17, 129–130
Scotland: reprint trade, 12; books exported from, 13, 163 n.3

Scott, Thomas (ed., *The Holy Bible*), 91, 133
Scott, Sir Walter, 90, 139
Shakespeare, William: publication of plays, 90, 97–98; stereotype editions, 113–115
Shareholding, 55–57
Simpson, Robert, 44–49, 170 n.18, 171 n.20
Small, Abraham, 33, 38, 49, 70, 151
Snowden, Richard (*The American Revolution*), 82
Sons of Liberty, 22
Spotswood, William, 29–30
Stanhope, Earl of (Charles Mahon), 95–96
Stationers' Company, 55
Steady sellers, 4, 16–17, 97, 129
Steam printing, 3, 94
Stephens, Thomas, 70
Stereotype plate printing, 3, 95–97, 113–114
Stewart, James, 41
Strahan, William, 163 n.8
Subscription publishing, 4, 18–19, 46–48
Supporter; or, Daily Repast, 33. *See also* Nicholson, John
Swaine, John, 82
Swedenborg, Emmanuel, 70
Swords, James, 174 n.67

Thomas (Isaiah) and Andrews (Ebenezer T.), 41, 56, 80, 123
Thomas (Isaiah) and Thomas (Alexander), 120–121
Thomas (Isaiah) and Whipple (Charles), 88
Thomas, Isaiah (*The History of Printing in America*), 93
Thompson and Wardlaw, 145
Thompson, John, 33, 49
Ticknor and Fields, 150
Ticknor, William Davis, 152
Truman and Smith, 189 n.77

United States Constitution, 5
Unites States Copyright Law (1790), 40, 53

Vertical integration, 4, 92–95

Waddell, Moses, 135, 186 n.40
Wait, Thomas B., 80
Walker, John (*Critical Pronouncing Dictionary*), 108
Walsh, Michael (*The Mercantile Arithmetic*), 101
War of 1812, 133, 146–147

Warner and Hanna, 88
Warner, Benjamin. *See* Johnson and Warner
Washington, D.C., as new capital, 7, 35
Washington, George, 25, 27
Watts, Isaac (*Psalms of David*), 19
Watts, John (J. Watts & Co.), 96
Webster, Noah, 54–56
Weems, Mason Locke, 54, 110, 128, 131–132, 147, 173 n.58, 186 n.21
West, John, 174 n.67
West, David, 55–56
Wheeling, Va., bookselling in, 140–141
Whitefield, George (*A Journal of a Voyage from Gibraltar to Georgia*), 19
Whiting and Watson, 96
Wholesale book distribution, 141–146
Wiley, John, 150

Wilson, James, 88
Wolf, Edwin, 185 n.17
Woodward, William W.: and country book distribution, 126, 129, 132–136; early printing career, 32–33; on exchange, 80; as publisher, 38, 70, 73, 151; and shared imprints, 91; surviving records for, 8; and trade associations, 50
Wrigley, Francis, 70, 72
Wroth, Lawrence, 162 n.16

Young (William) and McCulloch (John), 92; Young, William, 58–59, 83, 151, 187 n.41
Young, William P., 84

This book has been set in Galliard. Galliard was designed for Mergenthaler in 1978 by Matthew Carter. Galliard retains many of the features of a sixteenth-century typeface cut by Robert Granjon but has some modifications that give it a more contemporary look.

Printed on acid-free paper.